THE FLYING SQUAD

THE FLYING SQUAD

Neil Darbyshire
and Brian Hilliard

HEADLINE

First published in 1993
by HEADLINE BOOK PUBLISHING PLC

10 9 8 7 6 5 4 3 2 1

British Library Cataloguing in Publication Data

Darbyshire, Neil
Flying Squad
I Title
363.2

ISBN 0-7472-0685-6

Typeset by Keyboard Services, Luton

Printed and bound in Great Britain by
Mackays of Chatham PLC, Chatham, Kent

HEADLINE BOOK PUBLISHING PLC
Headline House
79 Great Titchfield Street
London W1P 7FN

Contents

Acknowledgements

My thanks are due to many people for their help in compiling this book, most notably to my friend Brian Hilliard, who researched and wrote the sections covering the 1960s and the Tony Lundy affair and was generally a pillar of support.

Inevitably with a book spanning such an extended period, first-hand witnesses of the early years were always difficult and in many cases impossible to come by and it was necessary to rely heavily on memoirs and press cuttings.

I am however grateful to Bernard Scarlett, who interviewed several founder members of the squad for a book he wrote with Norman Lucas twenty-five years ago and confirmed some of the detail of the squad's origin.

Tom Sandrock and John Weeks, two of my illustrious predecessors as crime correspondent of the *Daily Telegraph*, helped enormously with their recollections of the character of the Metropolitan CID in the 1950s, 60s and 70s.

A number of retired career criminals helped to fill in the opposition side of the story, including Bobby King, Bruce Reynolds and Ron Biggs. Quite a few others declined and at least one was re-arrested before I could reach him.

Sources of reference included the Commissioner's library at Scotland Yard, the Metropolitan Police Historical Society, the library at Bramshill and various newspaper archives.

At the *Daily Telegraph*, special thanks are owing to the editor Max Hastings for allowing me a month of paid leave and a month of holiday in quick succession, to the newsdesk for not complaining (much), to Marylin Warnick for her encouragement, to John in the library, Valerie who gathered together the bulk of the pictures and Stephanie at DT systems, who kindly printed the manuscript.

But most crucial at all stages was the assistance of many police officers, serving and retired, who with very few exceptions were always happy to pass on their knowledge and anecdotes.

John O'Connor, Brian Boyce and Mike Brooker I must thank for their detailed help, others such as Roy Ramm, Eddie Ellison, John Grieve, Graham Saltmarsh and Dan McCarthy for their stories over the years which made me want to write the book in the first place and George Ness and his deputy Bill Griffiths for their consideration.

Brian was indebted to Tony Lundy, Bert Wickstead, Bob Robinson, Gwyn Waters, Roy Herridge, Mick O'Leary, Peter Darke, Gerald MacArthur, John Simmond, John Swain, David Powis and Martin Short.

Finally, thanks to Celia Kent at Headline for her patience, to Caroline North for her copy-editing, to Patrick and Nicki for the seaside retreat, to Mark Lucas for persuading Headline to shell out an advance and to Isabel and Rosie for helping to spend it before it ever approached the bank.

1
Cops and Robbers

The armoured Securicor van pulled into a busy service station forecourt. On board was a collection of bags containing close to £1 million in cash, to be delivered to a number of branches of Barclays Bank in the area. It was 9.55 a.m. on Tuesday 27 November 1990 in the unremarkable Surrey suburb of Woodhatch. This was a routine weekly run which had previously been operated with no hint of disruption. The three guards manning the vehicle – June Wheeler, Ray Tuck and Brian Delamere – felt confident enough to call at a café behind the Texaco garage for coffee.

It was an unscheduled stop and one they knew would have been frowned on by their managers at Securicor. But it seemed harmless enough. They had stopped at the same café on past runs without incident and no one back at head office had been any the wiser.

Today was to be very different. At 9.57 a.m., as guards Wheeler and Tuck emerged from the van to collect the coffee, leaving Delamere to look after the cash, an open-backed Nissan truck suddenly accelerated on to the garage forecourt with headlights blazing. Out jumped a bearded gunman wearing a furry black wig and paint-splashed jeans. Wheeler was grabbed by the arm and told that if she did not cooperate both guards would be shot. 'Do as you're told and you won't get hurt,' the gunman said. A pistol was jabbed into the petrified young woman's back and she and Tuck were frog-marched back to the van.

A split second later three more sinister looking men, all armed with handguns and all in heavy disguise, sprang out of the bright red Nissan. One had his face blacked with boot polish and wore an

Afro wig and spectacles, another had on a Hallowe'en mask which made him look like a grotesque old man and the third wore a mask in the style of the Spitting Image puppet of President Ronald Reagan.

While 'Afro' and 'Reagan' provided armed cover in case of possible interference by any foolhardy member of the public, the other two assailants bundled all three guards into the back of the security van. 'Hallowe'en' held them hostage while the bearded gunman grabbed the ignition keys and got into the driving seat. Rather than looting the cash bags on the spot, which would have involved them standing around in full public view for anything up to ten or fifteen minutes, the gang intended to hijack the Securicor van and the guards, drive to a more private location and help themselves to the money at their leisure.

The robbery had been planned with what was later to be described at the Old Bailey as 'military precision' by a gang with access to enough weapons 'for a small war'. They had followed the Securicor van on at least three previous Tuesday morning rounds and each time they had registered that same unscheduled stop at the Woodhatch café. This was the point at which the van and its guards were at their most vulnerable. The gang was determined to exploit that vulnerability to the full.

What they did not know was that all the time they had been watching the Securicor van, waiting hungrily for the best moment to pounce, a pack of equally patient but stronger and better equipped predators had been watching them. The Flying Squad, Scotland Yard's shock troops in the war against professional armed robbery, had been following their every step – using a combination of static surveillance, telephone bugs and homing devices – for twelve long weeks. A bulging intelligence dossier had been compiled and the detectives, supported by police marksmen from the Yard's tactical firearms unit, were just waiting for the robbers to make their move.

From monitoring the gang's previous Tuesday excursions from their base in Dulwich, south-east London, detectives believed they were very likely to attack the van at Woodhatch although they could not be certain. Within the surveillance period the robbers had also taken a keen and unwholesome interest in the routines of two other security vans as they made weekly delivery rounds in Otford, Kent and Crawley, Sussex. Any of the three vans could have been the target. But on the evening of 26 November, the squad was given a strong hint that the robbery was to take place the following day on the Woodhatch 'plot'. That night, one of the gang members had driven a stolen car to a secluded spot near Woodhatch, which detectives were convinced was intended as an alternative getaway vehicle. They reasoned that the gang, instead of making their way back to London in the vehicle used for the robbery, which the police would be looking for, would switch cars in mid-journey.

So the early hours of 27 November saw a well-rehearsed strategic plan swing into action. It was marshalled by Detective Chief Inspector Mike Brooker and involved eight vehicles and more than thirty police officers, fourteen of them armed with 9 mm Browning semi-automatic pistols, Smith and Wesson .38 revolvers, or 7.62 calibre rifles. Brooker had secured the use of two adjacent first-floor flats overlooking the Woodhatch service station and its environs. From this vantage point he could watch the drama unfold and issue instructions to the rest of the troops over his radio.

Immediately he saw the red Nissan truck charge towards the security guards Brooker knew the game was on and shouted the order: 'Attack! Attack! Attack!' This was the signal for four squad cars, each containing a driver, a squad detective and two firearms officers, and two unarmed surveillance cars to advance immediately to the scene. The vehicles had been dotted around the location in anticipation of the robbery attempt and were supported by an attack van carrying a team of six more marksmen.

However, the police ambush was slightly thrown by the speed of the robbers' strike and the fact that the Nissan was not one of the many stolen vehicles the gang had previously used. It was unknown to the police, so they had not been able to track its movements prior to the raid. The result was that neither of the first two police cars on the scene after the attack order was given contained any armed officers. Both were surveillance vehicles containing unarmed squad detectives, one of which had been following the security van at a discreet distance. The other had been cruising the roads around the garage looking for suspicious activity. For the first few seconds of the ambush, four desperate robbers armed with revolvers, semi-automatic pistols and a pump action shotgun were confronted by three policemen without so much as a truncheon between them.

Displaying remarkable courage, Detective Sergeant Terry Hobbs drove his unmarked black saloon right up to the bumper of the Nissan, into which 'Reagan' and 'Afro' had now climbed back, both waving their guns. Then, having prevented them from driving off the forecourt, Hobbs got out of his vehicle and dived for cover. Meanwhile the other surveillance car, containing Detective Sergeants Christopher Smith and Donald Mackenzie, was driven hard against the front of the Securicor van to block the hijack attempt.

Moments later the artillery arrived and took over the attack. Marksmen William Hughes and John Benson drew up alongside the Nissan in their Ford Granada attack car. Hughes flung open the Nissan passenger door to be met by 'Reagan', levelling his 9 mm semi-automatic pistol. Hughes shot him once in the abdomen. Almost simultaneously Benson, believing his partner to be under attack, took up position at the front left of the car and shot 'Reagan' a second time, through the glass of the passenger side window. The rifle bullet hit him in the mouth and pierced his skull. He died instantly. 'Afro', in the driving seat, still with gun in hand, was hit in the shoulder by a second rifle round and slumped to the ground through the open door.

The two robbers in the Securicor van, realising the strength and ferocity of the opposition, quickly surrendered, but not before one of the police marksmen, fearing a hostage situation might develop, fired several shots at the bearded robber sitting in the front of the van. He was uninjured.

It had been a quintessential Flying Squad operation: long in the planning and breathtakingly rapid in the execution. From the time the Nissan appeared on the scene to the moment the final robber surrendered less than two minutes had elapsed. The time was now 9.59 a.m.

A man was dead, never a cause for celebration, but the policeman who killed him had been faced with little option but to fire. Firearms officers are trained to fire only when another life is in imminent danger, but once they decide to shoot they do not shoot to wound – they shoot to kill. In general terms the ambush, codenamed Operation Yamato after a celebrated Japanese military tactician of the Second World War, had been an outstanding success.

Now that the scene had been made secure, it was time for the squad detectives to unmask and de-wig the robbers to find out who was who. They had a good idea of the general make-up of the team but because of the disguises they still did not know who they had shot.

The dead man behind the Reagan mask proved to be Kenny Baker, at forty-five the eldest member of the gang. Kenny had been a well-known north London 'face' and had previous convictions for robbery and firearms offences. His close criminal association with the other three gang members, all from south-east London, had been relatively recent.

Next, a detective wiped some of the boot-black from the face of 'Afro' and removed his hairpiece and spectacles to reveal thirty-nine-year-old Mehmet Arif. He had clearly feared that something might go wrong with the robbery because he was wearing body armour. It had not saved him from a nasty shoulder wound but would have fended off a potentially more deadly shot. 'Hallowe'en' turned out to be his younger brother, Dennis Arif, thirty-four, and the fourth man was their brother-in-law, Anthony Downer, forty-three.

These were armed robbers of the highest calibre and the arrests prompted celebrations back at the south-east area Flying Squad office near Tower Bridge, from which Operation Yamato had been conceived and planned. The Arifs belonged to the most heavily investigated criminal 'firm' since the Krays, and to catch two of them red-handed on the same day was seen as a major achievement. Where the Krays were intensely territorial and specialised in extortion and racketeering, the Arifs were mobile. From a family of Turkish Cypriots who settled in Rotherhithe in the 1950s, they were principally interested in armed robbery and had developed it into something of an art. According to a confidential Flying Squad report on Operation Yamato, the convictions of Dennis and Mehmet Arif and the conviction, five months later on separate charges of another Arif brother, Bekir, another brother-in-law and three of their associates following a second squad ambush in Norwood, south-east London, 'ended an era of criminality'.

In a spirit of extraordinary optimism, given that he was caught holding three guards at gunpoint in the back of a security van loaded with cash, Dennis Arif pleaded not guilty to conspiracy to rob and his case was heard at the Old Bailey during November and December 1991. His defence was that Kenny Baker, to whom he owed £60,000, had threatened to kill him if he did not take part. The trial was accompanied by security measures normally seen only in the most sensitive terrorist cases, with armed officers guarding the court and full searches carried out on all those who entered. A special seventy-two-man police squad was set up to give twenty-four-hour protection to the twelve jurors.

Mr Michael Stuart-Moore, prosecuting, gave some indication of the perceived dangers posed by the Arif family in his pre-trial argument. He described them as a family of 'considerable influence in terms of money and muscle'. Making a formal request for jury protection, he told judge Heather Steel: 'There is every likelihood if protection is not granted that the defendant's family, or associates, will attempt to interfere one way or another with jury. They have done it before and they are quite capable of doing it again.'

Mr Stuart-Moore was referring to an alleged attempt to bribe and intimidate the jury in a previous trial involving Dennis Arif, who was jointly accused with his brother Bekir of an armed robbery conspiracy in Bromley in 1981. In the second week of the Old Bailey trial, a fourth Arif brother, Michael, was seen outside court at about 4.00 p.m. 'with a heavily built man', apparently waiting for the jury to leave. A black BMW car was observed cruising slowly down a nearby street with two more men inside. As the jury emerged, the car moved slowly in their direction.

'It seemed that at that stage Michael Arif spotted police watching him, and he and his associate jumped into the BMW and they all drove away,' Mr Stuart-Moore said. 'The registration number was taken and later the man whose car it was gave evidence in the defence of Bekir Arif.' More concrete evidence of a plot to 'nobble' the jury came the following day when an unknown woman approached a female juror as she made her way home on the underground and offered her money to engineer a verdict of not guilty against the Arif brothers.

The juror did not speak to the woman but reported the bribe attempt to the court the next day. She was given police protection, along with four other jurors who felt vulnerable. At the end of the trial, the jury could not agree on verdicts and the female juror who had been approached subsequently broke down in tears and admitted to police that although she was convinced of the Arifs' guilt she had pressed for their acquittal because she was terrified. As well as the woman on the underground, she had been intimidated by a large man who had fixed his gaze on her from the public gallery of the court throughout the case.

A retrial was ordered a few weeks later, this time with full jury protection from the outset. Both Arif brothers were convicted on what Mr Stuart-Moore called 'overwhelming' evidence. Bekir, who had recently come out of prison following a five-year sentence for an earlier armed robbery, was jailed for twelve years and Dennis for eleven, reduced to nine years on appeal.

The four aforementioned Arif brothers do not constitute the whole picture: there are seven in all. In descending order of age they are Yusuf (born April 1945), Ozer (born September 1947), Dogan (born February 1949), Mehmet (born December 1950), Bekir (born September 1953), Dennis (born April 1956) and Michael (born March 1961). Their sister, Susan, is the common-law wife of Anthony Downer, arrested with Mehmet and Dennis at Woodhatch.

Dogan, the former manager of the Vauxhall Conference League soccer club Fisher Athletic, was sentenced to nine years for drug trafficking in December 1990 following a surveillance operation by HM Customs. Two of his wife's brothers, Peter and Terry Cunningham, are currently serving eight and sixteen years respectively for conspiracy to steal, conspiracy to rob and firearms offences.

Ozer, who has bar, restaurant and other business interests, was acquitted in 1977 of the murder of a security guard in an armed robbery on a Securicor van on the A2 near Dartford, Kent, during which £103,000 was stolen. (Bekir was convicted of armed robbery during the same trial.) Ozer had previously had a number of relatively insignificant convictions, including one in December 1975 for a minor role in a west London bank robbery. Yusuf, eldest of the seven brothers, is the only one not to have been the subject of police attention.

It is also worth noting that during a secret eighteen-month Scotland Yard surveillance operation centred on the Arifs and their associates in 1981–2, codenamed Operation Kate, a south London robber called Michael McAvoy was photographed with a member of the Arif family. McAvoy was jailed for twenty-five years in 1984 for his part in the £26 million Brinks-Mat gold bullion robbery, still Britain's biggest proven robbery.

Dennis Arif's implausible yarn about being forced to bear arms and rob the Woodhatch Securicor van on pain of death cut little ice with the jury when he appeared at the Old Bailey in late 1991. At the end of the two-week trial, they took just over an hour to return unanimous guilty verdicts on the charges of conspiracy to rob and possession of a firearm with intent. The judge said Dennis, who gave his occupation as self-employed jeweller, was 'likely to have been the ringleader' and gave him two concurrent twenty-two-year sentences. Mehmet, described as a restaurateur, and Downer, a builder, had both pleaded guilty and were each sentenced to eighteen years on similar charges. As the three men went down the steps from the dock to the cells, Downer's parting words to the judge were: 'Thank you. Happy Christmas.'

The severity of the sentences reflected an understanding that the defendants came from the hard core of professional robbers to whom the sawn-off shotgun and .38 Special are tools of the trade. Characterised by nerve, cunning and resourcefulness, they regard arrest and imprisonment as occupational hazards and the infliction of injury on uncooperative opponents as sometimes unavoidable. But the potential profits are enormous. As the judge put it in her comments before sentence: 'You were playing for very high stakes.'

To combat this élite of organised crime, the police have had to display the same qualities as their quarry. Their planning needs to be thorough, their surveillance equipment of the highest quality, their nerve strong and, where possible, they must seek out inside information. In London and its outskirts, home base of the vast majority of Britain's most audacious bandits, the suppression of armed robbery is the task of the Flying Squad. The squad has set the standard by which the CID in this country has developed. Its detectives were the first in Britain to be assigned motor cars, the first to have radios, the first to be allowed to travel freely throughout the Metropolitan Police district without regard for divisional boundaries, the first to have a separate criminal intelligence section and the prime movers in the development of the 'supergrass' system. Squad officers were, and by some assessments still are, the *crème de la crème* of Scotland Yard's specialist operations department.

Since the late 1970s their efforts have been concentrated on the investigation of attacks on banks, building societies, security vans, jewellery shops, post offices and bookmakers. But for half a century before that they roamed across London, investigating whatever crimes took their fancy, without any real external supervision. Almost straight from their creation at the end of the First World War, they captured the public imagination. In 1924 Edgar Wallace wrote a thriller about them and four years later the composer J. Ord Hume penned a vigorous march tune in their honour.

Over the years, despite being racked in the 1970s by corruption scandals, the squad retained considerable popularity, and even have their own nickname in Cockney rhyming slang, the Sweeney (short for Sweeney Todd). The television series *The Sweeney*, which portrayed two squad detectives, Regan and Carter, as workaholic, hard-drinking, foul-mouthed, womanising cynics, was one of the most viewed drama series of the 1970s. 'It was sheer observation from the squad officers I knew,' said the series creator, Ian Kennedy-Martin. 'They had flaws but they were seen as an élite, a loose cannon against organised crime. They also seemed much brighter and much more clued up than the average policeman and had a good line in gallows humour. I suppose the series tried to explain that it was tough on the streets and that these were the men at the sharp end.'

In 1993 the squad, known at Scotland Yard by its branch code, SO8, comprises around 200 detectives and civilian staff working from four major area offices across London with almost unlimited access to a full range of motor vehicles and regular back-up from the tactical firearms and specialised criminal intelligence units. When first formed as a 'mobile patrol experiment' seventy-five years earlier, the squad consisted of twelve detectives borrowed from divisional police stations who had to make do for transport with two horse-drawn covered wagons. This book charts the development of the Flying Squad between those eras.

2
Backdrop

In the first week of October 1918, twelve Metropolitan detectives were summoned to Scotland Yard for a secret conference. Drawn from all areas of the capital, they had been selected for their familiarity with the arcane ways of the underworld, their proven abilities as 'thief-takers' and, above all, their physical toughness.

Presiding over the meeting was Chief Detective Inspector Frederick Porter Wensley, unquestionably the most distinguished CID officer of his generation. Born of Somerset yeoman stock, Wensley, then fifty-three, had a reputation as a hard, austere man and had spent twenty-five years serving in the East End before being posted to Scotland Yard in 1916. His career in the Metropolitan Police had begun in Whitechapel in 1887. In his first months of duty he had been one of the many uniformed constables assigned to assist the CID in the notorious Jack the Ripper murder investigation. The fact that the Ripper was never caught rankled with Wensley throughout his working life and the investigation of murder and other violent crime became an obsession.

He had one of the most impressive arrest records of the age and, in 1909, he became the first detective to be awarded the King's Police Medal. He won further praise and commendations two years later for courage under fire during the siege of Sidney Street, in which police and a platoon of Scots Guards fought a gun battle with two anarchists who had holed themselves up in a house in the East End. When one of his junior detectives was wounded, he rushed immediately into the street under heavy fire to save him. With the help of another junior officer, he was able to carry his

11

man to safety and the incident, depicted as a stirring case of leadership by example, made him a popular hero both inside and outside the police force. In the years to follow, he would become the first Detective Chief Superintendent at the Yard and later the first career detective to achieve chief constable rank. By the time he retired in 1929, he was head of all London's CID.

Journalists of the 1920s nicknamed him 'The Ace' and a retrospective *Daily Express* report of 1934 described him as:

> a terror to old-time East End gangsters. Stocky, bird-like, close cropped, slow of speech, brusque of manner; wears a stand-up stiff collar, [bowler] hat a size too small; a gourmet, hates publicity. Crooks call him, affectionately, 'Fred'.

When the twelve detectives called to the Yard for that October meeting realised that Wensley was involved, they would have known their mission was to be one of great importance. This belief would have been further reinforced when they saw the man at his side, Detective Inspector Walter Hambrook.

A man of Kent who had joined the Met at the turn of the century, Hambrook was of a more relaxed demeanour than his boss but his arrest record, too, was prodigious. A *Daily Telegraph* special correspondent's contemporary report described him as:

> the ideal officer. Quiet in speech, happy looking and primly dressed, he suggests amiable docility; but mention criminals to him and he becomes a very different man. He carries a cane, which, for celerity and sureness in action, he will back against a criminal's jemmy or automatic pistol.

After ushering the assembled men into an unmarked office and posting a guard outside the door, Wensley began to address them on the prevailing state of criminal activity in the capital. His tone was grave as he detailed alarming increases in robbery, house-breaking and racketeering. He offered an equally grim prognosis of the shape of things to come.

Of special concern were the growing signs that the end of the First World War was imminent. Armistice appeared to be close and the consequent demobilisation would release legions of battle-hardened Allied troops from the bloody theatres of the campaign. It was clear that many of these veterans would return to England embittered by their experiences. After suffering the horrors and privations of trench warfare, the returning warriors would expect to be welcomed with dignity and gratitude by their nation, if not as heroes. At worst they would hope to resume life as they had left it, in something approaching the relative prosperity of pre-war Britain.

What many would find was abject disappointment. The war had left world trade in a shambles, bringing in its wake a slump of proportions previously unimagined in Britain. In the days before the development of the Welfare State, this could only mean poverty for the massed ranks of the unemployed. Wensley told his detectives that bitterness would lead to anger and that that anger would be expressed by some fundamentally decent men in crime. Indeed, some soldiers who had already been released or deserted from the Front had turned to criminal activity to support themselves and their families.

In addition to the homecoming veterans, there was a new generation of young criminals whose strict parental control had been relaxed while their fathers were fighting for King and country. Encouraged by more experienced lags, deserters and profiteers, they had been easily lured into criminality and would not readily return to honest endeavour.

The net result of this social dislocation was already being seen in one of the first definable crime waves in post-Victorian London. Although the figures involved seem almost laughably low in a city which now experiences a million crimes a year, they were treated with all due seriousness by the police leadership of the time. Between 1915 and 1918, burglary, robbery, extortion, shop-breaking and offences against property involving violence had risen from 7,384 to 11,224 – an increase of more than fifty per cent. Theft, embezzlement, fraud and receiving stolen goods rose by almost 9,000 offences in the same period to a 1918 total of 71,979, according to the Met annual report of 1918.

Gang fights were commonplace in the traditional criminal areas of the East End, south London and the fringes of the City as different family-based groups grappled for territory. In and around Soho, a disparate group of unscrupulous Londoners, French 'apaches', Italians and east European emigrés competed for the lucrative proceeds to be made from vice.

In addition a war of growing ferocity was being fought out on the country's racecourses, with Epsom and Ascot, both tracks then under the jurisdiction of Scotland Yard for major meetings, experiencing the worst of the trouble. For important fixtures like the Derby and Royal Ascot, the mobs would muster from as far away as Leeds and Birmingham in a ritual flexing of muscle. On their home patches, the gangs' territories were fairly clearly defined and, in general, each gang would recognise the sovereignty of others in their given localities. At the racecourses no such protocol applied. Each meeting was a new adventure and a chance to 'mix it' with the enemy on neutral ground.

On the trains and buses carrying the punters to the racetracks the gangs would pick pockets or fleece ingenuous 'mugs' with variations on the three-card trick. At their destination, they would divide into con-men and enforcers, the former creating a sideshow of gambling pursuits to divert the spectators between races. Lottery wheels, box and ball games and 'housey-housey' stalls would be erected to tempt the gullible. All the games would have one thing in common – they were fixed.

But the real business of the day was engaged around the bookmakers' stalls. Here, the gangs' hard men would carve out spheres of influence in which they alone were allowed the privilege of 'protecting' the bookmakers *in situ* – for an appropriate fee, of course. The bookmakers were obliged to pay the fee if they wished to carry out their business unmolested. The best pitches went to the toughest gangs and the only way to work out the pecking order from meeting to meeting was by combat. Like fighting birds circling one another in a cockpit, the gangs would tread warily to begin with, sizing up the competition before wading in with iron bars, knuckledusters, coshes and occasionally firearms to determine supremacy by brute strength.

It was a war fought, at that time, largely beyond the control of the police, as even the most seriously wounded victims would seldom inform on their attackers. What was required was inside information. While Wensley stressed the need to bring the racecourse gangs to heel in the interests of public order, he conceded that most of their victims were either themselves of the criminal fraternity or dupes who became involved with their gambling swindles out of greed.

Far more worrying, politically, was the rising tide of house-breaking in the genteel suburbs and domestic burglary in the more affluent areas of central London. Here the victims were the middle classes – the natural supporters of law and order and the most voluble and influential critics of the police when they themselves came under attack. Similarly, commercial burglary had doubled in the three years since 1915 to almost 6,000 offences, and the business community was demanding action.

Such offences were increasingly being committed by travelling criminals rather than the old-style 'hooks' and 'blaguers', who would seldom stray far from their home patch and were comparatively easy prey for the diligent local detective. The Metropolitan Police was often hamstrung in dealing with mobile thieves and robbers because of deficiencies in its organisational structure and territorial jealousies. Each police division was run by a uniformed superintendent who regarded his plot as a fiefdom – and God help the officer who was caught pursuing inquiries on an alien division without specific permission, which was rarely given.

This imperialism worked in the favour of any thief who was prepared to broaden his geographical horizons. If he was not caught in the act while working away from home, the chances were that he would not be caught at all.

Most itinerant villains would travel to their targets by public transport, bicycle or horse and carriage, but a handful of the more enterprising and successful were beginning to realise that the purchase or theft of a motor car could bring untold returns. The Metropolitan Police annual report of 1918 made reference to 'frequent' thefts of motor cars and vans in London, blaming the problem partly on the 'carelessness' of owners and partly on the lack of a proper registration system. It is unclear exactly how many cars were stolen in that year (Scotland Yard did not publish specific car theft figures until 1921) or how many of those cars were used in subsequent crimes, but Wensley was well aware of the criminal potential of the motor age and the force's weaknesses, which he had first brought to the attention of Assistant Commissioner Sir Basil Thompson in 1916.

Wensley favoured a roving band of detectives under central command, who could transcend the parochialism of the divisional superintendent and attack the criminal wherever he roamed. He recounted an experiment some years earlier in which a small central unit had been set up at Scotland Yard to tackle an increase in counterfeiting in London. The squad had been deemed a great success after breaking up the two principal gangs of 'coiners' but had been disbanded when the problem was thought to have receded. Wensley argued that a comparable squad with appropriate transport and a brief to tackle all major crime was now overdue.

Sir Basil was sympathetic to Wensley's views but, with the war still dominating the body politic of the country, he was unwilling to recommend such a giant stride at that moment. A London-wide squad, possibly with eventual national implications, might conjure up totalitarian images to a public conditioned to seeing the police as a generally devolved confederation of local forces dealing with local problems.

For the time being, then, Wensley and his CID colleagues, whose ranks were already depleted because so many officers had volunteered for war service, were told there would be no new initiatives and no new recruitment. The war effort was paramount and they would have to make do with what they had.

Two years later, the political climate, the Commissioner of the metropolis and the public perception of rising crime had changed. The new Commissioner, General Nevil Macready, late of the Gordon Highlanders and a veteran of the Egyptian campaign of 1882, took office on 4 September 1918. The son of an actor, he was the latest in a line of soldiers and colonial servants to be handed the reins at Scotland Yard. It was not until well after the Second World War that the government would come to regard a career policeman as suitable material for the commissionership, despite the failure of many soldiers and imperial administrators to come to grips with the mechanics and the singular pressure of heading Britain's largest police force.

Macready inherited a force in profound crisis. His two immediate predecessors had had uncomfortable rides and had been forced to quit Scotland Yard in ignominious circumstances. The man he succeeded, Sir Edward Henry, a former inspector general of police in Bengal under the Raj, had taken over as Commissioner in 1902 from another professional soldier, Sir Edward Bradford.

Bradford was a superannuated warhorse who had served the Army with distinction during the Indian Mutiny and Persian Wars. In his younger days he had had a penchant for tiger hunting, which was curbed only when one of his intended bags had the temerity to fight back and bit off his left arm. From then on he confined himself to pig-sticking, holding the lance with his remaining hand and the reins of his mount in his teeth. Flamboyant and brave the one-armed hero may have been, but a successful commissioner he was not. After only a few months his competence and interest in his post began to be questioned in the press and within three years he was ousted by the Home Secretary.

Henry, a more reflective figure with a strong administrative background, was seen as a welcome change within the Home Department. He showed considerably more willingness and aptitude for his new task than the gallant Bradford but he too was to learn the hard way that running Scotland Yard was a world away from being a mandarin in the colonies.

Having survived an assassination attempt in 1912, he became rather withdrawn and his failure to keep abreast of the feelings and needs of his men certainly contributed to the acrimonious police strike of August 1918, which brought his downfall.

The would-be assassin was a man with a history of mental instability who had recently been refused a licence by the police to drive a taxi cab. He focused his deranged anger on the Commissioner, lay in wait for him and shot him as he stood by his car near Scotland Yard. Fortunately for Henry, the bullet wound was not fatal and the attacker was quickly overpowered. Henry, though shaken by the attack, believed it could have the positive effect of improving morale and respect for senior authority among his men, bringing home to them that all members of the force, including the Commissioner, were subject to the same risks. He was mistaken.

The strike, the most serious in the history of the police service, followed a claim for increased allowances by the National Union of Police and Prison Officers. The union, the forerunner of the Police Federation and regarded by officialdom at the time as a rallying point for subversive elements in the force, also demanded recognition as a legitimate negotiating body. When these demands were not met, half the constables and sergeants in London went on strike, besieging police stations and harassing their colleagues who had remained at work.

After three days of London being virtually unpoliced, the government yielded. The Prime Minister, David Lloyd George, gave a personal assurance to look sympathetically at the strikers' demands and Commissioner Henry was duly persuaded to resign.

When General Macready was sworn in as his successor, it was made clear to him that his twin priorities should be to nip any further industrial problems in the bud and to put the brake on rising crime. His strategy for quelling the dissent which had led to the strike was to win over the moderate elements in the force and gradually to dismiss the agitators. This would take a little over a year and was to prove an unqualified success. The union called another strike in August 1919 but this time only six per cent of the force responded. The strikers were dismissed and the union broken once and for all. It was dissolved and replaced by the officially sanctioned and more moderate Police Federation.

One of Macready's first tactics for turning back the crime wave, activated within six weeks of his arrival at Scotland Yard, was to embrace Wensley's proposal for a travelling detective unit. The meeting of October 1918 launched what was initially known as 'the mobile patrol experiment'. The twelve detectives summoned by Wensley would be seconded to Scotland Yard by their divisional superintendents and would form a team which would try to get to the root of London crime. Each had specialist knowledge of habitual criminals in his own area and, led at ground level by Hambrook, they would be given a free hand to patrol when, where and how they chose. Their only obligation was to get results.

The first transport for this revolutionary unit was less than glamorous. There were only two motor cars attached to the Metropolitan Police in 1918, both 10 h.p. Wolseleys with six-seater wagonette bodies. One was at the disposal of the Commissioner, the other of the Scotland Yard Receiver. The new unit would have to make do with a horse-drawn covered wagon rented from the Great Western Railway.

3
Beginnings

Early in 1919, just a few weeks after the signing of the Armistice which ended the Great War, Hambrook and the twelve detectives assigned to the mobile patrol experiment made their first foray from their headquarters at Scotland Yard.

The confidentiality of their new role was impressed upon them and information about their activities was to be made available strictly on a need-to-know basis. If their purpose were to become widely broadcast, it would be only a short time before their intended prey were alerted and placed on their guard. The detectives even went through the motions of signing on at the police stations from which they were seconded before travelling to the Yard to begin their real duties.

The covered wagon, looking like any one of thousands of commercial carriers trundling through the streets of London at the time, was driven out of the station yard at the back of Whitehall by two PCs in plain clothes. In the back, concealed behind the tarpaulin cover, were the detectives, squatting on bench seats and keeping watch through spy holes cut in the canvas.

Their *modus operandi* was to travel to an agreed location where crooks were said to be operating and cruise the streets looking for suspicious activity or known 'faces'. When a potential target was spotted, one or more of the detectives would get out and follow on foot. If a crime was seen in action, the officers would try to make their arrests at a distance from the wagon to maintain its anonymity. Despite its surveillance function, the wagon was essentially a means of transporting the detectives unobtrusively to their areas of interest. Most of the real work was still done on foot.

When not patrolling, the men were expected to visit criminal haunts, often pubs and other drinking dens, in an attempt to glean information. Although each detective had been selected for his knowledge of criminals on his particular division, the disadvantage of his previous successes was that he was probably too well known by members of his local underworld to move among them anonymously. It was therefore quite common for one of the twelve to identify a likely meeting place of thieves or robbers on his plot and for one of his colleagues from another police division to be sent inside to test the water. When a promising line of inquiry presented itself a decision was made by the detective concerned whether to go it alone, or to call on the wagon for support.

If a gang of pickpockets became the target, for example, and their next destination was known, the wagon could be of considerable use. The scene of operation would invariably be a place where a large crowd was gathered – a football match, racecourse, or exhibition of some kind – and more than one officer would be required to keep track of the thieves. The wagon could follow the gang, who would normally travel on public transport, and drop off a number of detectives where appropriate. If the gang members began their work on trams or buses on the way to their destination, up to twelve policemen would be on hand to tackle them. Where one officer might have been relatively easily beaten back, a group was a much tougher proposition.

In its first year of operation, 1919–20, the mobile patrol experiment recorded notable successes. While exact figures on the arrests they made in that period were not published, pickpocket offences and other thefts from the person were brought down to below their pre-war levels, theft in general showed a seven per cent decrease against a previously rising trend and the rates of increase of burglary and house-breaking (which differed from burglary for recording purposes only in that it was committed by day rather than by night) had been held down. The unit was credited with having made a significant contribution and was thought to have secured convictions against some of the worst habitual offenders.

The experimental period was extended and it was not long before the subject of improving the squad's transport and communications was raised. The wagons (a second had been provided a few months after the experiment began) were fine for surveillance duties and commuting between engagements, but they were ungainly and slow. It was successfully argued that the squad was at the forefront of the Yard's detective work and that the wagons had passed their sell-by date in an era in which the car was becoming a widespread mode of transport for public, criminals and police alike.

In mid-1920, the Metropolitan Police still had only six motor vehicles – the two cars used by the Commissioner and the Receiver and four dispatch vans. By July of that year two more had been bought for the exclusive use of the mobile patrol experiment. The 'new' machines were hardly state-of-the-art. Public funds were tight and it was not considered cost-effective to invest in brand new cars or vans to equip London's first motorised squad. With the end of the war, a seemingly endless supply of military goods which had become surplus to requirements was finding its way on to the home market. The goods were cheap and could be delivered immediately.

So it was that two Crossley motor tenders were bought from the Royal Flying Corps and delivered in due course to Hambrook and his men. Generally speaking, one vehicle would be used to patrol the London streets north of the Thames and the other south of the river. The tenders made their first outings in July 1920 and it could be said that it was then that the Flying Squad was truly born. Within a few weeks, the squad would be christened with the name it still bears today. The epithet was first published in the *Daily Mail* by the newspaper's aptly named crime reporter, G. T. Crook, following a series of highly praised arrests.

It was probably inspired partly by the Royal Flying Corps link and partly by the relative speed at which the squad was able to get around now its transport had been updated. The nickname stuck and was adopted officially the following year. On 22 September 1920, in a ten-paragraph article headlined 'Motor Car Detectives', Crook wrote:

> . . . Flying squads of picked detectives, with motor transport at their disposal, were based at police headquarters ready to go

23

anywhere at any time ... A vigilant watch was kept on old criminals and very important steps were taken to obtain a thorough knowledge of the many young men who have just embarked on a career of crime.

The results of these 'live' operations have been remarkably successful. During the past two months, scores of the most daring and dangerous criminals in London have been caught. They have been picked up by the flying squads at all hours of the day and night, some while actually engaged on a burglarious enterprise ... Criminals of all grades have had scarcely a moment's peace. They have been kept on the run all the time. By their new methods the detectives have fulfilled their primary duty of preventing crime – which is of infinitely more value and importance than the detection of crime – and thousands of pounds' worth of property has been saved.

In fact the tenders, welcome as they were to the detectives who used them, could often be outrun by the cars being purchased or stolen in increasing numbers by career criminals, particularly 'smash and grab' raiders and bank and post office robbers. The Crossleys had no front brakes, their thin wheels and tyres made for unwieldy handling, they were heavy, noisy and had a top speed of little more than 40 m.p.h. – and then only with a friendly gradient and following wind. Like the wagons they replaced, they had canvas hoods on the back which could hide up to a dozen officers.

The squad now comprised Hambrook as senior Detective Inspector, three other inspectors, four sergeants, eight constables and two drivers. Hambrook remained in operational charge of the squad with Wensley as the overall authority. In his autobiography, *Hambrook of the Yard*, he gives a flavour of the mobile criminal of the day. Given the frequency of violent crime in 1920 compared with 1993, his assessment now seems a little hysterical, but it is a measure of the alarm felt throughout society at the time about the post-war crime wave:

They launched themselves into all sorts of wickedness. Luxurious motor cars left unattended in busy streets were always available for their use. It was so easy to steal a fast and valuable car and to abandon it after it had served its purpose of carrying them swiftly and unsuspiciously to and from the scene of crime. The spirit of adventure increased as the risk of capture decreased and there was an unlimited area of operation.

Householders in town and country were terrorised by masked burglars; post offices were raided during the day and night and brave but helpless girl assistants were threatened at the point of a revolver; men and women cashiers were knocked down and robbed in crowded streets; banks were held up by armed thugs; defenceless women had their handbags torn from their grasp as they walked quietly homeward; jewellers in Bond Street and elsewhere were forced to put up stout steel grilles to guard against smash and grab raids; warehouses were stripped of valuable furs and silks and other merchandise; safe-breakers found it comparatively easy to transport heavy oxy-acetylene cutting apparatus; rival racecourse gangs blackmailed bookmakers and cut one another's throats; motorists were waylaid and threatened with death if they showed resistance; garages were pillaged for petrol, oil and cash; police officers were shot with automatic pistols and a few were murdered.

Such was the deplorable state of crime which the authorities had to combat and subdue . . . For practical purposes there [had been] no mobile force at all and criminals snapped their fingers at our impotent efforts to catch them.

The first major target, selected personally by Hambrook, was 'the Elephant and Camden gang', a band of travelling robbers and burglars who attacked houses and commercial premises all over London and the inner suburbs. They were so named because of their twin bases at the Elephant and Castle, a mile to the south of Southwark Bridge, and Camden Town, three miles to the north of Westminster.

One fully manned tender travelled to each location on a preliminary reconnaissance mission. They staked out the regular meeting places of the gang members and followed selected individuals. Two nights later they had identified the gang's southern hideout and began a twenty-four-hour watch on it.

Later that week, in the early hours of a humid Saturday morning in July, came the confrontation. A tender containing Hambrook and nine other detectives observed four members of the gang leaving a disused garage near the Old Kent Road. 'Tooled up' with crowbars, they climbed into an unmarked van and headed north. They were trailed to Westminster, where a further three gang members climbed into the van. The seven drove to a silversmith's shop in Victoria Street, where four of them took up positions as look-outs and the other three made towards the shop door with their crowbars.

Having 'cased' the shop, they apparently decided it was too well fortified to rob with ease, so they returned to the van and drove to a well-stocked clothier's store nearby. The police were not quick enough to stop the robbers returning to their vehicle and speeding off to the clothier's. However, the squad was lucky enough to have as one of its drivers a former transport officer from the Royal Flying Corps, Detective George 'Jack' Frost.

Frost had driven Crossleys through the muddy fields of France during the war, with shot and shell exploding around him. He was familiar with the vehicle's every feature, and driving on the hard roads of London, whatever the weather conditions, was as nothing compared to hacking across the Somme. Within seconds he had nosed in front of the van and forced it to a halt in Westbourne Street. Hambrook takes up the story:

A terrific thunderstorm broke. I jumped out of the back of our tender followed by all the other officers and opened the back door of the van. Before one could say Jack Robinson the men scrambled out armed with knuckledusters, loaded life-preservers (improvised coshes, usually socks filled with sand, or coins or other metal pieces) and daggers and attacked us right and left.

We suitably replied, and what with the thunder, the lightning and the rain and the yelling, it was small wonder that many of the residents flung open their bedroom windows to see the battle. I used my stick to great advantage but one of the men who shouted: 'Let's kill the blighter', managed to lay me low with his life-preserver. Another officer gave him tit for tat with a blow from his truncheon.

Hambrook escaped with relatively minor injuries and weight of numbers finally ensured victory for the squad. 'Not a single one of the criminals escaped. We bundled the whole lot into our tender and took them to Gerald Road [Belgravia] police station, where we must have presented a picturesque if bedraggled spectacle, with our clothes soaked with rain and our prisoners looking none too good after their encounter with our fists and truncheons.'

While these accounts may be thought to carry a hint of melodrama, they give a good idea of the physical qualities demanded of the squad officers at that time. Outside of large-scale public order incidents, it is almost unheard of in the 1990s for ten policemen to take on seven robbers in this type of street brawl, not least because it would be rare to find a group of seven robbers without a gun between them.

The Westminster magistrate, in committing the seven men for trial, said the capture was one of the most spectacular he had ever heard of. At the Old Bailey trial, the Flying Squad received the first of countless judge's commendations.

But it was not all blood and thunder. A less glamorised picture of the routine work of the team is given in the memoirs of Chief Inspector Frederick 'Nutty' Sharpe, who joined the Flying Squad in 1922 and rose to become its leader in the mid-1930s:

The two tenders used to patrol town all day and all night . . . Girls in Piccadilly and neighbourhood quickly observed us when we pulled up in the middle of the night and very quickly they would come round to find out just what this new fish was.

The driver, the only apparent occupant, had to do all the talking. He would tell them that we were a load of vegetables for Covent Garden or beef for Smithfield, or anything else that came into his head. Occasionally they would ask to be taken for a ride and he would have an embarrassing few moments getting rid of them. Meanwhile, we sat in the tender as quiet as mice.

We had a little light which could not be seen from outside

27

and we read by it. When things were particularly slack, the lads would play bridge while we waited for some alarm from the man keeping watch through the little hatch in the front of the van behind the driver.

When they were called upon in earnest, however, the squad detectives continued to impress their masters at the Yard with their prowess, and in 1923 they were honoured with another technological first in the annals of the British police service.

The first police telephone had been installed at Scotland Yard in 1888 and by 1918 there were emergency lines between headquarters and every divisional station in the capital. Once these installations were completed the Commissioner became interested in improving communications still further by utilising wireless radio-telegraphy, which had been invented in the 1890s and was eventually to revolutionise criminal investigation.

Five years after the rudimentary telephone system was completed, a fixed radio base was installed on the roof of Scotland Yard and a mobile receiver fitted to one of the Crossley tenders, making the Flying Squad not only the first police unit in Britain to be motorised but also the first to be able to send and receive radio messages while on the move, albeit only in Morse code to begin with. The receivers, which bore a remarkable resemblance to huge iron bedsteads, were clamped to the roof of the tender, the weight making it even slower and harder to manoeuvre than before. But the benefits more than made up for the disadvantages. Sharpe wrote:

What a change that little transmitter wrought in the business of catching crooks. One day the tenders were patrolling blind to what might be happening in the next street. The next, cruise where they might, they were in receipt instantaneously of whatever helpful information found its way into every department of the Metropolitan Police.

There wasn't then and never has been the much-dramatised 'calling all cars', such as we hear in films depicting the squad's American counterpart. Urgent messages are received just as efficiently in little dots and dashes which would be Greek to anyone successful in tuning into the Yard wavelength.

After initial tests proved successful, the second Crossley was also fitted with a bedstead aerial and the newly modified vehicles made their operational debut at the Epsom spring race meeting of 1923. By the middle of 1924, two more Crossleys had been purchased and the strength of the squad raised to thirty men.

Wensley continued to be the driving force behind squad policy and its chief supporter in official debates on funding and the procurement of new equipment. Despite the provision of transport and technical aids, however, he continued to stress to the men their individual responsibility for catching criminals. In 1929 he wrote:

> Facilities for quick information and instant action are of immense service . . . but it is a mistaken notion that fast cars, wirelesses, police boxes, or any other mechanical device can ever supersede the single detective. As a rule, the capture and conviction of a criminal must depend upon men and not upon things.
>
> The real function of the Flying Squad is very like that of all other detectives, to act upon information. Although its cars patrol the streets night and day, the percentage of criminals caught, so to speak, by accident, is ridiculous. The Flying Squad catches thieves because it knows thieves.

In keeping with this philosophy, the squad continued to admit to its ranks only those who had proven track records in divisional or central CID policing. Consequently it rapidly gained a reputation as the country's élite detective force, a reputation it held on to for at least fifty years, until the very familiarity with criminals so fostered by Wensley led to an abrupt downfall.

4
Early Opponents

Today, the Flying Squad is involved only in the investigation of serious armed robbery against banks, building societies, post offices, security vans, jewellers and betting shops. In the 1920s and for several decades thereafter, its brief was almost infinite. Any crime committed in London or the inner Home Counties which was regarded as a serious threat to the public well-being came within its remit. Wensley and Hambrook were determined that the new unit should develop into the cutting edge of the CID.

Wensley inspired admiration and loyalty from his troops for his dedication and work-rate. Always a committed detective, he had thrown himself into his work with even greater vigour in an attempt to come to terms with the tragedy of losing both his sons in the Great War. The younger son died of an illness shortly after the Armistice was signed without ever seeing active service.

Wensley was described by one former junior, Jack Capstick, who became a detective in 1926 and was to serve in the squad on and off for sixteen years, as:

one of the finest, if not the finest detective in the Metropolitan Police. A stout man, always smartly dressed and with extremely penetrating eyes, Wensley had a greater knowledge of thieves, their habits and their foibles than any other man in Britain. They feared him and if he entered a public house frequented by crooks of the underworld, there were always those who would gulp down their drinks and vanish within seconds.

Although he was a scrupulously fair man, Wensley also engendered a certain amount of fear among his own men, for he was a disciplinarian. He had no objection to his officers discarding their jackets on a hot day but always insisted that if they did so they must remove their braces. His comment: 'I expect you all to behave like gentlemen and you never see gentlemen in motor cars in their braces.' For Wensley, time had no meaning in the fight against crooks. If necessary, his men had to work around the clock without complaint and a fifteen-hour day was part of a normal routine.

Hambrook too demanded ever greater expertise and devotion from his men. He wrote:

The work of a Flying Squad officer demands many qualities of a high order. He must, of course, be thoroughly acquainted with criminals and their ways and have an unerring knowledge of criminal law and police procedure but beyond that he must have an unbounded love and unflagging enthusiasm for the work, be patient to endure many hours of silent watching and waiting, ever alert, stout-hearted, agile, cool in the presence of danger.

One of the first long-term tasks Wensley set for the squad in the 1920s was to tackle the race gangs, whose activities had now approached open warfare on tracks as far afield as Sandown Park, Uttoxeter, Goodwood and Bath. The most pressing problems were deemed to be at Ascot and Epsom. Chief Inspector Fred Sharpe remembered:

When we started looking into it at first, the sport of kings was more like the happy hunting-ground of knaves. There was scarcely any control of bookmakers; anybody could set up so long as he had a board and satchel, without any inquiry or fee. Welshing was common and regular mobs of thieves travelled to every meeting.
    Terrorism was carried out to such an extent that decent bookmakers and other racegoers were afraid to complain.

Gangs of pickpockets would surround punters placing bets. The bookmaker, who would recognise all of them as notorious characters, was expected to loiter about his work in order to give them an opportunity to pick his clients' pockets. If he didn't, a gang of thugs would rush in and knock bookmaker, stand and all flying.

By the spring of 1921, the situation was becoming desperate as the four main gangs – one from the East End, one from Leeds, one from Birmingham and the other a group of Italian toughs based around Clerkenwell and King's Cross, led by a particularly brutish immigrant named Darby Sabini – took up arms against each other with a ferocity that appalled the public of the day.

Their activities were no longer confined to the courses themselves. One of the leaders of the Birmingham mob was shot in London, having been lured to the capital on the pretext of 'peace talks' with the heads of both major London gangs. A junior member of the Sabini gang confessed to the shooting but it was widely believed he had been ordered to do so to protect his boss, the genuine culprit.

The Birmingham mob retaliated by attacking the east Londoners at Alexandra Park and later at a race meeting in Bath, where three men were beaten close to death with hammers and a gun was drawn by one of the victims in self-defence. Sabini himself was attacked at Greenford track by a dozen Birmingham men, escaping only after firing a shot into the ground in front of his assailants.

A bookmaker was murdered at Sandown Park, a policeman fatally injured in a mêlée at Epsom and a gunfight was played out at a Clerkenwell café frequented by members of the Italian gang in which one Sabini man was critically wounded. One of the East Enders was stabbed to death in Hampstead soon afterwards and as his funeral procession made its way through Aldgate, one of the mourners was slashed across the face with a razor in full view of a large crowd.

In the summer of 1921, on the last day of the Epsom Derby meeting, the Birmingham and Leeds mobs suffered a near-terminal setback, partly through prompt Flying Squad action but mainly because of a bizarre case of mistaken identity.

The two provincial gangs had formed a loose alliance and arranged to travel separately to Epsom Downs to launch a joint attack on the London gangs. The Birmingham contingent, numbering almost thirty, arrived first and set up an ambush next to the Brick Kiln public house in Ewell, a major staging-post on the way to the races. When they saw a large tender filled with men, they assumed it was one of their intended targets and attacked.

A fearful fight broke out, involving axes, iron bars, bricks and coshes, and casualties were heavy. It was not until some twenty men lay battered and bleeding in the street that the Birmingham mob realised they had waylaid their new allies from Leeds. The alliance had been so hastily arranged that the members of one gang did not recognise those of the other.

The Flying Squad had had intelligence that a battle was looming and were on the scene in minutes. They scooped up the wounded and a few stragglers at the scene and picked up the remainder a few miles away in Kingston-upon-Thames. Twenty-three men were eventually tried, convicted and imprisoned, bringing a temporary lull in racecourse hostilities.

Trouble was to break out again periodically up until the mid-1930s but the squad had begun to gain the upper hand and the situation was gradually brought under control. A few detectives were deployed full-time to combat pickpockets, both on and off the racecourses, and this eventually became a squad within the squad.

Just over a year after its victory at the races, the Flying Squad took on its first significant murder case in which the victim was not himself involved in the criminal fraternity. Although essentially a straightforward case of a wife conspiring with her lover to murder her husband, it was a murder which provoked enormous public comment and one which may never have been solved had the squad not been assigned to it.

Shortly after midnight on 4 October 1922, Percy Thompson, a thirty-two-year-old shipping clerk, was returning home to Ilford with his wife Edith after a night at the theatre. As the couple walked through a side-street less than a mile from their house an assailant wielding a knife burst out of the shadows. Edith was pushed to the side and Percy stabbed repeatedly in the back and neck. By the time help arrived, he had bled to death in the street. It was an apparently motiveless crime and Edith was unable to give any description of the attacker or describe the attack, which she said she must have blocked from her mind.

Wensley, recently promoted to Superintendent in charge of all central CID officers at Scotland Yard, was asked to take charge of the investigation and duly travelled to Ilford police station to begin his inquiries. He first interviewed Edith and although she still professed to remember nothing of the attack, she was not regarded as a suspect. Edith, aged twenty-eight, who managed a millinery wholesalers in the City of London, impressed Wensley. 'There was no doubt that her distress was genuine,' he remembered. 'She could scarcely have been called a pretty woman but she had a distinctly attractive personality. She carried herself well, was dressed tastefully and spoke with an air of culture. In moments of animation she must have been a woman of considerable fascination.'

It was not until the victim's brother was questioned that doubts began to grow in Wensley's mind. He spoke of a lodger, Frederick Bywaters, who had been staying at the Thompson home in Kensington Gardens, Ilford, and had struck up a strong relationship with Edith until Percy had objected to his familiarity and thrown him out. Edith was questioned again. Who was Bywaters? Why had she not mentioned him before? What had been the nature of her relationship with him? Edith remained calm. Bywaters was merely a boy of twenty she had known for many years and had helped out when he needed accommodation. He was a ship's writer, often away on voyages. She was not sure whether he was even in the country.

Further inquiries revealed that Bywaters was indeed in London but was about to leave on a foreign voyage any day. Wensley knew time was of the essence. If Bywaters was the killer, he would probably destroy any evidence of his crime before going to sea. Watch would have to be mounted immediately on all his known haunts. To do this through the normal channels would have required a series of requests and explanations to be passed to senior divisional detectives in various parts of London. At best the process would be slow. By using Flying Squad officers, then still the only detectives in the country outside the Special Branch who were unfettered by geographical barriers, Wensley was not obliged to contact anyone before launching the surveillance operation.

Within a few hours, Bywaters had been picked up at Edith's mother's house in Manor Park and escorted to Ilford police station. He had blood spots on his overcoat. As the young man was denying any knowledge of the murder and stressing the platonic and respectful nature of his relationship with Edith, another unit of Flying Squad officers entered his mother's house ten miles away in Upper Norwood, south-east London.

Mrs Bywaters took Detective Inspector Frank Page to Freddie's bedroom, where he uncovered six love letters from Edith, which left no doubt about the passion of their relationship and contained some significant undertones. One passage read: 'Yes darlint, you are jealous of him – but I want you to be. He has the right by law to all that you have the right to by nature and love. Yes darlint be jealous, so much that you will do something desperate ... Don't forget what we talked in the Tea Room. I'll still risk and try if you will.'

So, twenty-four hours after the stabbing, Wensley had two suspects, a motive, some slim circumstantial evidence and proof that Edith and Freddie had told some lies during questioning. However, he had nothing approaching proof of murder. The ace up his sleeve proved to be the fact that neither suspect had been told the other was in custody. When Edith caught sight of her lover in the interview room at Ilford police station, she sensed the game was up and dissolved into hysteria, crying: 'Why did he do it? I did not want him to do it. I must tell the truth.'

She gave a full statement admitting having seen Bywaters stab her husband and run off into the night. Although she did not admit her own involvement and Bywaters did not say anything to implicate her, both were charged with murder on the strength of the letters.

More of Edith's love letters were found among Bywaters' possessions on board his ship. They contained apparent references to previous unsuccessful attempts by Edith to poison her husband by putting arsenic and ground glass in his food. Percy's body was exhumed but no traces of poison were found.

Bywaters confessed to having killed Percy but there was still no evidence against Edith except the suggestions contained in the letters, which her counsel described as romantic fantasy. The Old Bailey jury, however, felt they were proof enough of conspiracy and both defendants were found guilty of murder and sentenced to death. Edith's case prompted a strong public cry for clemency but, in spite of a lengthy petition signed by many thousands of sympathisers, her appeal against conviction was refused. At dawn on 9 January 1923 Edith and Freddie were hanged, she at Holloway prison, he at Pentonville.

Wensley had little sympathy for either defendant. They had, he said, conspired jointly in 'a cruel and calculated murder in which it was hard to see a redeeming feature'. More significantly, he impressed upon his superiors at the Yard the indispensable role played by the Flying Squad in gathering and preserving the evidence which led to the convictions.

'I was in a position to see that instant action took place over a wide area without requests,' he said. 'Had Bywaters eluded us for twenty-four hours [he was caught about eighteen hours after the murder], he might have got away to sea and it is pretty safe to assume that the damning evidence which we ultimately managed to secure would have been destroyed and there would have been nothing to connect any person to the crime.

'Perhaps by this time he would have married Mrs Thompson and they would have been living in the odour of respectability in some neat little suburban villa.'

In its infancy, the squad was still in need of good internal public relations and the Thompson-Bywaters case did much both for its own image and for the concept of more freedom for the CID within the police. A few months later, the prestige of the squad was further enhanced by its leading role in the investigation during 1922 and 1923 of an unprecedented spate of commercial arson which had swept through scores of East End shops and warehouses owned mainly by Jewish businessmen.

Before the gang responsible was finally run to earth, some 300 fires had been raised, costing fifty insurance companies a total of

£250,000 in payouts to the apparent victims. Both the insurers and the police concluded that the fires were probably the result of traders trying to beat the economic slump by paying to have their own property burned out and making inflated insurance claims. But the fires were so skilfully set that no proof could be obtained.

Wensley took personal charge of the Flying Squad investigation, to which a number of experienced non-squad detectives were also seconded. Over a period of several months, a large body of circumstantial evidence was gathered against two men suspected of leading the arson gang. Joseph Engelstein and Julius Brust, both Jewish emigrés from Russia who had set up furniture businesses in east London, were known to have been in contact with several of the arson victims immediately before their premises were gutted and were also found to have made six insurance claims between them for mysterious fires at their own business premises and homes.

'These gentlemen, it was said, could arrange fires, or by way of variety fix up bogus burglaries, either for a fixed sum or for a percentage of the amount realised by the insurance,' said Wensley. 'A close watch was kept on the pair but although a great deal of moral proof was accumulated, for the time there was nothing on which we could act.'

On a May evening in 1923, Engelstein and Brust made a crucial, and almost fatal, mistake. They had approached a struggling cabinetmaker, James Bernard Stolerman, offering to burn down his factory in Columbia Road, Shoreditch to facilitate a bogus insurance claim. The building was insured for £3,700, enough to pay off Stolerman's creditors and start his business again from scratch. A bargain was struck and the three men went together to the premises. But for once, Engelstein's plans went sadly wrong.

In addition to placing his normal incendiary device in an appropriate part of the factory, Engelstein decided to make absolutely sure the building would be razed to the ground by spraying petrol around with a watering can. When a match was struck to light the incendiary fuse, it ignited the petrol fumes and created a premature explosion. The three men all suffered burns and were seen running from the blazing building by several witnesses, who were able to give full descriptions to the police.

Thanks to the thorough groundwork put in by the squad in previous months, the three were immediately identified from their descriptions, arrested the same night, charged and later convicted at the Old Bailey. Engelstein received six years but died before the end of his sentence and Brust four years, after which he was deported to Russia. Stolerman, also a Russian Jew, served five years but escaped subsequent deportation on the grounds that he had been a supporter of the White Russian cause and would be executed by the Bolsheviks if sent home.

Another intriguing early problem for the squad was an outbreak of cat burglary in two of the more exclusive areas of central London, Mayfair and St James's. The fashion for this type of crime appears to have been at its height in 1924 and Bob Fabian, then a young detective, who was to lead the squad during the Second World War, laid claim to having apprehended London's most daring and idiosyncratic cat burglar in that year.

According to Fabian's autobiography, *Fabian of the Yard*, which was later to be the basis for a singularly self-congratulatory television series, Robert Augustus Delaney was the quintessential cat burglar:

Delaney trod the crags and precipices of Park Lane's roofs with a nonchalant skill. Wearing faultless evening clothes, he could apparently climb the sheer side of a house. When the rich and noble residents of Park Lane were trooping splendidly into dinner, Delaney would crouch beneath their windows unwinding his gossamer rope . . . and robbed their bedrooms like a wraith and departed before coffee wafted fragrantly into the victim's drawing-room and cigar smoke hazed the wine.

In five weeks, Delaney, who carried a collapsible ladder concealed in a bundle of firewood, stole £30,000 in jewellery and cash in five separate raids, an enormous sum of money at the time. Flying Squad and local officers were told to concentrate on the case and surveillance was placed on a number of high-risk streets.

Fabian and a colleague were posted to keep watch on the streets at the back of the Ritz Hotel. After two nights, they saw a shadowy figure entering the gardens of a mansion block on Arlington Street. He vaulted a high fence and melted into the darkness. The two detectives gave chase, as quietly as possible, one alerting the residents and the other stalking around the outside of the building. The thief reappeared on the balcony a few minutes later and disappeared across the rooftops. 'All I had seen was the glint of a diamond stud in what was obviously a dress-shirt front,' Fabian wrote.

The next morning it was discovered that the burglar had managed to make off with jewellery worth £2,000 before being disturbed but had left two distinctive footprints on the balcony ledge. From the shape of the imprints, Fabian concluded that they had been formed by evening shoes. He was convinced the shoes must have been specially hand made, because the impression clearly showed the porous tread of crêpe soles, probably designed to give better grip than the smooth rubber soles normally used on dress shoes.

By a combination of dreary legwork and extraordinary good luck, Fabian found the maker within thirty-six hours. He had visited dozens of bespoke shoemakers in the Jermyn Street, Dover Street and Shepherd Market districts of Mayfair and St James's and finally found his man in Albemarle Street. The proprietor of the shop remembered having made the shoes for a customer because he had found it remarkable that 'any gentleman should require crêpe soles, however thin, on patent leather shoes', and was able to give Fabian the address immediately. Although it turned out to be a false name and the street number had been wrongly recorded, the street name was correct, and after a few further inquiries, Fabian tracked his suspect to an upstairs flat in Half Moon Street, off Piccadilly.

Delaney, of Canadian extraction, proved to be less glamorous than his working attire might have suggested – just another professional thief, although admittedly a nimble one, with big ideas. He received three years' imprisonment for the six Mayfair burglaries and by the time he died in Parkhurst twenty-four years later, he had been arrested and convicted so many times that he had spent almost twenty of the intervening years in police custody or in prison.

His initial successes inspired many imitators, two of whom fell to their deaths around the period of his arrest. That and other types of burglary, both residential and commercial, were to occupy a fair proportion of the squad's energies through the 1920s and 1930s. But it was as a mobile strike force against violent crime that their reputation was made. They became renowned for their physical courage against armed robbers and gangsters and in 1925 their status was assured with the publication of a novel by Edgar Wallace, the most popular thriller writer of his day, entitled *Flying Squad*.

Wensley was rewarded for his efforts in 1924 by being promoted to Chief Constable (CID), now roughly equivalent to Deputy Assistant Commissioner, a post specially created for him. One of his recommendations to Sir Basil Thompson in 1916, that the detective branch should be split into four super-regions, had come to fruition five years earlier and he had been placed in charge of the eastern quadrant, his spiritual home as a policeman. This was in addition to heading the central detective branch at Scotland Yard.

5
Permanent Status

The exploits of the squad continued to impress police, press and public through the early and mid-1920s and in 1927, a little over eight years after the mobile patrol experiment was launched, the Flying Squad became a permanent CID unit under the control of the Assistant Commissioner (Crime) at New Scotland Yard.

Brigadier General Sir William Horwood, General Macready's successor as Commissioner of the Met, proved himself to be an enthusiastic supporter and permanent status brought with it a new generation of squad transport. In his annual report to the Home Secretary in 1927, Horwood made the briefest of references to the elevation of the squad:

> The body of detective officers which has become known as the 'Flying Squad' has been augmented and equipped with motor cars to enable it to cope more effectively with the activities of criminals, especially those who themselves use motor vehicles in committing offences. Excellent results have ensued and still greater success is hoped for in the future.

Horwood's reassuringly matter-of-fact tone masked a genuine alarm at the rate of increase in motor crime and the use of stolen cars in robbery and burglary over the previous three years. The overall number of indictable offences recorded in Greater London in 1927 was 15,328, a small reduction on the previous year and the lowest figure since the post-war peak of more than 17,400 in 1920 and 1921. But car crime appeared to be spiralling out of control. In 1924, 278 cars were stolen in the whole of Britain. In 1927 that figure had multiplied more than five-fold to 1,515, of which 1,197 were stolen in the Metropolitan Police district. With so many cars in the hands of London criminals, robbery and house-breaking by mobile gangs had increased out of all proportion to the overall crime rate.

The speed of new cars was also increasing by the year and, although the Crossleys had served their function well, they were now frequently being left for dead by gangs determined to outrun them. The element of surprise was also long gone. Although the identities of the tenders were changed daily by sticking a variety of bogus commercial nameplates or advertisements on the sides, word had got around the criminal fraternity to beware of any Crossley seen cruising near the scene of an intended crime. Improvements in telegraphic technology meant that radio aerials could now be fitted inside the vans, so they were less conspicuous, but as strike vehicles the tenders were obsolete.

Major T. H. Vitty, head of the engineering department of Scotland Yard, was instructed to find an appropriate alternative and he detailed 'Jack' Frost, still the squad's crack driver, to travel to Coventry with him for discussions with the manufacturers of a number of high-powered sports saloons. In May 1927, the squad had its first cars: six Lea Francis 14 h.p. convertibles, each with a maximum speed of about 75 m.p.h.

'For the first time we had a literally flying squad, for the discussions in Coventry had produced the very first fast car to be used by the Yard,' said Frost. 'The question of strengthening the chassis had been considered and rejected because we did not want anything to add to the weight . . . It was decided to rely on speed rather than a massive chassis.

'Each of the cars chosen for the squad was of a different colour so that the crooks would not soon get used to seeing and recognising one. False number plates were carried, although there was no frequent necessity for their use. At the front was concealed an official Metropolitan Police sign which could be raised and illuminated. Each of the cars was fitted with radio and at the stage in the development of short-wave communication it was necessary to carry an aerial fitted in the hood. As at all times the hood was up to conceal the occupants, this did not matter very much and the aerial wires were concealed in the hood lining.'

The Crossleys, now numbering four, were kept on for several more years but their principal uses after 1927 were as mobile radio stations and basic transporters. The Lea Francis cars were to be the main police weapon against the travelling criminal.

It is an indication of the high aspirations held by the leaders of Scotland Yard for this new development that the six squad drivers were sent for training in the 'Leafs', as the Lea Francis tourers became known, to the world famous Brooklands racetrack in Surrey under the tuition of racing drivers from the Brooklands Automobile Racing Club. Officials measured exact wind speeds, tested the adhesion quality of the tyres on the concrete track and checked mean and maximum speeds in differing conditions. After a week, the cars and their drivers were ready to do battle on the London streets.

Just before permanent status was conferred on the squad, Hambrook had been promoted to Detective Chief Inspector and had transferred back to divisional duties. His replacement as operational head of the squad was Detective Chief Inspector Charles Cooper, who had worked with some distinction on the investigation of the Doctor Crippen murder and the infamous Seddon poisoning case.

In *Flying Squad* by Lucas and Scarlet, he is described as having:

> . . . a cherubic face, a pink countryman's complexion and an almost benevolent manner. He was a reserved and rather reticent man who, as he sat at his desk fingering his horn-rimmed spectacles, seemed more like a shrewd lawyer or bank manager.

His appearance apparently belied a strong aptitude for his chosen calling, for in the first year after delivery of the new cars, Cooper's squad, now forty-strong, secured 300 criminal convictions against robbers, burglars, vice rings and gangsters. Comparative figures for earlier years were not published but the total led to a string of newspaper features glorifying the achievement.

One particularly ecstatic series of articles, entitled 'Invisible Force', was written by a special correspondent for the *Daily Mail* in October 1928.

In the Flying Squad, Scotland Yard's newest arm, all the achievements of science that can aid authority have been mustered against the criminal classes. What is this romantic unit of which so much is heard and so little is seen? How does it function? Although there is much about it that must necessarily remain secret, many of the questions that have arisen in the public mind about it are answered below.

The articles, like many of the time, reveal little about the detailed workings of the squad but they are notable in one respect. Our intrepid reporter, after being given the thrill of a ride in one of the unmarked and unobtrusive Lea Francis cars, likened them to the 'Q' ships of the First World War – warships which were disguised as merchantmen to fool the enemy. The analogy caught the public imagination and squad vehicles became popularly known as 'Q' cars.

The new cars undoubtedly helped to swell the arrest figures but the squad detectives still relied for their success on being one step ahead of their opponents. Hanging around in seedy pubs and cafés in the hope of picking up titbits of information and cultivating small-time criminals as informants remained their bread-and-butter work. Sir Basil Thompson, the Assistant Commissioner of Police who had first discussed the creation of the squad with Frederick Wensley back in 1916 and commended it to the Commissioner two years later, wrote in his memoirs about the importance of pre-emptive tactics.

True, [squad] cars can patrol the streets night and day but the number of criminals caught red-handed without previous information is absurdly small. [The squad] arrests thieves occasionally because it knows thieves by sight and the thieves do not always know a Flying Squad car when they see it. In rare cases the man in the car catches sight of, say, a Hoxton criminal taking the air in a well-to-do residential district like Belgravia. 'Hallo! That's John Jackson from Hoxton. What's he doing down here?' The car is pulled up out of sight of John Jackson and its crew keep an unobtrusive eye upon him. As soon as he does something which a Hoxton man would not be doing in Belgravia unless his intentions were sinister, he is arrested as a suspected criminal, but such cases are necessarily rare.

A detective is as God made him. He cannot divine the intentions of a person whom he has never seen before and to make police inquiries about a person whose face does not please him would take up more time than he can spare. To send a number of men from the Flying Squad into a district where there is an epidemic of crime would be worse than useless if they went without any knowledge of the men they were to look for, for the thieves would get to know the detectives before the detectives got to know them and would betake themselves to another district.

In addition to seeking intelligence on burglars in the suburbs and the more exclusive areas of the City of Westminster, gangs in the outer urban areas of London and on the racecourses, and pickpockets, confidence tricksters and smash and grab raiders wherever they could be found, the squad began to move in more and more on the West End of London, in particular the sleazy criminal sub-culture of Soho and the rougher end of Covent Garden.

Prostitution rings, illegal gambling dens and, by modern standards, a small degree of drug trafficking were already well established in the narrow streets around London's theatreland. Many of these activities were in the hands of foreign nationals, largely Russian emigrés, Italians, French and immigrants from the eastern Mediterranean.

Towards the end of 1928 a crackdown was ordered and the Flying Squad were assigned to execute it. It is hard to assess whether the operation would have been quite so intensive had the seamy trade been run by good old British villains, but newspaper coverage of the arrests was frighteningly xenophobic. A *Daily Mail* report of 17 December ran:

The *Daily Mail* learns that Scotland Yard is subjecting the West End of London to a moral spring clean. This has driven

47

from the country in the last few weeks large numbers of unwanted aliens who have thrived for years on the ruin of other people. So thoroughly is this scavenging being conducted under Chief Constable Wensley and Chief Inspector Cooper that scores of undesirable aliens who still remain are also thinking of going without the impetus of deportation orders.

It has been realised that whenever gambling resorts and other haunts of such undesirables as drug traffickers, share pushers and blackmailers come under the surveillance of the police, there is usually an unwanted alien behind the operations. These aliens take the biggest share of the haul and run the least risk. These aliens, who have imagined for years that they have conducted their operations unknown to the police, were alarmed when they found that the authorities were tackling vice at the fountainhead.

They have thought that as long as their wretched and comparatively poorly paid dupes went to prison at regular intervals, the police would be satisfied that they were doing all they could to suppress the loathsome side of the West End that has grown year by year since the war. Only a few weeks have elapsed since the screens behind which these aliens worked were torn away. Already the West End of London is a better place.

Although the reporter did not realise it at the time, his allusion to the police being satisfied with catching smaller fry in the Soho underworld while the prime movers went about their business unhindered was to prove prophetic. A little over forty years later it would be alleged that detectives from the Obscene Publications Squad and the Flying Squad were actually fostering just that climate in return for the payment of substantial bribes by the barons of Soho vice. The allegations, many of them proved, were to lead to the destruction of the Obscene Publications Squad and prison sentences for several senior members and former members of the Flying Squad, including its Commander.

At that time, however, the Flying Squad could do no wrong and almost anything they asked for in terms of manpower and equipment was provided. They were glamorous, brave, hard-working and had achieved tangible success against some of the most dangerous and active criminals in London. Their work-rate and driving techniques took a heavy toll on their vehicles and after two years of scouring the 700 square miles of the Metropolitan Police district on the hunt for likely villains, the Lea Francis tourers were almost ready to be consigned to the scrapheap. Their engines became so worn that they could no longer be spurred on to anything like their full speed or acceleration and the squad began to lobby for replacements.

They were helped by a supportive press and in the spring of 1929 a number of stories appeared in most of the national newspapers hinting that unless new cars were brought in soon, the squad would lose its potency. This extract, from the *Daily Mail* of 4 April, is typical.

Under present conditions, the motor-bandit runs only a small risk of capture because a 'borrowed' car of high power is well on the way to safety before the police car can start in pursuit. Many of Scotland Yard's motor cars have been in use day and night for two or three years and are beginning to falter in tests of speed. The motor-bandit never uses a car that will not accelerate quickly into a mile-a-minute speed.

Other articles stressed the need to supply the squad with top-grade equipment to aid their fight against crime, a view which already carried considerable favour in the highest circles of Scotland Yard. It was not long before funds for new transport were made available, despite the public spending restrictions necessitated by the slump of the late 1920s, which was plunging daily closer towards the worst worldwide depression in modern history. And it was not just any old cars they would be given.

Before the purchase was made, the six squad drivers 'Jack' Frost, 'Ginger' Galley, Frank Cox, Marshall 'Bunn' Bunney, Arthur Melton and Bert Court were consulted. They had been happy with the general speed, handling and acceleration of the Lea Francis but a little concerned that its lightness could be a handicap

49

in the occasional cases in which criminals decided to try to ram or buffet it from the road during a chase. One smash and grab team was reputed to have had the chassis of its own car specially weighted to give it an advantage should it become involved in a spat with a police vehicle.

Ideally, the drivers favoured a car which would combine speed, chassis weight for a relatively low centre of gravity and manoeuvrability in extreme circumstances. In the search for the perfect machine, the Yard consulted a noted saloon car racing driver and motor engineer of the day, Captain 'H' Macklin, who suggested that the squad drivers should try out a high-performance Invicta. The 29.1 h.p., 4.5 litre tourer with a top speed of more than 90 m.p.h. and a list price of £632 was among the most coveted sports saloons on the road and had recently triumphed in the ultimate combined test of speed and endurance – the twenty-four-hour race at Le Mans.

Remarkably enough, the car offered to the squad by the Invicta company was the fully equipped racing model which had actually won the Le Mans event. The Yard was impressed and the car was bought. Certain modifications were ordered to make the Invicta weightier and more stable at high speed and the drivers returned to Brooklands to test it on the track. A few days later, 'Jack' Frost gave the car its first test run on a section of public road at Cobham, Surrey which had been specially sealed off by the police for the occasion. He was thrilled by the 'tremendous acceleration factor of ten to sixty miles per hour in less than ten seconds', and by the beginning of July, after further pilot runs on the Thames Embankment in Westminster, the car was ready for active service. Within days it had been involved in its first chase – and had had its first crash.

At around 10.00 p.m. on a hot and overcast Friday night, the Invicta, driven by Frost and carrying a rather heavy load of five detectives under the command of Detective Inspector Ted Ockey, was on gentle patrol in south London. At a late-night coffee stall in Kennington, the team recognised four men whom they suspected of being members of a smash and grab gang. When the men pulled away from the stall in a Vauxhall van the squad followed at a discreet distance. They were led across Westminster Bridge to

Parliament Square and through the intricate back-streets behind Westminster Abbey until the van stopped outside Studd and Millington's tailor's shop in Victoria Street. The suspects' purpose became obvious when the van was backed on to the pavement and chains were attached to the back of it. The plan was clearly to drag the steel security grille from the shop front, smash the window and make off with the fabrics and clothes inside.

Frost could hardly contain his excitement at the prospect of putting the Invicta through its paces in a genuine pursuit. 'I had kept the police car out of their sight by staying about eighty-five yards away, but I could reach sixty miles an hour in nine and a half seconds and knew this was the time for the fun to begin,' he remembered. He drove straight at the gang but they saw him coming just in time to jump back into their van and make a break for it. The chase sped through Tothill Street, along Petty France and into Buckingham Gate, where the powerful Invicta drew level with its quarry. At this point, Ockey made a gesture of courage bordering on foolhardiness. Frost wrote:

As we were both speeding level at around fifty miles per hour through the night streets, Ockey sprang from our car to the Vauxhall. Holding on with his left hand he grasped one of the crew round the neck but the Vauxhall increased speed again and two of the crew hit him on the head with a heavy jemmy. As I wrestled with the wheel to keep my car level, we prayed that Ockey would be able to jump back to safety but another member of the crew battered his knuckles with an iron bar so that he fell off. By God's grace I managed to avoid him as he collapsed into the road. That split second I have relived too often in my memory.

By braking and swerving to avoid the stricken Ockey Frost lost ground on the gang, but his determination was intensified by their savage treatment of his fellow officer and he was soon closing once more. In Ebury Street, the van slowed down to negotiate a sharp bend. Frost, fresh from his training course at Brooklands, put his foot down on the accelerator and rammed the Vauxhall amidships, turning it over against a wall. A brief fight ensued but the detectives' truncheons dealt quickly with the robbers and the gang was rounded up and marched to Gerald Road police station. They eventually received prison sentences of between three and five years.

The case made banner headlines and all the officers involved in the operation received Commissioner's commendations. Ockey, who miraculously was not gravely injured, was awarded the King's Police Medal for his bravery. The car had performed to all expectations and despite the crash was back on the road within a few days.

Major Vitty, the Metropolitan Police chief engineer, professed himself delighted with the Invicta and more were ordered. The next few years were to see the height of luxury and performance in squad transport – Bentleys, Lagondas, Railtons – nothing, it seemed, was too good for the men of the 'Heavy Mob', as they became known in underworld circles.

On 3 July, Vitty could not resist a small boast at the annual conference of the Chief Constables Association in Brighton about the great technological strides being made on behalf of the squad. Apart from the fast cars now being provided, wireless communication was improving all the time, he told his audience, and the time was coming when all forces would be in direct communication with one another on a permanent basis.

'There is no doubt that inter-communication by wireless is coming. The wireless installation at present in use at Scotland Yard has a radius of fifty to a hundred miles. There is no technical obstacle to that range being extended. Indeed, apart from the cost, there is no reason why every provincial headquarters in the country should not be in communication with one another and with Scotland Yard by wireless.'

Vitty used the Flying Squad as a perfect example of how radio could be employed successfully to tackle crime. All day and all night squad cars were sending and receiving Morse code messages to and from Scotland Yard. He gave two recent examples in which the radio communication had led to good arrests. 'A message was received at Scotland Yard at 1.05 a.m. that a motor car had been lost or stolen. This was immediately broadcast and by 1.15 a.m. the car had been recovered and the thieves captured by a police car which picked up the message while patrolling. In another case, information was telephoned to the Yard that a number of well-known women shoplifters were drinking in a public house. This was sent out by wireless and a patrolling car went to the public house and waited. As the women came out they were followed and the whole gang caught red-handed shoplifting in a large store.'

So innovative was the Flying Squad wireless set-up that it was used to listen in to selected radio frequencies thought to be being used by anarchists, Bolsheviks, Fenian terrorists and other 'subversives', on behalf of the security services and the Special Branch.

The pretence of official secrecy over the work of the squad was now gone. They had proved their worth and were increasingly flaunted as the Yard's special implement of retribution against career villains. The appearance of their cars, however, continued to be altered regularly so they could still work undercover. Colours were varied, registration numbers changed and radiator grilles switched. A car could have a completely new identity, including colour, within twenty-four hours.

The new Commissioner of Police, Field Marshal Lord Byng of Vimy, yet another highly decorated old soldier to be installed in the post, was most enthusiastic about the work of the squad. In October 1929, he decided to see whether he was getting value for the considerable amount of his budget he had authorised to be spent on updating squad equipment. He tested the speed of their reactions late at night by going into a call-box at Piccadilly Circus, ringing Scotland Yard and asking for a car to meet him as quickly as possible. According to the *Daily Telegraph* of 29 October:

He hung up the receiver, walked up the steps into the street and to his surprise a car was waiting for him. 'I have just sent a message for you,' he told the officer in charge. 'We have just received it, sir – just as we were coming up Regent Street.' This incident is a graphic illustration of the promptitude with which the Flying Squad, with its day and night service of fast motor cars and its wireless equipment, is now enabled to respond to calls for help sent out by radio from police headquarters.

That year, 1929, also saw the retirement of the founding father and early driving force of the Flying Squad, Frederick Wensley, an event greeted with an outpouring of sentiment from the press. He was lionised as 'the greatest of modern detectives' (*Evening News*) and extracts from his candid autobiography *Detective Days*, serialised the following year in the *Sunday Express*, were given the kind of prominence reserved these days for revelations about the Royal Family.

Not all the comment, however, was positive. Such was Wensley's intimate knowledge of Scotland Yard's secret stratagems and activities that a number of politicians believed the book had betrayed vital confidences, to the advantage of criminals and the detriment of future detection. Two MPs, Sir Nicholas Grattan-Doyle and a barrister and King's Counsel named Mr Holford Knight, urged the Attorney-General to prosecute Wensley under the Official Secrets Act. The Attorney-General, and the rest of the leading members of the government, appeared less alarmed at Wensley's disclosures. Presumably realising the public relations capital to be gained from press articles and a book which glorified the work and dedication of the police at a time when, for reasons which will be explained in the next chapter, they were under considerable public pressure, they backed Wensley to the hilt.

His reputation grew still further in the summer of 1931, when the authorities in New York, who knew of his work against violent crime in London, invited him to take up a consulting role in the United States to help them in their fight against the gangsters who had grown in strength and firepower during the Prohibition era. Typically, Wensley said he would consider the job only if he was placed in full control of policy and operations against the gangs. 'It is one thing to be able to advise on what steps should be taken and quite another thing to have the power to carry out your own suggestions,' he told the *Sunday Dispatch* (2 August 1931). 'I certainly do not think it is a superhuman task. Although it may not be generally known, we have had something of the same problem in this country and I don't think it can be said that we failed to deal with it.'

In an oblique reference to the success of the Flying Squad he added: 'Gangsters over there would never be able to win through if the problem were tackled in the same efficient way as we have done here. I have had some very nasty gangs to deal with – very desperate gangs, in fact. But they have never beaten Scotland Yard because we tackled the matter unflinchingly. I should not be averse to dealing with the American gangs either but, if that is to be done, the man who does it must be given absolute control of the forces fighting the gangs.'

The Mayor of New York was unwilling to risk bringing a foreigner in to lead his police force and the offer fell through. Instead, Wensley retired to his suburban north London home at Palmers Green to tend his vegetable and rose gardens and to regale his grandchildren with thrilling tales of police work in old London.

At about the same time as his departure, possibly in a move to maintain continuity of direction, Detective Chief Inspector Walter Hambrook, the other giant of the early years, was brought back from divisional duties to lead his men through the early 1930s.

6
Heroes and Villains

As the reputation of the Flying Squad climbed steadily through the late 1920s and early 1930s, the standing of the Metropolitan Police as a whole was plummeting rapidly in the opposite direction. Interestingly, it was to the squad that the Yard would turn for help in restoring some of the lost public confidence.

Accusations of shady practices and strong-arm methods had been building up in the press and some sections of Parliament since 1922, when the *Daily Graphic* published an attack, later partially retracted, on police in the West End of London. The piece included the allegation that the proprietors of illegal gambling houses were making so much from the wages of sin that they could 'afford to bribe the police to a certain extent' and carry on their nefarious activities without serious hindrance. The main thrust of the article was that the wide powers given to the police during the Great War under the Defence of the Realm Act had made them believe they had absolute discretion to carry on as they wished.

Intermittent press campaigns of criticism followed, based on a string of incidents over the next few years, which ranged from unnecessarily heavy-handed behaviour to out-and-out corruption. Three constables were convicted in unrelated instances of fabricating court evidence and a series of cases of wrongful arrest of normally law-abiding citizens, including three knights, an MP and an eminent archaeologist, for offences such as drunkenness and indecent behaviour, received a welter of publicity. There followed further claims, often made in letters sent anonymously to the newspapers and Scotland Yard, of bribery and intimidation, including the allegation that police in several areas of London were taking 'tributes' from street-walkers and illegal liquor salesmen.

By 1927, public disquiet was deemed serious enough for the government to order an independent inquiry, chaired by Mr Hugh MacMillan KC, into a list of cases of alleged impropriety. As a result of MacMillan's findings, five officers were brought before disciplinary boards and two were reprimanded. In a rather vague report, the tribunal found that police had acted injudiciously in one specific case involving the arrest on suspicion of indecent behaviour of an Indian Army officer (who was later offered £500 compensation for wrongful arrest), but offered a general endorsement of the police as a whole. 'We regard it as unfortunate that when a mistake does occur it should be made the occasion of a general attack on the police,' the report said.

Commissioner Horwood was more outspoken about the effect of loose gossip on the good name of the hard-working policeman. How would the critics fare if required to police the streets and parks of London themselves? If they felt they could do better they were welcome to try. 'As things are, [the policeman] has to carry out the law to the best of his judgement. If occasionally this fails him it is not surprising. In such cases he may be left to the mercies of a disciplinary board . . .'

With hindsight, Horwood might have wished he had been a little less strident in his reprimand of the rumourmongers. A few weeks later came another high-profile case of police intimidation which was to lead this time to a full-blown Royal Commission into police powers and procedure.

In May 1928, an eminent economist, the appropriately named Sir Leo Chiozza Money, and his friend Miss Irene Savidge were arrested on suspicion of indecency during a police sweep of Hyde Park after nightfall. The case was thrown out at the magistrates' court for lack of evidence; costs were awarded against the Met and a police inspector was ordered by the Director of Public Prosecutions to take a statement from twenty-two-year-old Miss Savidge to see whether she wished to pursue an action for damages, or even to seek criminal charges against the officers who arrested her.

The interview, held at Scotland Yard, was to be the source of an even worse fuss than the original arrest and acquittal. The police version of events was that Miss Savidge had been treated with cordiality and consideration at the Yard and had decided not to take the matter further. Miss Savidge told a rather different story. She said she had been bullied into a state of terror and had agreed not to press charges only after five hours of browbeating in a gloomy chamber at police headquarters.

The Home Secretary, Sir William Joynson-Hicks, adjudged that the case, taken in conjunction with the cumulative effect of previous alleged indiscretions, warranted a Royal Commission, and one was duly set up under the chairmanship of Lord Lee of Fareham.

While the Commission was sitting, yet another corruption scandal, by far the worst to date, was beginning to emerge. A number of letters, signed by a woman calling herself 'Richette', began to arrive at Scotland Yard alleging that police based at Vine Street were extorting money on an organised and regular basis from the owners of clubs, gambling houses and prostitution rings in Soho.

The controller of the protection racket was said to be a Sergeant Goddard, an officer with an apparently faultless record who was based at Vine Street and had for six years had responsibility for investigating infringements of the liquor licensing laws by West End clubs and for the suppression of illicit gambling houses and brothels. One of the main clubs Goddard was said to have been collecting from was the 43 Club in Gerrard Street, owned by the most celebrated Soho hostess of her day, Kate Meyrick. It was a lively and semi-respectable nightspot which offered lewd cabaret, unlicensed drinking and a team of hostesses who were employed to dance and keep company with single men and, for an appropriate consideration, engage in extra-curricular activities. A zealous policeman could have closed the 43 down on any one of half a dozen legal counts but Goddard allowed it to thrive. Spurred into action by 'Richette', who had also communicated some of her allegations to the press, Scotland Yard determined to find out precisely why.

There was only one natural choice for the assignment. It was a delicate job and required a publicly respected senior officer with full credentials of integrity and detective skill. The Commissioner had no hesitation in choosing Frederick Wensley, who in turn automatically brought in the Flying Squad. As an opening shot, a squad team led by Detective Inspector 'Nutty' Sharpe was ordered to raid the 43 and a second Soho club owned by Mrs Meyrick, the Manhattan in Denman Street. The instruction was that neither Goddard nor any other Vine Street officers should be told in advance of the operation and the aim was to collect evidence of graft against Vine Street officers from club staff.

It was the era of the 'bright young things', the monied and hedonistic youth so vividly chronicled by Evelyn Waugh, and the 43 Club was one of their late-night haunts. Sharpe wrote:

> Outside her place at four, five and six o'clock and on occasions even eight o'clock in the morning, you would see them going home. Undergrads with scarves round their necks, girls in gorgeous gowns climbing into open sports cars. It always amused me to contrast the artificial appearance of some of these people under the lights of the club to that when they appeared in court. My word, how some of those lovely red-lipped, mascara-eyed girls grew to mature womanhood in the cold light of the morning after the night before.

So respectful was Sharpe of the club's regular clientele that he dressed specially in an evening suit for the raid. 'I think the majority of them regarded it more as a lark, for it gave them a thrill, but they changed their view when they appeared before the beak,' he said. Kate Meyrick was charged with various offences and later received a six-month prison sentence but neither she nor any of her staff was prepared to implicate Goddard in any impropriety.

The raid, and the whole investigation, seems to have been regarded by Sharpe and his men as rather demeaning. They were used to fighting it out with desperate villains and seemed to have little stomach for turning over a nightclub full of people enjoying themselves. 'The fact was that nothing improper did take place in the 43. In the cabarets a little more body than you would see in a theatre was visible but there was nothing obscene... Kate gave her customers what they wanted and she got what she wanted; no one complained, and personally, I can't see that much harm was done. She didn't drive anyone to the 43 who didn't want to go there – anyway, she did break a law and we had to do our job.'

But Wensley determined to get at the truth about Goddard and decided the squad should examine his bank accounts. They quickly discovered that he was living well beyond the means of the average police sergeant. An expensive new car, a house worth £2,000, bank accounts containing £2,700 and two safety deposit box numbers suggested a substantial private income. Goddard initially tried to explain away the money as the proceeds of gambling successes, but under further interrogation he buckled and admitted that he had been taking bribes. His safe deposit boxes were found to contain £12,000 in cash. Early in 1929 Goddard was sentenced at the Old Bailey to eighteen months' hard labour.

Despite the implications for the wider image of the police, the Lee Commission reported that Goddard's was an isolated case and that much of the criticism of the Met was unfounded. Among 20,000 officers there were bound to be a few who fell by the wayside, but as a whole the force was manned by honest, competent and efficient men.

Sir John Moylan, the Yard Receiver, said after the Commission findings: 'The police have never escaped charges of taking bribes or levying illicit tribute but these have rarely been made in relation to their duties for the protection of the public and the prevention or detection of crime ... The facts with regard to police and nightclubs which were exposed in the Goddard case related to a very special sphere of police duty, and one of the features of this case was the practical monopoly, so to speak, of corruption in a singularly fruitful field for it, by one sergeant who secured for himself a sum more than sufficient to bribe a whole division.

'Those who from time to time believe that corruption is widespread among the police perhaps forget that a corrupt police force argues a corrupt community. A police force is a section of the community with the usual human failings and a great deal more than the usual allowance of temptations. Of no public servant can it be more truly said that he is what the public makes him. If the police take bribes, it is usually because they are offered them.

Even where this is not so and the evil is rather that where certain classes engaged in illicit occupations, or subject to supervision or licensing by the police, are exposed to extortion by unprincipled members of the force, the police authorities cannot stamp it out unless they have the fullest support and assistance from the public.'

What is significant here about the Goddard affair is that it was to the Flying Squad that the Yard turned to investigate it. As well as being regarded as shock troops in the battle against dangerous criminals, they also appeared to have developed an image as incorruptible and therefore the best weapon to use to root out corruption within their own force.

If Moylan's theory that the policeman most likely to be corrupted is the one closest to those with the greatest incentive to offer him bribes was correct, the choice of the Flying Squad as an anti-corruption unit was perhaps surprising. The squad's central purpose was to mix with criminals, befriend them, drink with them and live around their haunts in an attempt to get to the roots of crime. Who more than they would be likely to be offered bribes or other incentives to look the other way when a crime was being committed, or not to press charges afterwards?

The extent of the old-time squad detective's immersion in the underworld he was trying to police is clear from the recollections of many officers of the era. A certain mutual sympathy, respect, even affection grew between hunter and hunted. In *Forty Years of Scotland Yard*, Wensley tells of receiving a signed note on the day of his retirement from a professional criminal with whom he had crossed swords many times during his career. It read: 'I feel I must join with all other criminals and old lags in sincerely wishing you years of happiness and a complete rest.' Although the phraseology was open to interpretation, Wensley had no doubt the sentiment was genuine:

There are no born criminals. I have had to deal with many men who, in other circumstances, would have been fine and valuable citizens – men with great physical and mental qualities . . . Not all criminals are heartless ruffians.

Sharpe expressed similar fond memories:

On the day I retired as chief of the Flying Squad, I read how crooks spat on the ground when I walked by – hooey; every time I stroll through Piccadilly, Leicester Square and neighbourhood I get more handshakes from crooks and ex-crooks than any other class of people. I've met thousands of crooks and although you run into a real son of a gun now and then, most of them are pretty decent fellows.

So long as you play the game straight with them and let them know you mean business they respect you. They realise that you've got your living to get, same as they have, and when you pinch them they regard it as all in the game. They don't bear any malice and hard feelings.

This relationship did not change in essence for several decades. Bruce Reynolds, the professional south London thief who helped mastermind the Great Train Robbery, described the relationship between squad detective and established criminal as 'a diplomatic link'.

'There was a very thin dividing line between us. They were the opposition but there was generally a friendly rivalry and it was not unknown for us to be drinking with them. There were various pubs and clubs that you might go in where you would usually see policemen. There would be a nod and drinks would be sent between the two tables. I didn't encourage personal relationships with police but there was no animosity.

'The Flying Squad was seen as the cream of Scotland Yard and it was as well for crims to keep in with them for those times when you were arrested. For example, you might be able to get bail for not too large an amount of surety if you had a reasonable relationship with the police. It was not really corruption and I never had a situation where I was asked for money by a detective or had one put up a job in return for a payment. There were always mavericks on both sides but I remember the Flying Squad as being fairly straight. I always regarded myself as an "honest thief" and I think our relationship with the police was almost symbiotic.

'They knew we were at it but it was up to them to get evidence. By being in the places we used to go, they were keeping doors open and maybe hearing things and understanding things which would help them.'

It was to the credit of the squad that, despite the obvious temptations of living among the underworld and the malicious accusations from people they had arrested, there was hardly a single case of corruption proved against them until the 1960s. By then, the criminal fraternity had fragmented and the cosh and knuckleduster had given way to the gun. Huge profits were being made from vice and epic robbery and some detectives decided to take their cut of the action. The old ground rules which existed between policeman and criminal began to disappear.

The early 1930s were also marked by strong criticism of the police in general for their inability to make a lasting impact on rising burglary and shop-breaking figures. In a Commons statement in 1931, the Home Secretary was forced to admit that break-ins and smash and grab raids in the Metropolitan Police district had again become a cause for public alarm. Despite some good successes up to the mid-1920s, not least by the Flying Squad, the annual total of domestic break-ins had increased from 3,000 in 1913 to 8,000 in 1931. When shop-breaking offences were added, the figure was over 12,000.

The new Commissioner, Viscount Trenchard, who took over in November 1931, referred to the Commons debate and 'these remarkable figures' in his first annual report. Like many Commissioners after him, he laid the blame publicly on almost everything except police performance – the ease with which criminals could steal unattended cars; the poor protection of shop windows; householders failing to secure doors and windows; changes in statistical methods so that more offences were now recorded than in earlier years; and the general economic depression – the list of reasons would have graced a Home Office press conference today.

But privately, Trenchard was well aware of weaknesses within the police structure and set about a wide sweep of reforms. He will be remembered most for improving the education and training of the force and for the creation of the police college at Hendon. In 1931, less than a third of the 42,000 applicants to join the Met had any secondary school education and a large proportion were

64

virtually illiterate. Because the middle and higher managerial ranks of the police were staffed by officers who had come through the ranks, Trenchard believed many were not intellectually able enough to be effective leaders. By 1933, the police college had become established, taking in promising officers from an early stage in their career, moulding them, enhancing their education and training them in leadership skills.

Trenchard also recognised the virtues of technology and set up the scientific laboratory, driving school and wireless training centre. Police telephone-boxes, a large increase in the provision of 'Q' cars, the 999 emergency call system and automatic traffic lights, which freed hundreds of police officers from point duty to concentrate on more important aspects of police work, had all been devised under his predecessor Lord Byng but were enthusiastically brought to full fruition by Trenchard.

Even more latitude was given to the Flying Squad to curb burglary and robbery and the message: 'We don't need to know all the details, just get results' was reinforced. It is impossible to say precisely how much the welcome successes of the following years were due to the work of the squad and how much to other reforms, but the statistics for burglary, robbery and shop-breaking between 1932–3 and the outbreak of the Second World War made remarkable reading.

After twenty years of regular yearly increases, the frequency of break-ins began steadily to go down and then level off. From a high point of more than 14,000 recorded offences in 1932–3, the statistics did not rise above that figure again for a decade. Smash and grab raids declined by more than forty per cent in 1933 and the total of all indictable offences recorded in London, apart from a fairly sharp rise between 1936 and 1938, also began to stabilise. Detection rates also improved to around thirty per cent for all crimes and sixteen per cent for burglary and shop-breaking. The only crime which showed no sign of abating was car theft. In 1936, more than 5,000 cars were stolen in London alone, thirty per cent more than in 1935 and six times as many as ten years earlier.

The increase had more to do with the proliferation of cars in society than with any failing of the police, but the Flying Squad was gradually increased to fifty detectives and continued to be provided with state-of-the-art cars to combat the teams who stole vehicles specifically for armed robberies. The earlier practice of buying some squad cars second-hand to defray costs was discontinued because of concerns that an ageing fleet would not perform to the high standards required.

In 1935, the squad took delivery of the first of many Railton 4 litre, 8 cylinder open tourers, the car with which they would become synonymous for the next ten years. Built at Brooklands by the Thompson and Taylor company, the Railton's specially tuned engine was capable of a top speed in excess of 100 m.p.h. and the then fantastic acceleration potential of 0–60 m.p.h. in 8.5 seconds. A report to the Commissioner by the Yard engineering department described the car as 'unequalled at present in rapid acceleration', and its compiler added: 'In my opinion there is no car in the country that could pass it on the London streets.' It cost £521, and by the end of the Second World War the squad was running nineteen of them.

Operationally, the 1930s brought a number of then unusual investigations which were to prove a foretaste of things to come. In 1932, for example, came what is thought to have been the first instance of a gunman holding up a West End jeweller's in broad daylight and walking away with his pockets full of gold and gemstones.

Rudolph Franklyn had been hardened to violence as a young man in the trenches during the First World War, and instead of returning home after Armistice he accepted a post in the Palestine police. He finally arrived back in England in August 1932 with little desire to hold down an honest job. A month later he walked into an Oxford Street jewellery shop and threatened the manager and two staff with an automatic pistol. After locking them in a cupboard he helped himself to the best and most portable of the stock and calmly walked off.

Bob Fabian carried out the investigation into the robbery, and on a trawl of pawnbrokers and cafés in lodging house districts bordering the West End heard talk of a suntanned stranger claiming to be a former Palestine policeman who had been offering a gold cigarette case for sale in local pubs. Fabian contacted the Palestine force asking for the names of Londoners who had recently been discharged. Franklyn was one of the two names offered and he was eventually tracked down to a guest house in Gloucester Road.

Knowing that he was armed and potentially dangerous, Fabian asked his landlord to knock on his door and tell him that a registered package had arrived from Palestine. As Franklyn opened the door, Fabian and another detective jumped him and put him in handcuffs. They had not been over-cautious: under his pillow they found the pistol, loaded and fitted with a silencer.

Franklyn was one of a breed of armed robbers who thought they could prey with impunity on the vulnerable. By way of self-justification at his Old Bailey trial he said: 'The ancient Britons plundered when they were poor and hungry. It's a matter of nature. What else can a man do? You can't beg in the streets if you have pride.' The judge, Sir Ernest Wild, was unimpressed with Franklyn's selective view of history. Before sentencing him to three years penal servitude and twenty strokes of the birch he told him: 'A man too proud to beg should be too proud to steal.'

Safe-cracking was another class of crime which became a serious problem in the mid-1930s, and in 1936 the Flying Squad tackled one particular gelignite gang which had had rich pickings by blowing up safes in large cinemas late at night and stealing their considerable takings. They operated throughout the London area and their most lucrative raids had been at the Commodore, Hammersmith, the Forum, Ealing and the Astoria, Purley (twice). The gang was broken after one of their number was arrested outside a cinema in Cambridge in possession of house-breaking equipment, a small quantity of gelignite and some detonators. Three other men were picked up inside the cinema but it was still not clear how they had come by the explosives.

Squad detectives were informed of the arrests and discovered that one of those in custody had been an operator at the Forum cinema, Fulham. They travelled to Cambridge to interview the arrested man and managed to pressurise one gang member into disclosing that the gelignite supplier lived in the Gray's Inn Road area of London. Following more discreet inquiries they located his hideout and launched a midnight raid. The four remaining members of the gang were detained and the rest of the gelignite store found hidden under a sink. It was not perhaps the squad's most intricate operation, but it had shown quick reactions and good cooperation between Scotland Yard and a provincial force.

Rather more embarrassing was another investigation the next year into a spate of jewel robberies in central London. They had been carried out by night and despite a surveillance operation by divisional and squad officers, no clue could be found to the identity of the gang. Regular checks were carried out on the registration numbers of cars in the area where the robberies were most prevalent but to no avail.

It was only when one of the divisional officers on watch mentioned that a Flying Squad car had been spotted at the scene of one of the robberies shortly before it happened that the penny began to drop. A check on the movements of all squad cars revealed that no genuine patrol had been in the area at that time and more inquiries turned up the fact that the same car had been seen in the vicinity of several other raids and that surveillance officers, assuming it was a genuine police vehicle, had taken no further action.

A watch was kept for the rogue vehicle and two days later it was seen by a squad crew being driven along Piccadilly by a well-known jewel thief. They stopped and questioned him and despite having no firm evidence that he had been involved in the robberies they demanded to know how he had acquired the car. He replied that he had bought it legitimately at public auction. His story turned out to be true. When squad cars had finished their useful service they were simply sold off to the highest bidder, and the enterprising jewel thief had bought one. The incident led to a hasty review of policy and it was decided that from then on, cars identifiable as ex-squad vehicles would no longer be offered for public sale but sent instead to the police driving school at Hendon for training purposes.

7
War, Rationing and the Ghost Squad

There is a popular belief that during the Second World War even criminals were imbued with the defiant community spirit of the times. People could leave their doors open without fear of being burgled, robbery almost ceased to exist and the only danger on the streets was from Hitler's bombers, or so the story goes. Like so many stories born of nostalgia, it is a myth.

From the outbreak of war in 1939 the urban crime rate rose sharply and between 1943 and 1945 the total of indictable offences in London increased by an unprecedented forty per cent to almost 130,000. The blackout provided a perfect cover for criminal activity of all types, evacuation meant large numbers of empty houses were at the mercy of the more callous burglar, looting of shops and homes became common in the aftermath of bombing raids (4,500 recorded offences of looting in 1940, rising to 5,500 the following year) and the black market created by rationing of almost every desired commodity gave birth to the spiv, the 'Flash Harry' character who could supply almost anything at a price and would steal, or handle stolen goods, to facilitate his profiteering.

As policemen volunteered or were called up to the armed forces, the strength of the Met fell from just under 18,000 in 1939 to 12,500 in 1945. Although it was supplemented by retired policemen brought back into service, special constables and other war reserve officers, the force struggled to keep a hold on rising crime. As well as being stretched numerically, the police were distracted from normal duties by the need to engage in rescue work in the wake of bombing raids and the enforcement of endless new civil regulations relating to the state of emergency.

Like many members of the emergency services, the police performed heroically through the Blitz, digging victims from bombed or burning houses while air raids continued around them and saving many lives against formidable odds. One hundred and fifty Met officers received either the George Medal, British Empire Medal or King's Police Medal for their courage and public esteem was restored following the setbacks of the early 1930s. But the gallantry took its toll. Injury and sickness rates more than doubled among regular police and more than quadrupled among war reserve officers, depleting still further the force's crime-fighting abilities. If the roots of organised crime were to be attacked in these straitened times, it was vital that limited CID resources should be employed in the most efficient way and that key detective units gave of their very best.

Fortunately, when the war began the Flying Squad was better equipped than it had ever been before – fifty detectives, drivers, ancillary staff and twenty-one vehicles – and was at the height of its operational effectiveness. Because of petrol rationing and the need for as many vehicles as possible to be devoted to essential war work, the squad again became, as it had been in its earliest days, the only motorised detective unit in the Home Counties and was relied on heavily to take on major inquiries. Towards the end of 1939 a new man was placed in charge, Detective Chief Inspector Peter Beveridge. A tough Scotsman who had served during the Great War with the Seaforth Highlanders, he joined the police in 1919 and, like many of his predecessors, served his CID apprenticeship in the liveliest parts of the East End. He had particular contempt for spivs.

The term 'spiv' was first coined by the racecourse gangs around the turn of the century and derived from 'spiffing', the old slang word for spruce or splendid. It was originally used to describe a flamboyantly dressed member of the underworld but during the war it became a more widely used pejorative label for any shady character who lived dishonestly by his wits and always dressed sharply. The community of spivs was a loose amalgam of old lags, crooked businessmen, draft dodgers, deserters from the services and feckless young toughs, and the blackout and the black market were the worlds in which they thrived.

One of the most successful London spivs of the early war years was an east European refugee who had set up a legitimate wholesale business in Golders Green which he used as a cover for black marketeering and receiving stolen goods. He was known to all as 'Flash Izzy' because of his taste for expensive suits and ostentatious diamond jewellery. Izzy had enlisted the services of a number of lorry drivers to transport consignments of textiles from various manufacturers to the London docks for export. When they were moving large cargoes of expensive and generally scarce materials, they would inform him and he would arrange for the goods to be stolen and later sold under the counter to retailers in north London.

Detective Inspector Jack Capstick, a powerfully built, ruddy-faced, pipe-smoking Merseysider known to his colleagues in the Flying Squad as 'Charlie Artful', was assigned to investigate Izzy's operation after a huge lorryload of silks disappeared on its way from central London to the docks. On the first day of his inquiry, he was tipped off by one of his many informants that the lorry driver used by Izzy for the theft was a deserter from the Royal Army Service Corps (now the Royal Corps of Transport), and that most of the stolen goods were to be sold to businesses in Camden and Kentish Town. A second informant led Capstick to a woman known to be the girlfriend of an RASC deserter who seemed to have plenty of money to spend, and a decision was made to place her under twenty-four-hour surveillance.

The next day the woman travelled from her home at Paddington to the police court at Clerkenwell, where she visited her man. Unknown to the squad, he had been recognised by local police only the previous day and arrested as a deserter. This arrest proved to be Capstick's breakthrough in the inquiry. The driver would do anything, including going to prison, to avoid returning to the army, so Capstick assured him that if he cooperated with the squad inquiry, he would be convicted of conspiracy but a word would be put in with the judge so that his sentence would almost certainly be reduced. Having served his relatively short prison term, Capstick said, there was every likelihood that the army would give him a dishonourable discharge.

The driver liked the sound of the deal and said he would comply, so Capstick arranged to have him temporarily released into police custody. He plied him with food and large quantities of drink at a restaurant near Scotland Yard and the driver eventually told him that the stolen silks had been delivered to a farm in Horsham in Sussex, chosen by Izzy as a quiet place for storing and repackaging the merchandise ready for redistribution to retailers.

Capstick and another detective named MacDonald took the lorry driver to Horsham in an attempt to identify the farm and after almost two days they found it. The farmer told the detectives he had rented out some outbuildings to a man with a London accent who had wanted them for temporary storage of a quantity of wooden packing cases. The farmer had no idea what they contained and had not asked. On searching the outbuildings, Capstick and MacDonald discovered the remnants of a fire on which the cases had been burned and also found a fragment of silk identical to that from the load which had been stolen. The gang, however, appeared to have left.

But a routine check on the house nearest to the farm paid handsome dividends. When Capstick knocked on the door it was answered by a London thief whom he had arrested on more than one previous occasion. The thief claimed he had not been involved in the theft of the silks but offered the name of another career criminal nicknamed 'Big Bill' as one of the real principals. Capstick went back to London and picked up Bill at his home in Tufnell Park, taking him to the local police station for questioning.

Big Bill denied any knowledge of the silks until Capstick happened casually to mention that they were probably worth up to £15,000 on the black market. Bill was so incensed that he had been paid only a few hundred pounds for the job, having been told by Flash Izzy that the load would not fetch much more than £1,000 on resale, that he agreed to inform to get his own back. A Flying Squad crew took Bill to Golders Green, where he pointed out Izzy's large house. Izzy, 'dressed in a suit which must have cost fifty guineas and wearing more diamonds than a prima donna arrayed for a gala performance', was arrested as he returned home in his huge American car from an evening on the town and he, the driver and Bill were charged at Old Street police station with stealing and receiving the load of silks. A Kentish Town dress manufacturer who rejoiced in the name of Sammy Starshine and a Russian wholesaler from Islington, who made up the rest of the gang, were arrested later and all were convicted. Izzy was sentenced to five years, the driver to four (which would take him up to the end of the war and fulfil his hopes of not being returned to uniform), and the other three to two years. A number of other merchants who had bought the silks from Sammy and his Russian associate in the knowledge that they were being sold on the black market but not realising they were stolen, received heavy fines for breaches of Board of Trade regulations.

Forgery and theft of ration books, coupons for such items as petrol, clothing and sweets and identity cards also became big business, and by 1942 threatened the virtual breakdown of the whole rationing system in London. Beveridge was asked to concentrate his attentions on the major players in this criminal arena and began a crackdown, first on the smaller fry to gain intelligence, and then on the bigger fish.

Three or four main criminal syndicates were believed to be responsible for organising the racket, all basing themselves in the West End. The most active gang included a number of vicious army deserters, some armed with guns, who were not averse to branching out into armed robberies and smash and grab raids. In addition to their considerable muscle, the crime syndicate had the great advantage of retaining a uniformed policeman on the payroll.

The trail that led the squad to the corrupt constable and eventually enabled them to break up the gang began in the far north-east of England, in the Northumberland town of Morpeth. One gang member named Smith had gone there to hide out after taking part in the theft of £10,000 worth of clothing coupons from a Board of Trade office in Bloomsbury. Believing he was untouchable so far from the scene of the crime, he became increasingly cavalier in his behaviour and drew particular attention to himself one night in a local pub by lighting cigarettes with pound notes.

A local police inspector heard of this show of bravado and discreetly approached Smith's wife, who admitted under questioning that her husband had been involved in a raid on 'a big white building near Pentonville prison'. Morpeth police informed the squad and Detective Sergeant John Gosling was ordered to investigate. He assumed that the building in question was the Board of Trade office but was puzzled that no theft of coupons had been reported. When he visited the offices, however, officials admitted that the coupons were indeed missing and said they had not reported the theft for fear of encouraging others to try the same trick.

There had been a total of four thefts of coupons from storerooms in the same building and the only common factors were that they had all taken place at weekends and the same doorman had been on duty on each occasion. The doorman, an alcoholic retired sergeant-major named Edwards, was visited at his home in east London and soon broke down. He confessed that Smith and another man, both employed as heating engineers at the office, had been behind the thefts and that he had been paid £500 on each occasion to turn a blind eye.

Smith himself cracked soon after his arrest and named several members of the ring who handled and distributed the coupons. More arrests followed, including a taxi driver and two well-known bookmakers who had been distributing the stolen coupons, and the squad found itself at the heart of a major West End gang it had been chasing for several months. One question remained, however. The deserters who made up the gang's shock troops all carried a full set of army discharge papers which they could produce in the event of being challenged by the police to prove their identities. Although they were filled in with false names, they were genuine papers and it was crucial that the squad should find out who was providing them.

Gosling had the numbers of the identity cards checked with the National Registration Office, and discovered they were part of a batch which had not yet been issued officially. He was given the name of a town hall clerk to whom they had been forwarded some weeks earlier. The clerk was interviewed and told Gosling he had been made to hand over the blank documents to a policeman, who had been selling them on to deserters attached to the black market and robbery gang. The policeman was arrested on Christmas Eve and later sentenced to two years in prison, and five other men received sentences of up to five years. So the back of this particular gang was broken, but the squad would continue to be active against other black marketeers until the abolition of rationing.

In addition to their work infiltrating black market gangs, the squad still had to continue with their more familiar role of investigating armed robbery, smash and grab raids, major burglary, and occasionally murder. Their success rate grew through the early war years, with 663 arrests in 1940, 767 in 1941 and 862 in 1942. But as the war drew to its close, the ranks of London criminals were swelled by a deluge of fresh deserters from several weary Allied armies, and after VE Day by returning veterans wanting to make some money in a hurry by any means at their disposal. The crime rate soared and illegal firearms, many brought back from the war in Europe, proliferated.

The Flying Squad made gallant efforts to control the worst of the criminal excesses but were hampered now by the state of their vehicles, which had been almost run into the ground during the six years of war. New vehicles had been impossible to come by and a shortage of spares for the old ones had made it difficult to keep the fleet in service. Not long after the war ended Bob Fabian, who took over from Peter Beveridge as Detective Chief Inspector in charge of the squad, sent a plaintive report to his masters at Scotland Yard.

How could the Flying Squad be expected to function against the flourishing motor-bandit, he asked, when its cars were in such poor condition? Almost all the ageing Railtons had covered well over 100,000 miles under the hardest of driving conditions and one of the vans, a Ford V8, was so decrepit it now had virtually no brakes and its smoking engine could muster a top speed of no more than thirty miles per hour. Fabian went on to describe specific instances in which the squad had lost dangerous robbers during chases because their cars could not keep pace. A few of the vehicles could be salvaged if the proper spares were made available, but most would have to be replaced as a matter of extreme urgency.

The Yard's Assistant Commissioner (Crime), Sir Ronald Howe, consulted the Metropolitan Police transport department, who told him that the squad cars were in no worse shape than the bulk of police vehicles. There was simply no money in the kitty to update the squad fleet and that was that.

But the squad was not prepared to let the matter rest there and they called on the support of their friends in the press. A series of articles appeared on the theme that the Flying Squad was 'unable to fly' and that criminals throughout the Home Counties were capitalising on their infirmity. It was again indicative of the reputation the squad had built for itself that when the Cabinet was made aware of their plight, they were immediately made a special case for *ad hoc* funding. A month after Fabian made his report, the Ministry of Supply contacted the Commissioner, Sir Harold Scott, to tell him that twenty of the squad's twenty-four vehicles would be replaced within eight weeks.

The new cars, mainly 18 h.p. Wolseleys and Humber Super Snipes, were rather more modest in appearance and relative performance than the Railtons, but they were received with gratitude and quickly put to good use. Squad arrest rates over the next two years increased by twenty per cent, contributing to a general fall in overall crime rates which had seemed in 1945 to be hurtling out of control.

A more subtle development in tactics, arguably the ultimate refinement of the squad's essential purpose of getting to know criminals and their habits in the interests of proactive detection, also occurred shortly after the war. On New Year's Eve 1945, in a soundproofed room at Scotland Yard, a secret meeting was held which had distinct echoes of Frederick Wensley's original 1918 gathering at which the Flying Squad had been launched. In the chair this time was Assistant Commissioner (Crime) Sir Ronald Howe, backed by his top lieutenant, Chief Constable Percy Worth, head of the Yard's CID. Four hand-picked squad detectives had been called to the meeting – Detective Inspectors Jack Capstick and 'Nobby' Clark and Detective Sergeants John Gosling and Matt Brinnand. Like their forebears in 1918 they had been chosen for their shrewdness, skill at cultivating and handling informants and intricate knowledge of criminal behaviour.

Their mission was to detach themselves completely from official police work and 'go down into the sewers' on the hunt for criminal intelligence. They would live among the criminal fraternity, never making arrests but simply obtaining and storing information. Once gathered, the information would be passed quietly to the Flying Squad or divisional CID for further action. In Worth's words they would 'carry the war into the enemy's camp'. He told Capstick, who was placed in charge of the small unit: 'Neither you nor your men will give evidence in court. As far as the underworld is concerned, you will have no more material existence than ghosts. How you manage it is your own affair but we want results – fast!' For internal purposes the unit would be known blandly as the Special Duty Squad. To those who knew of its real work it was named the Ghost Squad.

The Ghost Squad was an extraordinary innovation in a police force which was then, even more than now, run along rigid command lines. Four relatively junior detectives were given *carte blanche* to roam wherever and whenever they chose and would not be obliged to explain themselves to any senior officers except Worth and Howe. Even they were barely interested in the fine details. The creation of the unit could be said to mark the point at which the Flying Squad really began to develop into an exclusive and almost autonomous 'firm within a firm'.

The Ghost Squad was given a private office at Scotland Yard to which only they and their office manager, an ageing uniformed constable named Archie who would be their main point of central contact when they were out undercover, had keys. It soon became known around the Yard that the office was being used for a special operation but no one could work out what its purpose was. The initial rumour was that the detectives had been recruited as an anti-corruption squad, which suited them because it meant they were given a wide berth by their suspicious colleagues. They were also provided with a single battered Austin 16 car, a far cry from the Bentleys and Railtons they had been used to.

Gosling, in his autobiography *Ghost Squad*, described the task facing the police at the time the unit was born:

Against the depleted ranks of the police was ranged a new type of criminal, cunning, ruthless and well informed. Many had served in the armed forces – some with distinction – and many more were deserters. They were younger, fitter, harder, more resourceful and more energetic than the pre-war criminal.

All Britain was the province of these new criminals. Time, money and distance were no object if the pickings were good. They swooped almost every night. Lorryloads of tea, sugar, butter, clothes, cigarettes and whisky disappeared from the streets or were stolen from warehouses. Jewellery and cash vanished from private houses into the pockets of thieves who worked like phantoms. Furs and rings, clothing and petrol coupons, carpets, lipsticks, typewriters, razor blades, shoes – anything with a ready cash value was loot for the army of the underworld. The figures of stolen property rose to astronomical proportions.

Capstick's main areas of expertise were Soho and the clannish territories of south London; Gosling and Clark were experts on the East End and Brinnand's talents would be concentrated broadly on the West End and north-west London. The four would be joined a little later by a fifth detective, Sergeant George Burton, whose favourite stamping-ground was the western approaches to town, especially the shabby urban jungle around Paddington and the Harrow Road.

Gosling was a burly Suffolk man, quiet and immensely strong. According to Capstick he never needed to struggle with criminals he was about to arrest – 'he just put out a ham-like fist and grabbed them'. Capstick was also mightily impressed with the chain-smoking Gosling's bar-room talents. 'He could put away a pint of ale in one swallow, as a lesser man might take a whisky. Sometimes he looked almost sleepy – and that was when he was at his most dangerous.'

Clark, the only native Londoner of the original four, was regarded as an expert in disguise but also seems to have been more than familiar with the pub culture of London's less salubrious districts. Again according to Capstick, he was not averse to a good brawl when the situation called for it. 'Though smaller than most Metropolitan policemen, he was a terror in a rough-house, with a punch like the kick of a mule.'

Brinnand was a Cumbrian, tall, lean and wiry with a particular gift for following a target for many hours without being spotted. Gosling described him as 'utterly tireless' in his pursuit of crooks. 'If he had been on an all-night job he would sleep sitting upright in a chair in his office rather than go home and risk being late on duty in the morning.' Unlike Gosling, who nurtured his informants with some degree of kindness and consideration, Brinnand opted for tougher tactics. 'They came to him trembling, to tell him of this job or that job that was afoot.' But in spite of their differing approaches to police work, Gosling and Brinnand were firm friends and had worked as something of a team in the Flying Squad. They used their 'Mr Nasty-Mr Nice' approach to good effect and in 1944 had made more arrests, individually and jointly, than any other Flying Squad officers.

By his own account, Gosling had a large body of informants on whom he could more or less rely for sound information. All were or had been petty criminals and all seemed to have colourful nicknames. Their pedigrees give a good insight into the type of individuals courted by the Ghost Squad. Bert the Lorry was a scrap metal dealer of dubious ethics who rented out his lorries to thieves and receivers to transport stolen goods. Having taken their money, he would sometimes inform on them to Gosling for a further fee. Slicer Fred was a thief who began informing to break up a relationship between his daughter and another thief to whom she was about to get engaged. By telling Gosling of his prospective son-in-law's activities, Slicer managed to get him arrested, which led to the break-up of the affair. He was grateful for Gosling's assistance and gradually became a more regular informer. Hymie the Gambler lost consistently on the horses and at the card schools. He was one of Gosling's best 'snouts' and informed purely to finance his gaming pursuits. Stir-Happy Lou, on the other hand, was a monumentally unsuccessful thief and handler who had spent much of his adult life in prison. He continued to be caught regularly for minor offences and usually tried to trade information on bigger fish than himself for continued liberty.

The major criminals of the day had nicknames which were no less colourful – Boss-Eye Curtis, Willie the Face, Gelignite Gus, Holy Hal and Strong-Arm Vic, to name but a few. The trick for the Ghost Squad was to blend into the background, keep their eyes

79

and ears open and milk their informants without giving them or themselves away. It was a precarious existence and one which divorced the officers more and more from their controllers and colleagues at the Yard. When the chips were down they were on their own. In 1947 questions began to be asked about the large amounts of money the Flying Squad and Ghost Squad were paying to their informants. They were getting results – 157 arrests of top-grade criminals through the work of the Ghost Squad alone in 1946 – but it was expensive. The Yard has never published the precise amount paid in any one year to informants but it is clear that in 1947, the Metropolitan Police Receiver thought the total was excessive.

The four Ghost Squad men and their Flying Squad colleagues were so incensed that their methods and expenses were being queried that they staged what was effectively a work-to-rule. They wasted no time in telling their friends in the press about the disgraceful financial restrictions the Receiver wanted to place them under and on 4 July 1947 a prominent article appeared in the *Daily Mail* under the headline: 'CID Men Seeking Decision'.

It told how squad detectives had sought a crisis meeting with the Met Commissioner to clarify their discretion in the payment of informants and hinted that the Home Secretary, Mr Chuter Ede, was also being approached. The correspondent wrote:

There is no suggestion that the Yard men are relaxing any efforts in the drive against crime but I understand that no major arrests have been made for ten days. Detectives, it is believed, are carrying out their duties strictly to routine.

The financial status of individual CID men may be examined. Experienced officers declare it is impossible, on the meagre expenses they are allowed, to obtain vital information from underground channels. The scale of expenses also prevents those working on West End inquiries from patronising hotels and restaurants where leaders of black market activities are to be found.

Nothing is recorded of the outcome of the work-to-rule but it certainly did not damage the squad's image or impede its progress.

In 1948 the Flying Squad was detached from the wider body of CID officers under the control of the Commissioner's Office at Scotland Yard (known collectively as COC1) and became an independent central branch of its own, codenamed C8 (later S08). Instead of being led by a chief inspector, as it had been since its inception thirty years earlier, the squad was given a superintendent as its new chief, confirming its enhanced status. The new man was Superintendent William 'Cherub' Chapman, a forty-eight-year-old murder squad detective with twenty-six years' CID experience. 'It was his round face and twinkling eyes that won him the title of "The Cherub" among his colleagues', the *Daily Mail* reported on 22 May 1948.

Chapman was also given permission to recruit an extra thirty detectives and wasted no time in recalling some old boys from divisional duties to the Alma Mater to fill the vacancies. On 18 July 1948, the *Sunday Dispatch* reported:

> A number of senior CID officers in charge of divisional offices have been drafted into Scotland Yard's Flying Squad in the last few days as a first step in an all-out drive to smash up London's gangs of criminals.
>
> They are all ex-Flying Squad men who since their early days in the squad have been in charge of every type of crime in the West End and the inner suburbs of London. Headquarters have decided to use their experience and knowledge of the criminals of Greater London to guide the large number of younger men now being brought into the squad under the new expansion policy. This strengthening of the Flying Squad is preparatory to the launching of an all-out drive to smash London's black marketeers, razor gangs and 'confidence men'.

Within a few weeks of taking over, Chapman achieved his first high-profile success against a gang of armed robbers who had intended to steal a consignment of gold bullion worth £250,000 from a BOAC warehouse at Heathrow Airport. When the details of the plot were passed to the squad by an informant, an ambush was planned and fourteen detectives were planted in and around

81

the warehouse, posing as anything from mechanics to security guards. Another two were concealed inside the van which brought the bullion to the airport *en route* to its eventual destination in South America.

The gang had relied for information and assistance on an inside man, a warehouseman whose principal job was to drug the tea and coffee of the guards looking after the bullion so that they would be unconscious when the raiders arrived. But the warehouseman could not go through with the plan and informed BOAC security. He was instructed to carry through the operation right to the stage where he was to telephone the gang and tell them that the guards had been drugged and were asleep.

Unaware of all this, the eight robbers, armed with iron bars and coshes and with nylon stockings over their heads, entered the warehouse to see the three 'guards' slumped in their chairs. The real guards had been given the night off and had been replaced by Flying Squad officers. As the robbers searched for the keys to the strong-room, the squad declared its hand. The three bogus guards were reinforced by eleven other detectives and a bloody fight broke out which led to all eight robbers and several policemen being laid prostrate. It had been a delicate operation, but it proved an unqualified success. The robbers received on average sentences of ten years.

The policy of expanding the Flying Squad was quickly shown to be a shrewd one and the rate of serious crime continued to decline through the late 1940s and early 1950s. The average annual total of Flying Squad arrests topped 1,000, due in no small part to the clandestine beaverings of the Ghost Squad. Between 1946 and 1949, the Ghost Squad generated information leading to the arrest of 789 criminals, the clearing up of 1,506 crimes and the recovery of property valued in excess of £300,000. They continued to operate with as high a degree of secrecy as possible but it is likely that most Flying Squad detectives knew of their purpose within a few weeks of their first operation. As their faces became better known in criminal circles, the Ghost Squad detectives were moved back to normal Flying Squad duties and were replaced by other experienced thief-takers. Only Gosling remained throughout the four years of the Ghost Squad's existence.

In February 1947, one of the 'ghosts' received information that a gang of north London thieves was planning a raid on the Kentish Town branch of the Midland Bank. They had been watching the movements of the bank's manager for several weeks and were intending to kidnap him, steal his keys and help themselves to the money in the bank vaults. The Ghost Squad was able to establish when the manager was to be waylaid but not precisely where. They passed their intelligence on to the head of the Flying Squad, then Detective Chief Inspector Bob Lee.

Lee decided on a daring course of action which would require courage and nerve from the detective selected as the central player. On the evening planned for the hold-up, the bank manager would be substituted by a policeman of roughly similar height and build, who would act as a decoy. In this way, the bank manager would not be placed at risk but the robbers would still be brought into the open. Detective Sergeant William Deans volunteered for the operation and on the bitterly cold evening of 14 February he left the bank in the manager's clothes, bowler hat and a pair of false spectacles, and walked in the direction of Kentish Town station. Other Flying Squad officers maintained a watch on the bank but Deans was effectively isolated. These were the days before hand-held police radios and if his colleagues tried to follow him too closely the gang would be alerted and would scatter. A compromise was reached whereby one of the squad's few women detectives, Winnie Sherwin, and Detective Inspector Leonard Crawford would travel the same route as Deans but would keep out of sight.

Deans reached the station and continued on the bank manager's usual journey. As he left Woodside Park station and walked along a footpath towards the manager's home, he was approached by three men. He watched as two of them rushed in front of him and heard a voice behind him say: 'Right.' Almost simultaneously he felt a stunning blow on the side of his head, delivered with a sand-filled cosh. He was then beaten and kicked unconscious and, to the horror of Crawford and Sherwin, who witnessed the end of the beating, a van roared up and Deans was thrown into the back of it.

A scarf was tied over his eyes, sticking plaster was placed across his mouth and his hands and ankles were tied together. He was relieved of the keys and thrown, still unconscious, into a pile of snow on the roadside. Fortunately for Deans, who could easily have died from exposure or suffocation, a female motorist caught a glimpse of his huddled figure in her headlights and stopped to help him. He was taken to a local doctor's surgery and treated for concussion and hypothermia.

Meanwhile, a frantic search had been mounted by one squad team to find Deans while another team continued to keep watch at the bank. Within an hour of Deans being dumped, one of the gang arrived at the bank, took out a set of keys and began to let himself in. Half-a-dozen detectives flew at him and demanded to know where Deans had been dumped and the whereabouts of the rest of the gang. The terrified robber, a window cleaner by day, was in no position to demur and immediately told the furious detectives all they wanted to know. The five other gang members – a chauffeur, a mechanic, a demolition worker, a joiner and a market trader – were rounded up at a hideout in Walthamstow and Deans was sent home for a short period of recuperation.

The robbers received between three and seven years and Deans was awarded the King's Police Medal and commended by both the trial judge and the Met Commissioner, Sir Harold Scott, for his bravery. Sir Harold described Deans as having displayed 'cold-blooded courage'.

By 1949, the Yard was beginning to have second thoughts about the wisdom of maintaining the Ghost Squad. Its detectives were becoming closer and closer to their criminal opponents and senior officers became worried about possible accusations that the police were acting as *agents provocateurs*. Divisional CID chiefs were also beginning to complain that only the Flying Squad was benefiting from this expensive exercise and argued that their criminal intelligence should be more fairly spread. When the serious crime figures for 1949 showed their fourth fall in successive years, sending them back down to pre-1944 levels, Sir Harold Scott decided that the Ghost Squad experiment had run its course. The detectives were posted back to general Flying Squad duties and the unit was disbanded, to be succeeded a few years later by the Criminal Intelligence branch, a more general surveillance and intelligence-gathering unit which would serve the whole of the CID.

8
Wild West End

Of the many journalists who chronicled the Flying Squad's progress through the 1950s and 1960s, probably the best informed and most trusted was T. A. Sandrock of the *Daily Telegraph*. Sandrock joined the newspaper in 1935 and in 1952, when his predecessor Stanley Firmin fell seriously ill, he became its chief crime correspondent, a job he held until his retirement thirty-four years later. So close did he become to the inner workings of the squad that he was used regularly by them as a supernumerary driver, transporting detectives to and from jobs in his own car when they needed a vehicle in a hurry, or one which would not be identified as a police car.

'From the time I started on the crime beat it was obvious to me that it was the Flying Squad who were doing all the best work,' said Sandrock, now in his seventies. 'They were getting villains and they were getting the results, so I had to stay near them, sometimes all day and all bloody night. I was virtually part of the team. Their ability to move across divisional borders was still the big thing and they had an incredible network of informants across London.

'They mixed with a lot of criminals to get information but you have to remember that you were dealing with a different kind of villain in those days. If he got caught he got caught and accepted it. He didn't pull out a gun and try to shoot his way out. So there were some sort of rules between villains and squad detectives. They could mix and they did mix and often I mixed with them. The argument was made even then that by mixing with these people the police were opened up to corruption but it's not really valid. You will always get bad people, policemen or anybody else, but in the main the squad officers were all very straight, although they didn't always work by the book. They would cut some legal corners if it was going to lead to good arrests but I don't think of that as being corrupt. They were bloody grafters.

'If I was to sum up a squad man of those days I would say he had to be devoted to his job, to be able to drink a fair bit without getting drunk, prepared to sacrifice a great part of his family life, and he had to stick as close to the rules as he could but be sufficiently experienced and knowledgeable to be able to bend those rules slightly when necessary to achieve results against organised teams. He did not have to be crooked and the vast majority were very honest people who worked entirely for the benefit of the public.'

One of the first people to whom Tom Sandrock became close after becoming a full-time crime hack was Detective Superintendent Reg Spooner, who led the Flying Squad from 1953 to 1958. Spooner was a quiet, unpretentious Cockney with thick black-framed spectacles and a languid gait. During the war he had been selected for secondment to MI5 and was involved in the arrest and interrogation of the infamous Nazi propagandist William Joyce, alias Lord Haw Haw. In 1946, as a murder squad detective, he had helped catch the sadistic Air Force officer Neville Heath, who murdered and mutilated two women in a case which horrified the nation.

As head of the Flying Squad, Spooner set up a branch office in the St Stephens dive bar off Whitehall, in the shadow of the old Scotland Yard buildings. 'He would have his seat in the corner and he would sit there talking to his men as they came in and out,' Sandrock said. 'I'd go and sit next to him and as the men came in to tell him what jobs they had had off that day, he would tell me whether I could print them or not. He would be there for hours drinking quietly and never eating anything.'

By this time the squad was arranged into eight sub-squads of eight or nine detectives and a headquarters unit of like size. There would normally be at least three or four teams out on the road at any given time, while at least one would be on standby at the Yard. Although there were no strict geographical divisions, a team might do more work in a particular area of London than others because one or more of its detectives had a good network of

The Flying Squad launched Operation Yamato to catch the men who robbed a Securicor van in 1990. Kenny Baker, right, was killed in the shoot-out (*Scotland Yard*)

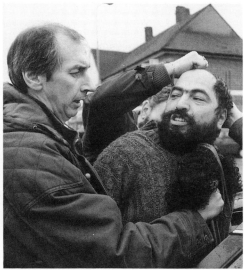

Dennis Arif ('Afro') was arrested . . . (*Scotland Yard*)

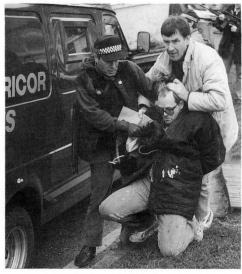

. . . as was Anthony Downer (*Scotland Yard*)

Mehmet Arif being patched up after being shot during the Squad ambush (*Scotland Yard*)

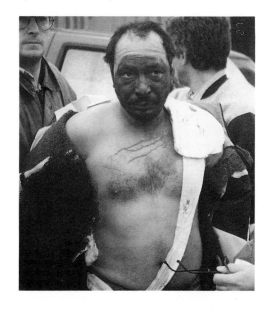

CID men in and out of disguise
circa 1910 (*Metropolitan Police*)

Progenitors of the Flying Squad – a special undercover team set up by the Yard to combat pickpockets and other thieves in London *circa* 1916 (*Metropolitan Police*)

Chief Superintendent Walter Hambrook, left, with a Flying Squad colleague (*Hulton Deutsch*)

Hambrook, then a detective inspector, on special duty at the Chelsea Arts Ball (*Metropolitan Police*)

Awards for bravery: Inspector Ted Ockey, right, who gallantly jumped on the footboard of a bandit's car and Detective Jones, left, congratulating PC Lewis Hoare, centre, who saved two girls from drowning at Brighton in 1929 (*Hulton Deutsch*)

Chief Constable Frederick Wensley – 'Father of the Flying Squad' (*Hulton Deutsch*)

Right: The Crossley Tender with its 'bedstead' pattern wireless antennae, first used on Derby Day 1923 at Epsom (*Metropolitan Police*)

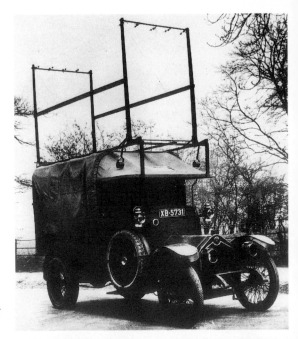

Below: Police vans leaving Poplar after a raid by the Flying Squad

The Lea Francis squad car used in 1927 (*Metropolitan Police*)

Invicta 4½-litre used by the squad in 1930 (*Metropolitan Police*)

Looking as sinister as the men they chased, detectives with a Bentley used in 1930–31 (*Metropolitan Police*)

A 1938 Railton Special Saloon (*Metropolitan Police*)

Jack 'Spot' Comer who controlled large parts of the West End underworld in the 1950s (*Topham*)

Frankie Fraser, a member of Billy Hill's gang who later teamed up with the Richardsons

Albert Dimes, a 40-year-old bookmaker, celebrates with his wife after he was found not guilty at the Old Bailey of wounding Jack Comer with intent to do him grievous bodily harm (*Topham*)

Billy Hill, Comer's West End gangland rival, arrives back in Britain in June 1955 after being refused permission to settle in Australia (*Topham*)

Jack Comer, right, and producer Michael Goodman on their way to Dublin to shoot a film on 'crime does not pay' in 1962 (*Topham*)

Above left: Detective
Superintendent Reginald
Spooner on the day he was
appointed Chief of the Flying
Squad, 3 February 1955
(*Topham*)

Above right: Superintendent
Jack Capstick, left, at Scotland
Yard with Sergeant Dennis
Hawkins and County Inspector
A. Kennedy of the Royal
Ulster Constabulary CID
(*Topham*)

Detective Chief
Superintendent Herbert
Sparks, head of the Flying
Squad 1958–61 (*Metropolitan
Police*)

informants there. Most of the work was self-generated and relied on inside track. The squad had a name for working hard and playing hard.

'In those days they didn't pack up at six o'clock and go home. I would join in with fifteen or twenty of them regularly in the Red Lion or St Stephens dive bar, talking about the job, having a drink together and a laugh and a joke. Percy Lawless was one of the team leaders and he always wore a trilby hat. He would put it on the bar and everybody would throw in an 'Oxford' – five bob – and they would have a few drinks until the money went. They weren't pissed out of their minds or anything like that. It was like a big club based on work. They were taking on the toughest and they had a real camaraderie.'

Having left the pubs around Whitehall in mid-evening, the squad officers would then peel off to drinking haunts in other parts of London and continue socialising and picking up local gossip until the early hours. Sandrock remembered: 'I have been with Flying Squad teams in various pubs which were used by villains and although each knew what the other was, there was a form of respect. If you take the Trinity or the Albany Tap down in south London, you would go in with two or three squad men and before you got to the bar there would be five beers lined up for you. A certain distance was usually kept but there was never any animosity. The criminals respected the squad and they feared them because they were hard men and they were a bit like the Mounties – they always got their man. If a team of robbers got wind the squad was on to them they would abandon the job rather than face them. This was their power because of their success rate. It wasn't a bluff, they were the single most efficient crime fighting body there was at the time.

'The pubs used to shut eventually but there would still be places you could go on to, especially in the West End. You'd be up there drinking among the barrels until three o'clock in the morning, all before the breathalyser days, of course. The squads had a charisma and it was accepted in areas with a lot of restaurants and clubs and pubs which had trouble every so often from criminals of some sort that the owners of these places would do anything for the squad and the squad would always try to help them. It was expected. In some places you would get a bottle – gin, whisky or whatever – with a scale marked on the side. When you had finished, the amount you had drunk would be marked off and the bottle would be kept behind the bar for you until you came in again. The coppers would usually pay something for their drinks but it would be at trade price. It was a sort of perk. But they always kept watching, looking to see who was coming and going and who was spending.'

The West End, particularly Soho and its surrounding streets, had developed its own criminal pecking order since the war years and two men had risen from the sordid heap of pimps, hustlers, extortionists and thieves to become self-styled 'kings of the underworld'.

Jack 'Spot' Comer was an East End streetfighter of Polish-Jewish stock who had made a name for himself as a young man for leading a commando-style raid on Oswald Mosley and his anti-semitic Fascist followers when they marched through Cable Street in 1937. In an act of blind daring, he ran up to Mosley's chief bodyguard, 'a six-foot-six bruiser', and knocked him out with blows to the head from a sofa leg filled with lead. 'Crowned him on the nut – boomp,' the cigar-smoking Comer later told the *Daily Express*. 'Big hero, came from up north somewhere. Blood all over the place. He lay on the floor screaming like a woman.'

Comer had learned to fight at an early age in the ghetto streets of Whitechapel. One side of his home street was populated by Jews, the other by Irish, an explosive mix. 'Been fighting all my life,' Comer said. The Mosley incident brought him celebrity status and his career moved swiftly from the East End to the West End, first as a bookie and leader of a group of young gipsy toughs, which he would hire out to others, and later as a club-owner, protector and 'fixer'. He maintained cordial relations with the police while taking a rake-off from most of the scams and rackets operating in Soho.

His only serious competition was a thin, mean-faced, sober character named Billy Hill. Quietly spoken and invariably dressed in a dark double-breasted suit with matching tie and handkerchief, Hill had been a thief and burglar in his formative criminal days but by the mid-1950s had achieved a secure base in the West End, thanks to a body of hard 'enforcers' including 'Wild' Billy Blythe, who had a conviction for slashing a Flying Squad detective in the face, and 'Mad' Frankie Fraser, later to become notorious as chief henchman of the Richardson gang. Between them, Hill and Comer carved up the West End, extracting a tithe from ordinary criminal activity, illegal gambling and vice. With so much money at stake, neither needed a gang war which would bring the police down heavily on both of them so, with a few minor lapses, they maintained a sullen peace.

But it was never more than a marriage of convenience and on 11 August 1955 the peace was shattered in spectacular fashion. The circumstances which led up to the 'Battle of Frith Street' are shrouded in a haze of conflicting versions of events, but what is certain is that 'Italian' Albert Dimes, one of Hill's top soldiers, engaged in a ferocious knife and stiletto fight with Comer which very nearly proved fatal for both. It was an unmistakable signal that Hill was making a bid for sole supremacy.

A bookmaker by trade, Dimes was of Italian descent and brought several other tough Italian gangsters into Hill's camp. The American Federal Bureau of Investigation would later allege that Dimes, who called himself Dimeo when in the company of his countrymen, had connections with the Angelo Bruno Mafia family of Philadelphia, a development of serious concern to Scotland Yard.

The combat between Dimes and Comer began at 11.40 a.m. on the pavement of Frith Street, Soho and developed into a running battle, in full public view, through a fruit shop along the road and into the doorway of a second shop. Both men suffered serious stab wounds and were arrested after undergoing medical treatment. Each was charged with making an affray, wounding the other with intent to commit grievous bodily harm, illegal possession of a knife and unlawfully fighting. The trial, however, was a farce. Neither defendant was prepared to give evidence against the other and even though the affray happened in broad daylight at a time when Frith Street must have been fairly crowded, the police could not persuade a single witness to testify to having seen anything amiss. The case was dismissed, but Comer now knew his position was under grave threat and decided to call on some extra muscle.

The collapse of the case brought strong criticism of Scotland Yard in the leader columns of several newspapers, including some of those normally most sympathetic to the police. The thrust of the editorials was that the Met had not tried hard enough to nail Comer and rumours abounded that it was because he enjoyed a corrupt relationship with certain West End detectives. A leading article in the *Daily Sketch* described the case as 'the most flagrant miscarriage of justice for many, many years' and called for a full public inquiry:

> The authority of British law is at stake. The good name of Scotland Yard is at stake. Ugly rumours are going round and each day the rumours grow. Each day there are more people ready to believe them. Can anybody be surprised? Criminal elements in Soho have openly threatened the police with blackmail. If the police interfere with Jack Spot, then the Jack Spot Protection Society will blow the gaff on corrupt policemen.

The *News Chronicle* also joined the clarion call for an inquiry, as did the *Daily Mail*, which described the Battle of Frith Street sarcastically as 'the fight that never was'. Faced with this barrage, the Yard instructed the Flying Squad to get to the bottom of the Soho feud and take the perpetrators out of circulation.

In the early spring of 1956 the major London gangs gathered for a big race meeting at Epsom. The mob violence which had characterised such meetings in the 1920s had been brought under control long ago but underworld figures still came together occasionally at the top race fixtures to look one another over and see who was associating with whom. Bookmakers still allowed themselves to be 'protected' but now more out of tradition than necessity. The profits to the minders were relatively small and their presence was largely symbolic.

But the tilting of the power balance in Soho was illustrated to those in the know at that Epsom meeting by the fact that Hill and his boys had been allowed to commandeer the best bookmaking pitch near the winning-post, while Comer had to content himself with slightly less prestigious positions lower down the course. However, Comer did provide a talking-point by inviting two newcomers with growing reputations as underworld hard men to join him at the meeting. They were twins from Bethnal Green who had both been promising amateur boxers before realising they could make more money by diverting their energies into crime. Their names were Ron and Reg Kray.

The twins, who were then based at a billiard hall in the East End, had come to the races as a favour to Comer and because they wanted to see what went on there, but they appeared completely disinterested once they arrived. The meeting passed off without incident but the inference was drawn that Comer was prepared to fight to hold on to his Soho interests.

A number of minor fracas occurred between men associated with Comer and Hill over the next few weeks but the dénouement came in May 1956. Blythe, Fraser and at least four other Hill henchmen lay in wait for Comer and attacked him with razors as he returned to his flat in Hyde Park Mansions after a night out with his wife, Rita. They held him and slashed him mercilessly across the face, head, chest and neck before leaving him bleeding profusely in the gutter. Surgeons at St Mary's Hospital, Paddington worked through the night to save his life and put seventy-eight stitches across his gaping wounds. Comer would later joke that 'There were so many stitches the doctors ran out of thread, so I put them in touch with my tailor.'

The Flying Squad, who had been keeping a close eye on the feuding parties, moved into action that same night. Hill, Fraser, Blythe and other gang members were arrested. Detective Inspector Tommy Butler, later to head the squad, and Detective Sergeant Peter Vibart led the inquiry, and although they still could not persuade Comer to name his assailants, Rita decided enough was enough and was encouraged by Butler to make a full statement.

Tommy Butler was to become one of the most famous of all squad detectives, though he was not a typical squad man. A non-smoker and moderate drinker, he was a life-long bachelor who lived with his mother in the genteel west London suburb of Barnes, though his work-rate was such that he rarely saw the inside of the house before dawn. He had one of the most meteoric rises through the CID ranks of any detective, progressing from detective sergeant to chief superintendent in less than ten years. He was known to spend long hours studying photographs of career villains and his infrequent holidays were usually taken alone in foreign locations where crooks congregated. But he also had a soft spot for the dependents of the criminals he arrested. A *Times* correspondent wrote of him:

> He has never made a secret of his dislike for thieves and criminals but has always been known to go out of his way to help their wives and children.

In the 1960s, Butler's successful pursuit of the Great Train Robbers won him the popular nickname of 'The Grey Fox'.

He was obsessively secret, keeping all his information to himself, and sending his officers out on missions with hardly any form of briefing. Despite this, he had the full respect of all the officers that worked with him.

'Tommy was completely without airs and graces. "Hello, mate," was his usual greeting when you joined the squad,' said one of the 1960s squad officers. 'Absolutely dedicated to the job, and no idea of what an eight-hour shift was. If you worked hard, he stuck by you. There were only two people close to him, his mum and his girlfriend – the job came before either of them. He'd stay on long after everyone else was finished, and if he thought you were a bit under pressure, you'd come in in the morning and find that Tommy had done all your paperwork for you. Yes, I've heard the rumours that he made a bit from the Great Train Robbery. All I can say about that is this: Tommy got rid of two or three blokes he suspected of being on the take. No messing, straight back to division. When he died, he left £7,000, hardly a fortune, and he was so naive about his own money that he hadn't thought to insure himself for his girlfriend's flat. When he died, she had to get out.'

The day after Comer was attacked by Hill's thugs, he was visited in hospital by Ron and Reg Kray. The twins told him they had amassed a small arsenal of firearms and other weapons and offered to mop up the key members of Hill's gang who had escaped arrest. Spot was in no doubt they were offering help in order to take over both his and Hill's empires for themselves. The violence had already been terminally bad for business, having brought the Flying Squad down heavily on both gangs, and Comer had lost all stomach for a fight. He refused to sanction the twins' desire for a final battle and concentrated on his convalescence. At that stage, Ron and Reg did not have the power to take on the Soho gangs without an influential ally, so they went back to Bethnal Green to pursue other criminal avenues. Mass bloodshed had been averted and the squad set about dismantling the two Soho gangs.

Hill himself was released from custody but Blythe, Fraser and the others eventually received prison sentences of up to seven years for the attack at Hyde Park Mansions. The Flying Squad was authorised by the Home Secretary to tap Hill's telephone after his release, a rare move in those days, and Butler, Vibart and the other members of the C8 team harassed the rest of his gang remorselessly until their business became untenable. Even Hill's barrister, Mr Patrick Aloysius Marrinan, was denounced at the Old Bailey by Butler for having had an improper relationship with Hill and other members of his gang, and for advising at least one defendant in the Comer case to escape rather than face trial.

Marrinan was disbarred by the Benchers of Lincoln's Inn. He later accused Butler and Vibart of maliciously setting him up and sued for defamation but the action ended in abject failure. At the High Court, Mr Justice Salmon ruled that the two squad officers had made their allegations against Marrinan during the course of a court case and therefore enjoyed absolute immunity from subsequent legal action. The judge also had a veiled word of contempt for the hapless lawyer. 'This immunity exists for the benefit of the public, since the administration would be greatly impeded if witnesses were to fear that any disgruntled and possibly impecunious persons against whom they gave evidence might bring costly litigation against them,' he said.

Butler's actions had been completely vindicated but there was some disquiet about the fact that the squad had been allowed to tap Hill's telephone and that transcripts of some of the calls they had taped were used against Marrinan at the disciplinary hearing in Lincoln's Inn. A Privy Council Committee was set up under the chairmanship of Lord Birkett to inquire into the whole question of telephone intercepts by the police. The Birkett report, published in late 1957, gave guidelines on the future use of taps which are still in force today. They include the necessity for the Home Secretary personally to authorise the tap by specific warrant and the instruction that information discovered should be used only for generally assisting investigations rather than as court evidence. No information from the taps may be passed to outside individuals or organisations.

Billy Hill hung on in Soho until the early 1960s but he knew he was beaten, so he took his money out of the West End, bought a new yacht and flashy American car and built himself a luxurious retirement villa in southern Spain. Spot Comer bought a furniture business in Marylebone, the beginning of a rapid decline in his fortunes. The business did not prosper and within two years he was made bankrupt. He was evicted from his home and the former East End hero suddenly found himself friendless. In the mid-1960s, shortly after a humiliating magistrates' court conviction for stealing meat worth a paltry thirty shillings from the Cadby Hall headquarters of J. Lyons, he left Britain for the Irish Republic and ended up as a bookie's runner, the very job in which he had begun his rise to power in the East End.

Comer was deeply embittered by his experiences. In a particularly mournful interview with the *Sunday Times* in 1965 he said: 'I should have known they'd get me some day. Once they get you you've had it. Your're on your own. You suddenly realise that all your right-hand men aren't about any more. Twenty-four hours a day my phone would ring. It don't ring at all now. I spent money like water. Hand-made suits, my own shirtmaker, my own shoemaker. You're all hand made. I went everywhere. Mae West was always on at me to go to parties at her suite at the Dorchester . . .

'I made Billy Hill. He wrote to me when he was in jail, wanted me to help him . . . so I gave him some clothes and made him my right-hand man. Then he got over the top of me. If it wasn't for me he'd never have got there. I should have shot Billy Hill, I really should. I'd have got ten years for it but it would have made me happy and I'd be out now – laughing.'

Notwithstanding his alleged links with the Mafia in the United States, Dimes retired from any personal involvement in violent crime and made an apparently honest living from his bookmaking interests until his death in 1972. He also struck up a friendship with the actor-director Stanley Baker and advised him and his production company on two 1960s films entitled *The Criminal* and *Robbery*.

After serving his sentence for the attack on Jack Spot, 'Mad' Frankie Fraser joined up with Charles and Eddie Richardson in their now famous south London fraud, extortion and protection gang. His later career is covered in Chapter 11.

The Flying Squad came out of the Hill-Comer affair with plaudits from all sides and Butler and Vibart became known in the press as 'the terrible twins'. Such was their reputation that they were selected to visit Cyprus to advise police on the island how best to combat the activities of the nationalist terror group Eoka.

Other members of the squad had also been far from idle and between January and October 1957 they chalked up a record total of more than 1,000 arrests. According to Tom Tullett, chief crime reporter for the *Daily Mirror* and himself a former CID man, this was 'the most spectacular performance ever of the famous squad of eighty-two detectives bossed by the shrewd Chief Superintendent Spooner – the squad the underworld call the Heavy Mob.'

Tullett focused on the squad's success in recapturing escaped prisoners who had gravitated back to London and attempted to melt into the underworld. They were, Tullet said, 'the most dangerous and ruthless of criminals. The names of the men read like the Old Bailey calendar.' It was a mark of the squad's information network that most were caught within a few weeks at most.

One who held out longer was Teddy Rice, a safe-cracker and warehouse burglar who managed to remain at large for two years after breaking out of Strangeways with five other men. He had set up home in a modest bungalow in Kilburn and lived a life of outward respectability but was finally betrayed by a squad informant. Charlie Parsons, a violent payroll bandit who broke out of Wormwood Scrubs, was picked up at a caravan park near Torquay. Anthony Hawkes, a notorious fraudster and confidence trickster, was traced to Newcastle-on-Tyne and his partner Dennis Stafford, known curiously as 'The Bandaged Toff', was arrested 5,000 miles from London in Trinidad. George 'Taters' Chatham, who went over the wall at Brixton prison, was recaptured closer to home at a luxury flat in Kensington. The impression was that no wanted criminal was safe from the clutches of the squad, however far he travelled to escape them.

To most observers, the squad appeared to have done a comprehensive job of cleaning up Soho, though this was inevitably an illusion. The two main gangs were broken but criminal elements continued to be attracted like moths to a flame by the huge profits to be made from illegal gambling and vice. The immediate effect was that criminality became fragmented and ironically more difficult to police. In the next few years more gangs would emerge, particularly from the Italian and Maltese communities; the Krays would make a comeback, the pornographers would flourish and, sadly, increasing numbers of policemen would succumb to the temptations of corruption.

The spectre of police corruption did rear its head in a highly publicised case in October 1957 but on this occasion it was a provincial force that stood accused and the Flying Squad was drafted in to help investigate the allegations. Again it was Butler and Vibart who handled much of the most delicate work.

Charles Ridge, the Chief Constable of Brighton, and two of his top CID men were accused of taking bribes and consorting with criminals. It was a case which shocked the nation because of the high rank of the senior officer involved. The basis of the case was that the defendants had sought and accepted favours and money from various shady characters in return for not arresting them or for helping them in other ways to circumvent the law. The nine chief prosecution witnesses, interviewed in the main by Butler and Vibart, were described at the Old Bailey as 'a procession of crooks', but their stories were consistent enough to convict the two more junior officers. Ridge was acquitted but dismissed from his post by the Brighton Watch Committee.

Butler and Vibart were accused by one of Ridge's co-defendants, a bookmaker named Samuel Bellson, of fabricating statements but neither judge nor jury gave the accusations more than cursory consideration. The attitude of the court was that they were members of the most respected police unit in the country and would not demean themselves by 'fitting up' a lowly bookie.

9
Swinging Sixties

At the beginning of the 1960s there was a small but ominous signal that Flying Squad officers could not always rely on their reputation to be certain of winning cases. A jury in a libel case returned a verdict which could only mean that they did not accept the evidence of the squad's senior officer.

The matter began in 1953 when a seemingly reformed criminal, Alfie Hinds, was convicted of a burglary at Maples Furniture Store in Tottenham Court Road. As a young man, Hinds had been convicted several times of safe-breaking, but he had not come to police notice since 1946. The evidence against him in the Maples burglary came from his alleged accomplices, from forensic evidence – the dust alleged to have been found in the turn-ups of a pair of his trousers – and from some alleged verbal statements. Chief Superintendent Herbert Sparks, then in charge of the Flying Squad, led the investigation. Hinds denied all the allegations against him, admitting only that he had been in Tottenham Court Road a few days before the burglary buying a carpet in a pub from one of the co-accused, to whom he had lent his Land Rover. The jury at the trial did not believe Hinds, who was sentenced to twelve years.

Hinds, who had an IQ of 150, escaped from prison three times and ran a leaflet campaign to protest his innocence. During one escape he was at liberty for over two years. In 1961, back in prison but on the point of being released, Hinds read an account of the robbery in the *News of the World*. The account, by one of his co-accused, admitted that Hinds had not been involved in the burglary. A few months later Sparks, who had just retired as the

101

Detective Chief Superintendent in charge of the Flying Squad, gave his version of the investigation to the *People*. Naturally he held that Hinds was guilty. Hinds, now out of prison, sued for libel.

In the subsequent civil action he was able to present alibi witnesses who had not been called at his trial. He was also able to overturn the forensic evidence and convince the jury that he was innocent. The jury ignored the judge's summing up and awarded Hinds the then substantial sum of £1,300 in damages. Reporters who were in court thought that the jury were more impressed with Hinds' quiet self-confidence than with Bert Sparks' aggressive answers, which at one stage led the judge to ask him to control his temper. This was a definite indication that the word of the world famous Flying Squad would no longer be accepted without challenge.

Yet on the whole, C8's reputation was comparatively untarnished. To be chosen for the squad was still every detective's ambition. To be recalled to the squad having spent the traditional year back on division as the result of a promotion was as good as a medal. There were then eight separate squads, each composed of a detective inspector, two first-class sergeants, two second-class sergeants and two or three detective constables. In addition each squad had three drivers, usually Class 1 uniformed drivers working in plain clothes, men who had proved their worth driving what were then known as area cars, but today would be called fast response vehicles.

In 1962 the officers at the top of the squad became concerned about the number of teams of criminals who were being arrested in which one of them turned out to be a police informant and was therefore either not prosecuted or was allowed to 'escape'. Ernie 'Hooter' Millen, then the Chief Superintendent, issued a 'no more participating informants memo' that brought the practice to an end.

Another concern for those in charge of the squad was the admission by one of its detective sergeants that he had lied to a magistrate to obtain a search warrant. Such warrants were granted before the opening of the court in the morning, or quite often, when it was a matter of urgency, at the home of the magistrate. In either case the officer applying for the warrant was required to formally swear that 'the contents of this, my information, are true and correct to the best of my knowledge and belief'. Information in this context is the formal term for the short report that the officer prepares for the magistrate outlining the reasons for his needing the warrant.

Detective Sergeant Frank Jiggins and Detective Constable James Shearon from the Flying Squad had worked with three British Transport Police officers in the arrest of a man who was stealing property from King's Cross railway station. The man had admitted the thefts but had alleged that Jiggins and Shearon had helped themselves to part of the property as well as stealing almost £100 from him. The detectives were charged with theft and faced trial twice, with the jury unable to agree on either occasion. On the third trial the prosecution offered no evidence, and the officers were dismissed. During the second trial, Detective Sergeant Jiggins admitted to the judge that he had lied to the magistrate from whom he had obtained the warrant. He claimed he had had to lie to protect an informant's identity.

The case not only hinted at the tendency of some squad officers to cut corners, but also underlined their known need to rely on informants. Two of the squad's best known characters in the 1960s founded their reputations on the range of their informants, some of whom provided information for money, some for the sheer sense of power it gave them, and some to pay off old scores or remove competitors.

Detective Inspector Tommy Butler, who had played such a key role in cleaning up the Soho gangs, was perhaps the most respected Flying Squad character of the decade. Detective Sergeant Alec Eist established two reputations. One was as a specialist in the arrest of lorry hijackers, the other as one of the most corrupt officers of his era. Eist was a man of great charm, a good after-dinner speaker, the ideal drinking companion, and a dedicated racegoer. He was recognised as the best in the business of investigating thefts of lorries and their loads. He had a record number of arrests for this type of crime, but his tendency to celebrate a particularly good capture by taking a day off to go to the races upset even the easygoing squad supervisors, and he was eventually returned to division. Some of his admirers admit that Alec had a thing about going to court. He was an expert at setting up jobs for other people to carry out arrests. That way he kept out of court and avoided a great deal of paperwork.

There was only one case in which Eist demonstrated a willingness to go into the witness box, and that was an arrest which attracted international attention. In 1968, James Earl Rae, wanted for the assassination of black American leader Dr Martin Luther King, was arrested at Heathrow Airport. His name and description had been given worldwide circulation as the FBI's most wanted man, and a suspicious Special Branch officer stopped Rae as he came through customs. His suspicions were verified when he found that Rae was travelling with a gun and a false passport. After a delay during which he protested his innocence and fought against extradition, he was taken back to the US under police escort, one of whom was Alec Eist. Rae was still protesting his innocence, but Alec gained his confidence during the journey and arrived in the US with the allegation that Rae had told him: 'Course I shot the nigger. They're just making too much fuss about it.'

Cynical colleagues who knew of Eist's desire to avoid court saw this as a ploy to get him another trip to the States for the eventual trial. Unfortunately for him, however, Rae pleaded guilty, and he was not required to fly back to America to give evidence. Even at Wood Green, the station to which he was transferred from the squad, he continued to haul in lorry thieves from the nearby North Circular Road. His second reputation, as the most corrupt officer in the Met, was established in the world of journalism and persisted even after he had been tried and acquitted on charges of corruption and conspiracy. Even journalists who believed he was corrupt admitted that bribes taken from one criminal were often used to pay informants to catch bigger fish. Former colleagues are hesitant to discuss his possible corruption. One man who knew him very well commented: 'Well, if he made money, it never showed. He was always hard-up, and he definitely didn't bring anything extra back home. Any time I saw him with money, he was giving it away. If one of his thieves got six months, Alec was round to the wife and kids giving them a few bob to see them through till he came out.'

In 1963 C8 was expanded by another two squads. Tommy Butler

had five DCIs between himself and the troops, but he made certain that he knew every officer on the squad, his – or occasionally her – family and background. The squad's main targets during this period were lorry thieves, pickpockets, high-class burglars, and 'pavement artists' – the robbers who attacked as money was being transferred across the pavement from van to bank. This type of crime was replacing the smash and grab raids of the late 1950s in which a team of villains would drive up to the front of a jewellery shop, smash the window, help themselves to the contents and then drive off. These raids rarely took any longer than a minute, there was little if any violence, and the property was immediately rushed to a fence.

The pickpocket or 'dip squad' worked in such locations as Epsom for the Derby and Westminster for the state opening of Parliament as well as among the daily crowds at the changing of the guard and the major underground stations. The squad picked its own jobs, and set its own objectives: no one assigned it to any particular crime or type of crime, and as ever almost all its successes came from the network of informants that individual officers had built up.

Peter Darke, who retired as Detective Chief Superintendent in charge of the murder squad, gives an example of how vital informants were: 'I was a detective constable on the Flying Squad in the late fifties. We were left completely on our own and had to bring in our own work, so we depended almost entirely on informants. In fact, it was almost impossible to get selected for the squad or to stay with it if you hadn't got a handful of good snouts. There were certainly some strange ones about. There was one snout in south London. We were never sure what side he was on, and I don't know how he survived. He lived in Peckham and wore a kilt.

'Just after I came off the squad in 1960 on promotion to detective sergeant, there was a robbery in Mitcham at the Coop Dairy. A team of four got away with quite a lot of money. As they were leaving, a milk lorry came in, and for no reason at all one of the bastards shot the lorry driver. I was working at Harrow Road, and one of my snouts rang up to tell me who the killer was. A bloke called George Thatcher. I passed it back to the squad. They nicked him and then let him go. "Wrong bloke, Pete," they told me. "Got a good alibi. Your snout must have got it wrong."

'Now my informant was first class. He didn't make mistakes. He only passed on certainties, not rumours or hunches, so I was pretty upset. Not nicking Thatcher was like telling my snout that he was lying. Instead of going home that night, I went out for a drink. I was quite depressed about it. If you've got a good informant, you owe him a sort of loyalty, and here was a certainty that the squad wasn't doing anything with. I thought the squad weren't doing their job. Anyway, I went to this club off Edgware Road. The bloke who ran it was also a grass for me. He saw I was fed up and I told him why.

'"That team," he says, "they were in the club the night before the job. They all signed the visitors' book." I looked in the book and there were four names. Thatcher had signed in as George Hatch. This time we were able to trace them all, and nicked them all at the same time with Thatcher. They went down for it, and that visitors' book was vital evidence that they had been together just before the robbery. Maybe it was a bit lucky, but it shows just how much we depended on informants.'

At a later stage the squad had to be ordered to share its information with divisional officers. Naturally, the only information passed back related to the less likely crimes and the more complicated inquiries. John Simmonds, who was a detective sergeant on the squad in the 1960s, said that their involvement in major crime was a matter of choice.

'We were chasing our own targets, but whenever there was a major crime, or it was felt that a particular villain was getting out of order, we'd have a swoop, bring the bodies, "the usual suspects", into a local nick, and then leave it to some unfortunate detective constable to get the evidence together. We were clocking up a high rate of arrests, and keeping the underworld on its toes, but I don't think there were many actual results in the way of convictions. But the villains certainly knew that the squad was about.'

Another detective sergeant of that time, Gwyn Waters, remembers the 1960s as an eternal round of court appearances: 'We were bringing in a lot of armed robbers. At one period I spent two and a half years – yes, years – in the Old Bailey, often giving evidence in three trials at the same time. And at the end of each day you were still expected to turn out for ordinary squad duties. It wasn't done for the overtime, either. In those days, detectives were not paid overtime.'

However, the squad philosophy, as outlined by John Simmonds, as well as persistent rumours about the corruption of certain officers caused some outstanding men such as Bert Wickstead, who retired as a commander, to refuse to join. Bert, who was responsible for the arrest of some of the gangs that tried to take over from the Krays, as well as for solving the still disputed 'legal and general' murders (so-called for the combination of the occupation of one of the murderers, a general dealer, and Alec Eist's legal backing), ensured that his personal file was marked in red ink 'Not C8' to make sure that no office-bound administrator transferred him.

'You couldn't call them detectives,' he claims. 'They were little more than aides to CID swanning around in cars, depending on informants, and arresting perchers. They did no investigating at all.' Aides to CID were uniformed officers anxious to transfer to the CID who had to prove their worth by making frequent crime arrests; a percher was a petty criminal who allowed himself to be arrested in place of a major villain, the result of a corrupt deal between police and criminals in which the police could be shown to be tackling a problem, while the major criminal could continue in business.

One of the unwritten objectives of the squad was the maintenance of its own reputation as a body of hard crime-fighters. John Simmonds remembered one routine operation that went wrong at first, before being righted in typical squad style.

'We had information about a raid on a post office van in Tottenham Court Road. The informant was spot-on, but the organisation of the ambush at the scene of the robbery was a bit faulty because the villains changed their plan at the last minute. Our practice was never to go in short-handed. You always made sure that you outnumbered the robbers. That way there was no violence, and professional criminals recognised that they had been caught bang to rights, offered no resistance, and usually pleaded guilty.

'So we had enough men there, but two of the lads in an observation van found themselves at the scene of the robbery itself. The post office van had taken a different route, and the villains had decided to attack at a new location. Our lads had no choice but to step in. And they really copped it. This was still in the days when neither police nor robbers carried firearms. This team was carrying pick-axe handles, and they laid into the two squad blokes. Broken bones, smashed faces, blood all over the place. And the robbers got away.

'The press, in their perverse way, loved it. It was not often that the squad came off worst. The Commissioner, Joe Simpson, came into the squad office next day, and one of the lads, Alfie Durrel, told him fairly forthrightly that when we caught the villains responsible, we'd give them what they'd given our two colleagues. Alfie got a bollocking from Ernie Millen for speaking out of turn, but he probably expressed what we all felt.

'We knew who we were looking for, but it took a long time. All the informants the squad had, and many more on division, were put on to tracing the four suspects. It became our highest priority. No one ever escaped from a squad ambush, and with the addition of two badly injured officers, it was essential that our status was restored. Then one Saturday morning there was a call over the radio for all central units to drop whatever they'd been assigned and to go to D99, the squad office. As we were approaching Derby Gate, the entrance to Cannon Row, we saw a detective inspector standing on the pavement. Now a detective inspector in those days was slightly more important than the Pope and very close to God. Anyway, here was this DI standing outside the Red Lion at the corner, waving down each squad car as it approached. That was a mark of the job's importance.

'"Penge nick, like the clappers," he was calling out to each car. Couldn't pass the message over the radio because the suspects might have been listening in. I don't think our driver even slowed down. When we arrived at Penge, every squad officer on duty in London was there. The streets around the station were blocked with their cars and it was standing room only in the nick. They'd found where the robbers were hiding out – information again – a semi-detached house in Clock House Road. There must have been twenty officers posted to the front of the house, twenty to the side, and another twenty to the back. Thank God we weren't armed. There were four suspects, Terroni, Jeffrey, Scrutton and Walker.

'At a signal we dived in. Doors came off their hinges, windows were smashed and dragged from their frames. If the walls could have been pulled down, down they would have come. In no time we had three bodies plus some guns. Terroni, lying on a settee, had a loaded revolver under a cushion and took a bit of handling. While we were there, the phone rang. It was the fourth suspect, Walker, asking if it was all clear. The DI who answered the phone told him it was, and then there was a mad panic to get all the squad cars out of sight and put the outside of the house in some sort of order.

'It worked. Walker drove into the road, walked up the garden path, and the two DCs who were holding the front door in place (it had been torn from its hinges) dropped it and grabbed him.

'There was a bit of unofficial revenge for a victim at Penge nick when Alfie Durrel interviewed Roy Scrutton. "Roy, you remember the robbery you did at Handley Page? Poor old night-watchman, seventy years old? Went down on his knees and said 'Don't hit me, lads,' and you whacked him over the head with a pick-axe handle? Well, I promised the old man I'd sort you out when I caught up with you. So this is for him . . ." and Alfie knocked him unconscious.

'They all pleaded, and received heavy sentences, around eight years. Scrutton made no complaint about Alfie, and I don't think after that a squad officer was ever assaulted again. I remember going on another ambush, about ten years later, and Terroni, the tallest and heaviest of the robbers, was out of prison by then and turned out to be one of this team. When they saw they were surrounded by the squad, his mates were ready to have a go for it. Not Terroni – he stood in the centre of the pavement, and raised his hands well above his head.

'"No trouble from me, gents," he shouted, "no trouble from me."'

It is interesting to contrast this first-hand account of a squad operation with the description of the same incident in Sir Richard Jackson's *Occupied With Crime*. Sir Richard, who was Assistant

Commissioner (Crime), clearly based his piece on the sanitised official report which gave no hint of the urgency and violence involved in dealing with armed criminals.

The Flying Squad's overall reputation for going in hard was maintained by the behaviour of one individual unit well known for internal scrapping. The combination of a Scottish detective inspector and Welsh and English sergeants produced excellent results when they were all sober. Unfortunately, they tended to celebrate victories by drinking heavily, which almost invariably led to what would today be classed as racist behaviour. None of the team was averse to referring to his colleagues in racially stereotyped terms. Returning from one night's drinking in the West End clubs after a day of arrests, the Welshman said something to the DI about the amount of work he was expected to do, while the Scot sat back and took all the glory. The DI chinned him, and the Welshman grabbed the DI round the neck and threw him to the floor. The Englishman intervened and was attacked by both, who left him lying unconscious in a wrecked office.

'Bloody English. Always sticking their noses into other people's business.'

The night duty detective constable, nationality undeclared, cleared everything up, and the squad reassembled the next day without any reference to the previous night's fight.

The post office robbery and the internal scrapping reflected the typical attitudes of the squad in the decade, with the majority of officers giving a full, honest professional commitment to their work – 'professional', in these times, implying a certain amount of corner-cutting. Most former Flying Squad officers accept that there was a small percentage of their colleagues who were in it for the money.

'But they were well known,' said one of the honest majority. 'You just didn't work with them. You didn't get involved in their jobs. You didn't drink with them. It's OK saying they should have been shopped, but who do you shop them to? In the sixties there was no complaints department, and when you see what happened later, it could be just as dodgy going to a senior officer.'

* * *

The three major police successes of the 1960s were the Great Train Robbery and the arrest of the Richardsons, and later of the Krays. The latter two investigations must have raised some questions in the Met hierarchy about the uses to which the squad was being put. The Criminal Intelligence section, C11, was formed to coordinate intelligence for the squad, and C10 was set up to look after stolen vehicles. In his book *The Queen's Peace*, David Ascoli comments: 'It was the start of a new game, super cops against super robbers.'

The prosecution of the Great Train Robbers in 1963 owed much to non-squad officers, but was seen as very much a Flying Squad victory. The Richardson and Kray gangs, in full control of their own territories, were finally arrested towards the end of the decade without too much squad help. But the pattern had been established for the setting up of special squads to deal with particular gangs. The Tibbs and the Dixons, two family gangs waiting for the opportunity to replace the Krays and Richardsons, were dealt with by Bert Wickstead and his specially formed Serious Crimes Squad which carefully excluded almost anyone with Flying Squad experience. The powerful London gangs had been operating without squad intervention since the early 1960s, and there have been few explanations for the failure of the squad's traditional reliance on local knowledge and informants to provide any weapons to use against these first signs of organised crime. Gerry MacArthur, who began the investigation into the Great Train Robbery, and later headed the team that arrested the Richardsons, said: 'It was almost as if everyone was afraid of them, as if they were seen as too big for the police to deal with. Everyone knew what was going on, but no one tackled it. The squad was very good at acting on information, but not good at gathering it.'

Another former squad officer had this to say about it. 'There were people trying to get the Krays when the top lot eventually realised just how dangerous they were becoming. At least one skipper got the chop for taking a backhander from them. Tommy Butler spent six months over on the Blind Beggar shooting when it seemed that very little was going on locally. But the Richardsons – who had heard of the Richardsons before Charlie was arrested? There's always been a lot of talk about gangs and gang leaders, but

111

gangs don't exist until the press give them a name after someone has been arrested.'

The only sign that C8 had taken note of the gangs came in 1966 when Tommy Butler arrested the Krays for the murder of George Cornell (see Chapter 11). The murder was being investigated by the local CID who knew that there would be no witnesses willing to speak out against the Krays. Butler decided to arrest them anyway, and put them on an identity parade. They were not picked out, and had to be released.

Years later, when 'Nipper' Read was investigating the Krays, he found that nothing had been added to the intelligence files on the brothers since his own contributions earlier in the decade. Butler, who had arrested the Krays in the interval for the murder of George Cornell, had kept all his information to himself, and had added nothing to their files. However, Gilbert Kelland, then in charge of the division in which the murder occurred, claims in his book *Crime in London*, 'The facts were recorded and put on file at the Yard.'

10
The Great Train Robbery

The squad's major triumph of the 1960s was undoubtedly the tracking down and conviction of the gang which planned and carried out the Great Train Robbery. Nipper Read, a divisional detective seconded to the investigating team, described the officers involved at the outset of the investigation into the robbery as being eager to establish individual reputations.

Each wanted to be seen as the instigator of this or that line of inquiry, preferably when it turned out to be a successful one.

Bob Robinson, who was a detective sergeant on the squad in the final stages of the investigation into the Great Train Robbery, describes this desire for fame as the 'Big Five Syndrome'. 'The press had this thing about Scotland Yard's Big Five, so whenever there was a major crime or a murder investigated by the Yard, the officer in charge was always described as one of the "Big Five". Some of the senior officers were very keen to be known as "one of the Big Five", so there was always this pressure on reporters to describe the investigating officer in this way. Remember that all senior detectives in those days had a group of tame reporters to whom they fed stories to keep their own name in the papers.'

Nipper Read confirmed the 'tame reporter' theory in his autobiography, in which he referred to Friday night drinking parties on the fifth floor of Scotland Yard, where senior officers passed on highly confidential information to friends in the press in the hope that they would be given favourable publicity on some future occasion. His own up-to-then secret inquiry into the Krays was blown open in this way in two Sunday newspapers.

Read was also critical of Tommy Butler's obsession with secrecy. More than once in investigating the Great Train Robbery he found himself dispatched with a colleague to interview a suspect without any information about what evidence there might be against him. One of Read's colleagues had this explanation for Tommy's attitude: 'Once you've had one or two jobs blown to the press, or even worse, to the other side, you can't be blamed for being as secretive as he was. There were even large-scale operations on which he would tell no one where they were going, even refusing to tell the drivers if they needed full tanks. Once we were twenty miles outside London before he told us where we were headed.'

This might be a reflection on Tommy's obsession with confidentiality, or a very unflattering comment on the integrity of this highly esteemed body of men. Alfie Durrel, who had taken a vigorous part in the arrest of the Tottenham Court Road post office van robbers, was said to have such close connections with some of the suspects that Butler ensured that the unit in which he worked never became involved in the Train Robbery investigation.

The Great Train Robbery took place on 3 August 1963. Its planning clearly took some time, and there is still doubt about the identity of the main organiser, and what happened to all of the £2.6 million stolen that night. Tommy Butler, as a result of his network of informants all over London, knew that something big was being planned and had a number of phone intercepts set up. But Jack Slipper, then a detective sergeant with the squad, wrote in his autobiography:

> One of the things that set the Great Train Robbery apart from other crimes was how little information leaked into the underworld before it was committed. Really, it was astonishing. As far as I'm aware no informant working for the Flying Squad had a whisper about the robbery in advance. And even when police started getting fingerprints, it still took a lot longer than usual to locate the villains we knew we were after.

However, Nipper Read had a more accurate perception:

> The Great Train Robbery was a job which had been hawked like a film script around the underworld for some time ... It had been on offer for so long that when it happened a number of people were not surprised.

The robbery was centred on the night mail train from Glasgow to London. The train was stopped by a fake signal at Cheddington in Buckinghamshire, and the two mail coaches were detached by a gang of about ten men. The train driver was 'coshed', and died of his injuries seven years later. The robbers, expecting tens of thousands of pounds, found that they had stolen over £2.6 million. They had bought a deserted farm near the scene of the robbery and took the cash there, expecting to be able to share it out at their leisure. A radio broadcast announcing that police were convinced that the robbers were still within thirty miles of the scene of the crime prompted a panic exit – one of the team escaped on a pedal cycle with £3,000 in his pockets. Within three days of the robbery they had all left. In another four days the farm had been discovered by a local labourer suspicious of the van and Land Rover that had been left there.

The first investigators were Detective Superintendent Malcolm Fretwell from the local force and Detective Superintendent Gerald MacArthur from Scotland Yard's C1, the man 'in the frame'. This was literally a frame, with one senior officer at the top of a 'ladder' of other officers allocated to take a call for assistance (usually for a murder investigation) made by a provisional force. MacArthur's part in the investigation has always been under-valued, and it is perhaps significant that he left the Met to become Assistant Chief Constable of Hertfordshire, where he gained such a reputation for trustworthiness that he was the only police officer to be approached by victims of the Richardsons (whose reign is dealt with in Chapter 11).

MacArthur immediately called for a records search to find which Criminal Records Office men might have formed part of the robbery team, especially those who might have taken part in earlier, similar robberies. He kept tight hold of the routine

115

investigation, while Tommy Butler, the Flying Squad Commander, took charge of the operation on the agreed assumption that only a gang of London criminals would have the experience and resources to mount such an operation.

The inference has always been that MacArthur did the very necessary paperwork while Butler, who kept his suspicions about who was involved to himself, engaged in sorties to arrest selected suspects. Butler and MacArthur worked under the overall supervision of Commander George Hatherill, the senior CID officer at the Yard. MacArthur has always valued the Flying Squad's contribution to the investigation. 'They were the hunters,' he explained. 'We told them who we wanted, and they went off and found them.'

The hideaway at Leatherslade Farm was discovered on the day that Butler was put in charge of the Flying Squad, and it was at the farm that most of the evidence that would later convict the robbery team was gathered by Detective Superintendent Maurice Ray and a team of fingerprint experts. One of the many question-marks over the organisation of the robbery has always been the way the farm was left by the robbers, who had been living there for a week. Speculation that they left it secure in the knowledge that they had hired someone else to burn it down after they had left, to destroy all clues, has been countered by the established fact that many of the team wore gloves during their three or four days at the farm, and spent their last twelve hours wiping down all surfaces that might have carried fingerprints.

Searching fingerprint files is a long business, and it could have taken weeks or even months for the prints found at the farm to be matched to known criminals. But Tommy Butler had a short cut. He had known that a big job was in the offing well before the robbery took place, and he knew who the principals were. In typical Butler fashion he kept his suspicions quiet and did not immediately let Fretwell and MacArthur know who he had in mind. Bob Robinson explained.

'Tommy Butler had the best network of contacts in the Met. He made a lot of friends inside the job through things like the Flying Squad's annual dinner. If you got invited to the top table there, you were really in. So he knew the best people to ask for favours when he needed them. He also had the best informants in the Met. Well before the train robbery came off, he knew that there was a big job being planned by some good-class villains. He would have put them on the tinkle [intercepted their phones] and his snouts would have told him who was meeting who.

'So the robbery takes place, and a week later they start lifting prints. Now normally the prints would go back to the Yard and even if they were given priority it might take weeks before there's a result. Tommy, however, bowls into Fingerprints, gives them a list of twenty names and says "Try these first". Of course, quite a few come up straight away. Charlie Wilson, Bruce Reynolds, Biggsy. In fact Tommy knew who he was looking for two days before the info got back to Gerry MacArthur. Fingerprints, on the other hand, were over the moon. Tommy had saved them a hell of a lot of work, so whenever he wanted a quick favour, he went to the head of the queue.'

The first arrest (achieved without the help of fingerprints) was of Roger Cordrey, who had been recruited to the team on his record of robbing mail trains in the south of England. He took his 'whack' of £150,000 to Bournemouth, where with a friend, Bill Boal, he rented two garages to hide the cash in two second-hand cars. (Boal was later sentenced as one of the robbery team on fairly thin evidence.) He rented the garages from a police widow, displaying a large roll of banknotes. The widow, who along with the rest of the nation had been reading about the Great Train Robbery in the national press for the past week, told the police, and Cordrey and Boal were arrested.

A few days later, a couple in Surrey came across some cases containing banknotes hidden in a wood. There was £100,000 plus a receipt from a German hotel in the name of Field. One of the solicitors at the firm which had handled the sale of Leatherslade Farm was Brian Field. Field had also acted for Gordon Goody, now a suspect through his previous connection with the 1962 London Airport robbery. Around the same time, Surrey police making inquiries about strangers who might be staying in the vicinity of the hoard were directed to a caravan at Box Hill. Inside panels had clearly been replaced. Behind them, police found £30,000 and the fingerprints of one Jimmy White. (After White's

117

much later arrest, they searched the caravan more thoroughly and found another £9,000.) Back at the farm, Detective Superintendent Ray's team had found the fingerprints of Charlie Wilson and Bruce Reynolds.

There was now a disagreement among the investigators. Hatherill wanted to publish the photographs and descriptions of the suspects who had been identified from fingerprints. MacArthur and Butler wanted to keep them back and to attempt to trace the suspects through the Flying Squad's network of informants. The senior officers won, and the identity of the three suspects made the front pages.

Wilson was arrested through Tommy Butler's informants a few hours before his photograph appeared in the newspapers. Then Gordon Goody, who was in Leicester, was arrested as a result of a coincidence. The receptionist at the Leicester hotel where he was staying thought he looked like Bruce Reynolds and informed the police. He had booked in using the name of a publican, Charles Alexander. A quick check in London revealed that Alexander was still behind his bar. Goody was arrested and taken back to Aylesbury by Flying Squad officers. He was interviewed by Tommy Butler and released with apologies. Even more strange, Butler and one of his officers were kind enough to drive Goody back from Aylesbury to his flat in Putney. Then Ronnie Biggs, who had left prints on a Monopoly board and a sauce bottle, was arrested. Fingerprints also led to the eventual arrests of Roy James and John Daly.

Jim Hussey's arrest was straightforward squad routine. He was associated with some of the other suspects. Every Criminal Records Office sheet has an entry for the subject's associates, and they are the first to be questioned when the subject is hard to find. Hussey was traced, kept under observation and arrested by Jack Slipper. Confident that he had left no fingerprints, he was happy to bluff it out, and made no objections to having his palm prints taken. They matched a palm print on the tailboard of one of the lorries left at the farm. Tommy Wisbey, knowing that police were questioning almost every active criminal, happily volunteered to return from Spain when he had heard he was wanted for questioning. Unfortunately for him, he also had left a palm print on a bath rail at the farm. Then Brian Field, his brother Lennie, and solicitor John Wheater, all involved in the purchase of Leatherslade Farm, were arrested by Tommy Butler. Field's guilt had already been established in a visit by Malcolm Fretwell, who had decided there was more to be gained by leaving Field free at an early stage to avoid panicking his fellow conspirators.

Six weeks after the robbery, police were still looking for Bruce Reynolds, John Daly, Buster Edwards, Roy James and Jimmy White. They still suspected Gordon Goody, but had no evidence against him. But a forensic expert, Dr Ian Holden, was examining clothing and shoes taken from Goody at the time of his arrest. Goody's shoes, underneath the mud and dirt on the soles, bore traces of yellow and khaki paint. The paint was identical to that used on two of the lorries at the farm. Goody was arrested on 3 October. At about the same time, Bob Welch was arrested on the strength of a fingerprint on an empty tin, a fingerprint which had been transferred through a hole in a glove.

In his book on the robbery, *The Train Robbers*, Piers Paul Read alleges that Welch was first warned that he was a suspect by a police officer, and was then offered his freedom for £70,000. This might have been a ploy to get him to admit that he had that amount of money, but Read also recounts that earlier an unnamed squad officer had offered to make things easy for Tommy Wisbey 'if someone sends round a parcel'.

John Daly was arrested after being grassed on by a man he was paying to hide him. Roy James was arrested in a large-scale squad operation in which his flat was surrounded and he was chased across the roof before jumping thirty feet to the ground. A detective who was there says that James was immediately knocked unconscious by one of the waiting detectives and carried to the police car. It may be a sign of those times that neither James nor anyone else connected with the case has ever considered this worthy of comment.

There was still little sign of what had happened to the greater part of the money. There was a strange episode when £50,000 was left in a West End phone-box. It was supposedly there as the result of negotiations between Frank Williams, Butler's second in command, and Buster Edwards and a man who has been identified by Read as Alf Thomas. Edwards, connected to the robbery by fingerprints, and Thomas, some of whose friends had been charged with handling a few banknotes from the robbery, had promised to surrender if they could be guaranteed a fair trial and to this end they promised to restore some of the stolen money. They wanted a deal in which the police would accept their plea of guilty to being accomplices who went to the farm after the robbers left it to clear up.

Thomas, according to Read, was arrested, and released for want of evidence. None of the former squad officers who had any connection with the robbery investigation, including Gerry MacArthur, have any knowledge of Thomas, but certainly two sacks of banknotes were left in a phone-box, as he had promised. The sacks were accepted by the squad as containing £50,000 and senior squad officers were photographed with them for the press before they were taken to Aylesbury.

The first trial of those arrested up to this stage lasted for eight weeks and ended with sentences of between fifteen and thirty years for everyone but John Daly, who was acquitted. (In *My Manor*, Charlie Richardson points out that criminals who had seen sentences of twenty-five years handed out for a robbery in which only one club was used took to using shotguns on the assumption that even if they were caught they would not get a longer sentence.)

Bruce Reynolds moved to Croydon and narrowly escaped arrest when two uniformed officers passed his flat minutes after it had been burgled and they saw a ladder against a window. His girlfriend dissuaded the police from a thorough search by pretending that she was a married woman, and that Bruce was her lover. By the time the officers had returned to the station, and had discovered that the address supplied by Reynolds had been false, he had taken the suitcase containing his share of the money and moved on. By the time the inevitable appeals by their fellow robbers against conviction had been rejected, he and Buster Edwards had left the country, and Charlie Wilson had escaped from Winson Green prison.

Wilson planned his escape carefully, even though he was kept under the tightest supervision, which included the removal of all his clothes from his cell at night. But just a year after the robbery, he

120

was released by three armed men who opened his cell at 3.00 a.m., handcuffed him, and led him past one unconscious warder, and through a seemingly unpatrolled prison to a rope ladder over a wall and down to two waiting cars. The organisation behind his escape has never been satisfactorily explained. He retracted the story first told to Piers Paul Read about the involvement of a Fascist group in the robbery. He had claimed that the Fascists plotted his escape to get access to their share of the loot. Whatever the circumstances, and Wilson had many powerful criminal friends capable of such organisation, he laid low in London before joining his wife and daughter in the south of France.

Ronnie Biggs, serving his time in Wandsworth, used part of his 'whack' to finance his own escape. A pantechnicon was bought and a scaffolding tower built inside it. On a prearranged day the pantechnicon stopped alongside Wandsworth exercise yard. The tower was raised and one man with a shotgun stood on top of the wall while another dropped a rope ladder into the yard. Two other convicts who had been bribed by Biggs jostled the warders who had seen him running towards the wall. Six weeks later he was able to get to France and later to Australia.

Buster Edwards, well aware that he was wanted, was still living with his wife in London under an assumed name. It was during this period that the curious negotiations involving the £50,000 left in a phone-box took place. However, after an interval in which he went to Germany for plastic surgery, he left with his family for Mexico.

Jimmy White was still free – at a price. A succession of supposed friends and fellow criminals were charging him thousands of pounds to provide lodging for him, his wife and child for a week at a time. At one point the child was taken away 'for safety', and Jimmy realised that he would be bled of all his money before the 'friend' thought it would be 'safe' to return the child. He got his child back by sitting on the doorstep of his 'friend's' house and threatening to call the police, give himself up, and implicate the friend for harbouring him.

He still had enough money left to buy a hill farm in Derbyshire, which he shared with another family who had helped him. He paid the other family £10,000 and then found that the husband had attracted attention by placing £500 bets. The Whites fled to Kent with only £7,000 left, and talked about buying a boat to go abroad. But £4,000 later, Jimmy was recognised from a wanted poster, arrested and sentenced to eighteen years.

News of Jimmy White's comparatively short sentence and the rate at which his own money was disappearing in Mexico persuaded Edwards to return to England and give himself up. He made a statement, backed by the squad's second in command, Frank Williams, claiming that he had been hired as a cleaner-up at the farm after the real robbers had left. But he was convicted of robbery and received fifteen years. Charlie Wilson moved to Canada; he had always wanted to live in a country in which English was the main language. Bruce Reynolds, also disturbed by the cost of living in Mexico, joined him, but alarmed by the suspicion aroused when he made inquiries at the immigration office, fled once again to France.

Charlie Wilson was betrayed by a friend who was supposed to be looking after his last £30,000. When he asked him to bring the money out to Canada, the friend turned up with £10,000 and a tale that the rest had been lost in investments. The 'friend' then tipped off Tommy Butler, who postponed his retirement to travel to Canada to arrest Wilson. It was a quiet affair. Tommy waited until Charlie had dropped his children off at school and then, accompanied by two Canadian police in plain clothes, walked up to his car.

'Morning, Charlie,' he said.

Charlie, equally low-key, nodded and answered, 'Morning, Mr Butler.'

Tommy now needed only Ronnie Biggs and Bruce Reynolds to complete the set.

Bruce Reynolds, no longer confident that his money in England was being properly looked after, returned with his wife and daughter to London. As London's top criminal he thought he would be offered the pick of the city's criminal projects, but Butler's determination and resolve had communicated itself to the underworld, whose members saw him as a liability. Only the small-time unsuccessful villains wanted to work with the last of the Great Train Robbers. He bought a house in Torquay where, in November 1968, Tommy Butler found him and took him back to

Aylesbury. Much of the work to trace Reynolds was carried out by Bob Robinson.

'Tommy called me in, and told me to go to Torquay and look for Reynolds, who he knew was living there under one of four names. I was to go round estate agents posing as a detective from the Fraud Squad and seeing if they had sold a house to one of the four names. Estate agents are always willing to help out in fraud cases that don't involve them. Tommy's info was as good as ever, and I found the house within a few days. He'd given me a description of Mrs Reynolds and one of the children, and I was lucky enough to see them going back into the house together. I gave Tommy a bell and we lifted Bruce that night. It was a sheer coincidence that the house in which he was staying was owned by a woman who had been brought up on Leatherslade Farm.'

John Simmonds was 'night provs' at the time (one unit of the Flying Squad was kept on standby to assist provincial forces or to make arrests outside London. The unit was known as 'early/late', or 'nights provincial'). 'Tommy came into the squad office and said that he wanted the three squad cars that were instantly available, including the 'night provs' car. He wouldn't say what they were wanted for or how long they would be away. The drivers asked if they should fill up with petrol and Tommy told them not to bother, there'd be no need for that, just to follow his car. About ten miles out of London, he pulled into the forecourt of a garage and told them to fill up and follow him to Torquay. He looked quite shocked when someone asked where they should stop to have a meal. The job always came first with Tommy.' In the early stages of the train robbery investigation, when the team had been working twelve hours a day, for twenty-eight days without a break, Tommy had been equally shocked when someone suggested there should be a rest day.

Reynolds was sentenced to twenty-five years, but Tommy Butler retired and died without getting Ronnie Biggs back. He had postponed his retirement until he had captured Reynolds, and when he finally left the force he died within the year.

Ronnie Biggs and his wife had settled in Australia, and he had given up hope of ever seeing any of the money he had left in England. Then he was recognised from a photograph in a magazine and moved on to Brazil. From Brazil he arranged to sell his story to the *Daily Express*. The paper tipped off Scotland Yard, and Jack Slipper, by now a detective superintendent, went out to arrest him. Biggs was taken into custody by the Brazilian police, and Biggs' Brazilian mistress revealed that she was expecting his child. Fathers of Brazilian children are immune from extradition. Ronnie Biggs is still in Brazil.

By no means all of the Great Train Robbers were arrested solely through the work of the Flying Squad and its informants. Roger Cordrey and Bill Boal were victims of a police widow's suspicion; Brian Field left his name in the suitcase found by Surrey police. White, Reynolds, Wilson, James, Daly and Biggs were identified by the intensive work of the fingerprint team. Goody was first arrested because of the suspicions of a hotel receptionist and later trapped by forensic evidence. Wisbey came back from Spain of his own accord, and Edwards surrendered. The investigation was certainly not the solo Flying Squad triumph that some police historians would like it to have been, but squad officers of the time maintain that it was their reputation and the knowledge that the squad would never give up until all the robbers were arrested that provided the psychological pressure which resulted in the arrests. Whatever the strength of their contribution, no one ever discovered what had happened to the whole of the £2.6 million; only £400,000 was ever recovered.

There have long been rumours, spread not only by journalists, but also by fellow officers, that certain corrupt officers on the squad took a considerable part of the proceeds that were found in the field in Surrey, in the caravan, and in the phone-box. But it may be significant that none of the convicted robbers have ever made direct allegations, although Welch and Wisbey claim they were asked for money.

Yet, as later events proved, there was a seam of corruption running through the City of London, and the Met CIDs, during this period, and while the Train Robbers made few allegations, Charlie Richardson, the next of the sixties *cause célèbres*, assumes in his autobiography that the whole police service, from the bobby outside his scrapyard to the most senior detective, was bent. But if you accept that premise – for which Charlie gives no proof and offers no names – you must also accept Charlie's other premise that he was nothing more than a very forceful businessman, innocent of the allegations of torture made against him, and was fitted up by the police whom he had not been given an opportunity to bribe.

11
Family Firms

Charlie Richardson once described himself as 'a businessman who had to protect his interests'. At one stage there was a magistrate on the board of some of his companies. Later he worked with an alderman. He had hoped that his flair for business might even have gained him a seat in the House of Lords. His brother Eddie, who spent time in prison with some of the Great Train Robbers and was involved with them in an aborted escape, had a knight on his firm's letterheads. Charlie had offices in the City of London and mining rights in South Africa. He had built up his small empire from a scrapyard. Eddie, who owned a large south London supermarket, was attempting to establish his own empire in the West End through hiring out gaming machines.

But the Richardson brothers' methods were not those of Marks and Spencer. Nor, despite their criminological grouping as 'The Richardsons', did they work together in the way that the Krays did. In fact, their careers are more easily followed separately. Each of them might be viewed by the press as a 'super robber', yet while there is little sign that they were caused any aggravation by super cops, there is equally little sign that they were caused any aggravation by their local CID officers in south London, who must have had a much better idea than the Flying Squad of what was going on.

By the mid 1950s Charlie Richardson, not yet twenty-five, owned five scrapyards. His first had been started with borrowed money which he made no attempt to repay. He claimed when the police came to investigate him that the matter was settled for £150. He branched out into drinking clubs and headed an 'association' (Charlie was not fond of the word 'gang') for the protection of mutual business interests. Protection of mutual business interests sometimes involved meeting other similar associations and beating them unconscious, as well holding informal trials of association members who might have cheated or failed to declare their real profits. Debtors could also expect to be beaten. On the few occasions on which victims took their troubles to the police, witnesses suffered strange lapses of memory in court. Charlie's vision of himself was as the Robin Hood of south London, 'smacking' petty criminals who burgled the poor, and giving Christmas presents to the local pensioners.

In 1959 his witness policy failed when he got six months for receiving, and he was arrested almost immediately on leaving prison for receiving stolen metal. He escaped to Canada while on bail. Eddie took over his business until his return, when another epidemic of witness amnesia freed him again to start long firm frauds (in which villains would buy goods on credit, store them in a warehouse, sell them on and vanish from the warehouse without paying the suppliers) and insurance fires. In the course of one tricky business negotiation Charlie found that he had to take Eddie and a third associate to 'smack' a Brian Mottram. The smacking was not as effective as Charlie might have wished, and a minor gang war developed which ended with Charlie paying Mottram compensation, and Eddie branching out into the supermarket business. George Cornell, later to be murdered by Ronnie Kray, joined one of Charlie's firms with Brian Mottram, and the scrap metal business was doing well enough to be awarded Ministry of Work contracts.

Then, in 1964, the Richardsons' 'wooden box' made its first appearance, or its first alleged appearance. Jack Duval, who operated one of Charlie's companies, had been cheating everyone with whom he came into contact, which obliged Charlie to fake a break-in at the City office to cover up a series of debts. Charlie also alleged that it cost £1,500 to ensure that the police did not look too closely at the break-in. Duval disappeared and another associate, Lucien Harris, was brought in to explain to Charlie and Eddie what had gone wrong.

Charlie, in between sending someone out to buy scampi and assuring Eddie that everything would be over in time for him to watch television, attached leads from the wooden box to Harris' bare feet, turned the handle a few times, and Harris was knocked to the floor. When the box seemed to have lost its effect, Harris was tied securely and gagged and the wires were attached to his penis and anus. The handle was turned repeatedly. When that was over, Charlie stabbed Harris in the foot. Then he was given a glass of whisky and £150 and told to find out where Duval had gone. A second man, Bunny Bridges, was given the same treatment in the quest to trace Duval.

Eddie, perhaps bored with business life, had formed another association, with Frankie Fraser, one of the better known faces of south London crime, a leader of the Parkhurst prison riot and one of the few south Londoners to have Soho connections. The new firm specialised in gaming machines, and more specifically in persuading club owners that the machines they were currently renting were far inferior to those that Eddie and Frank could supply. One of their early ventures took them to Southport, where they were involved in a fight while trying to take over a gaming club there. They were charged with GBH and Eddie was released on £15,000 bail. When the case came to court, the club-owner, whose face had been cut open with a broken bottle, could remember only that he had been drunk at the time and might have started the trouble himself.

Charlie was now negotiating with a Bedfordshire alderman for the acquisition of some South African mining rights. He saw it as an opportunity to smuggle diamonds, but his associates persuaded him that there was more money to be made in a legitimate mining operation. Charlie quarrelled with one of his partners, Thomas Waldeck, who was shot dead in his own home. Another of Charlie's associates, John Bradbury, was arrested by the South African police but not charged after being held for three weeks.

A potential investor in the South African scheme told Charlie that a man called Taggart owed him money. Taggart was forcibly reminded of his financial obligations by Frankie Fraser and a new associate, Charlie Clark. The same forcible reminder, made this time with a knotted wet towel, was handed out to an attendant at Heathrow car park who was cheating Charlie, who had a hand in the almost traditional fiddling of parking fees.

Charlie's career ended through a series of coincidences. He claimed that Frankie Fraser, on his way to look at a West End bank which had just opened (one of Charlie's ambitions was to be a banker), ran into Taggart, whom he had beaten up a few weeks earlier. Fraser followed Taggart until, again by accident, the latter came face to face with Richardson. Taggart's version was slightly different. Richardson and Fraser arranged to meet him in the West End. When he found that they wanted him to make inquiries about the new bank, he jumped into a cab, and the following day went to see Gerald MacArthur, the former Met Detective Superintendent who had opened the investigation into the Great Train Robbery and who was now Assistant Chief Constable of Hertfordshire and head of the newly formed Regional Crime Squad. Taggart assumed that whoever he spoke to in London would pass the information on to corrupt officers, from whence it would get back to Charlie.

Gerald MacArthur, however, has a more charitable explanation for Taggart's action: 'Taggart had a girlfriend who had been a witness in a case I was investigating in south London. She had been extremely brave in coming forward to give evidence, and we provided her with twenty-four-hour protection up to and during the trial. When Taggart found himself in trouble with Charlie Richardson, she persuaded him to come to me for advice. It was simply that I was someone she knew and trusted from the past.'

MacArthur will not be drawn on the honesty or dishonesty of police officers who should have been investigating Richardson. 'The facts are these. Once any report is committed to a Yard file, it becomes accessible to anyone who wants to draw the file. There were certainly City of London officers who took an unusually close interest in files that had apparently little to do with them, and it is a matter of record that one man, beaten up by Richardson and his associates, complained to local police, and a week later was shown a copy of the statement he had made to police by Richardson himself, who beat him up again.'

Back in South Africa, John Bradbury had confessed that he and Charlie had shot the latter's business partner. Another of Frankie Fraser's victims had joined the queue to speak to ACC MacArthur about Charlie's business methods, and on 7 March 1966 one of the Krays' associates was killed in a club in which the Richardsons were taking an interest.

Mr Smith's club was a cut above the single-room drinking dens that passed as clubs in much of south London. It had a restaurant, gaming tables, and a dance floor. It was being looked after by the Haward brothers (in the sense that the brothers and their friends had free drinks in return for preventing trouble breaking out). Eddie and Frankie Fraser thought they could do a better prevention job, and at the same time install their gaming machines. Everyone seemed agreeable to the new arrangement, but the change had to be explained to the Hawards. At 2.00 a.m. the club had emptied apart from Eddie, Frankie and their supporters, and the Hawards and their friends. The two groups were drinking together amicably, although it was later stated in court that Bill Haward had a shotgun under his jacket, and that Dicky Hart, a friend of the north London Krays and of the Hawards, was carrying an automatic. Nobody appeared to think this unusual.

At 3.00 a.m. Eddie called time, and when there was some dissent made it clear that he was now in charge, and was the only one who could order drinks. A friend of the Hawards attempted to grab a bottle and serve himself (the only remaining barmaid had already been told to go into the kitchen). Eddie Richardson grabbed hold of him and started to punch him, Hart fired his gun, and the two gangs started the fight that the whole evening had been building up to. Hart lost his gun in the battle and was chased out of the club by Frankie Fraser. One of the Richardson associates attempted to calm things down outside the club, foreseeing that the neighbours would be dialling 999. He was shot in the groin for his trouble. Fraser was seen kicking the now prostrate Hart, and when the police arrived, Hart was already dead, his face smashed in. He was later found to have been shot in the face. Fraser himself had been shot in the leg, and Eddie Richardson had been shot in the leg and backside. A Henry Rawlins, on the Richardsons' side, had been shot in the arm. Eddie and Frankie were arrested, and Frankie was charged with Hart's murder.

Charlie, who had been in South Africa, returned to help the

witnesses with their recollections, but some of them preferred to remember things their way rather than Charlie's. Attempts were made to nobble the jury at the trial in July 1966 and there were mixed verdicts. Fraser was found guilty of affray but not of murder, and was sentenced to five years. One of the Hawards received eight years, and Eddie Richardson, on a retrial, received five years for affray.

Between the fight at the club and the arrests came the murder that eventually led to the downfall of the Krays. Eddie's new associate, George Cornell, who had not been involved in the battle at Mr Smith's, crossed the river to see a friend in hospital. He took the opportunity to have a drink in The Blind Beggar in Mile End Road and was shot dead by Ronnie Kray, outraged by this trespass by a senior Richardson associate into what was recognised as Kray country. The incident seems to have lacked significance at the time. In *Crime in London*, Gilbert Kelland, who was the officer in charge of the area at the time, refers to it only briefly, and gives no explanation of why Tommy Butler chose to arrest the Krays and put them in an identity parade when it was absolutely clear that no one was going to give evidence against them. It may have been nothing more than an exhibition of how the squad rounded up the usual suspects without worrying too much about evidence.

Charlie Richardson was arrested with six or more associates on 30 July by a combined Metropolitan and Hertfordshire police squad. The Met contingent included some hand-picked officers from the Flying Squad. Gwyn Waters, one of the chosen officers, emphasises that it was not the usual routine of allocating one or two squad units to an investigation: 'I was called in from the street and told to go to Scotland Yard. There were officers there who had been pulled in from C11 and the Fraud Squad. It was clearly not going to be a squad operation. While we were taking statements in the Richardson case, we also began hearing bits and pieces about the Krays. At one stage, the Krays had come mob-handed on to the Richardsons' territory. Charlie claims that his skills as a negotiator prevented what would have been a commercially undesirable fight in the street.

'I wasn't on the Kray inquiry,' recalled Waters, 'but I have no doubt that Charlie Richardson was much cleverer than the Krays,

132

and, left alone, would have become much more dangerous.'

Richardson's South African friend, John Bradbury, had already revealed the secrets of the informal trials of debtors, while Harris and Taggart had provided further details. Gerald MacArthur, having painstakingly gathered all the evidence needed, and having convinced witnesses that they could make statements without any danger of the contents leaking back to the Richardsons, timed the arrests carefully, first letting it be known that he was taking a holiday in Austria. Richardson was found asleep, alone, in a house with the back door open. He claimed that he had been warned of the raid the previous day, but it is difficult to believe that had he known he was about to be arrested he would not have taken precautions, at least to have his own witnesses present to prevent the 'fit-ups' that he constantly alleges happened when the Met made arrests.

Gwyn Waters, who made the actual arrest, confirms that Charlie was completely unaware that he was to be arrested. Clearly the police contacts that Richardson claimed to have had failed to pick up any idea of what MacArthur's plans were. Between then and the trial in April 1967, witnesses were again approached and asked to change their evidence. This time three people were convicted of attempting to bribe a witness following a separate investigation by the Flying Squad under Tommy Butler. Richardson's victims, no doubt reassured by this positive police action, gave evidence against him. He was not only accused of using electrical torture but other victims came forward to allege that their teeth had been pulled out with pliers, or their feet nailed to the floor. Charlie and Frankie were sentenced to twenty-five years each.

'At one stage,' said Gerry MacArthur, 'we had over a hundred officers on jury protection duty. Not only for the twelve jury members, but also for their immediate families. The protection extended to the weekends. Once two of the lads had to travel to Nottingham with their man because he wanted to watch a football match there.'

Eddie Richardson received another twenty-five years in 1990 for drug smuggling. In 1991 Frankie Fraser was shot in the head coming out of a north London nightclub. He refused to give police any assistance, and gave his name at the hospital as Tutankhamen.

* * *

There may have been reasons for the Flying Squad not seeing the Richardsons as a major menace, but it is difficult to appreciate their lack of interest in the Krays. The twins and their elder brother, Charlie, had worked hard at establishing their reputation since the mid-1950s, when they helped the old-style racecourse gangs. The ex-boxers used their reputation for violence to take over small clubs, drawing a 'pension' from the takings and installing their own colleagues as bouncers and managers. One of their fights with rival gangs brought Ronnie three years' imprisonment. But their empire continued to grow. Anyone who wanted to open a club in the East End found it advisable to consult the Firm, as the brothers were now known. Consultation invariably meant a weekly 'pension' to the Firm plus the wages of the minder appointed by them. Their club interests spread to Soho and Chelsea, and their business protection was extended to scrapyards and pubs. Members of the Firm also assisted Peter Rachman in extorting rents from his slum properties in Notting Hill.

In 1964, the Metropolitan Police looked at the Krays for completely different reasons. The *Daily Mirror* made it known unofficially that it had photographs of a peer and a prominent gangster. The owner of the photographs was granted an injunction to prevent the *Mirror* publishing them. The *Mirror* countered with an editorial about a London gang so powerful that the police could not touch it. The Commissioner ordered an inquiry into the alleged relationship between a homosexual peer and a gay gangster.

A week later, the photo was published in a German magazine. It showed Lord Boothby sitting next to Ronnie Kray. The *Mirror* had to pay damages after Boothby issued a statement denying that he was homosexual or that he was a friend of Ronnie's. Nipper Read, then a detective inspector, was told to investigate the Krays. He claims that up to that time the CID had left the Krays alone on the grounds that they could never get any evidence against them. Nipper went round the East End looking for evidence before making any move against the Krays. He found out that they were well into long firm frauds, and as a result prosecuted some minor criminals without getting near the Krays themselves.

The officer in charge of the Flying Squad, Commander Ernie Millen, tried to close the investigation down. 'It's getting nowhere,' he told Nipper, attempting to intimidate him by rank, but Nipper persisted until he had enough evidence and sufficient willing witnesses to prosecute the twins for levying protection on a West End club. The Krays were arrested and held in custody until their trial (Lord Boothby expressed concern in the House of Lords for their loss of liberty). The case fell apart in court with witnesses either not appearing or failing to give the evidence contained in their statements. The Krays were acquitted.

In 1965 Reggie married. His bride committed suicide two years later. The brothers ostentatiously made a list of all those who had failed to send flowers to the funeral. They also moved towards a confrontation with the Richardsons and took to wearing bullet-proof jackets and being attended by bodyguards and look-outs. At one meeting between the two gangs, George Cornell called Ronnie 'a big poof'. Ronnie, who never liked open references to his homosexuality, shot Cornell dead the next day in The Blind Beggar public house in Mile End Road, the heart of Kray territory. Ronnie claimed that the killing was in retaliation for the death of Richard Hart, shot in the fight at Mr Smith's club, but many commentators felt the real motive was Cornell's 'poof' insult.

The Krays also wanted a counter to the Richardsons' Frankie Fraser and arranged the escape from Dartmoor of Frank Mitchell, a mentally handicapped giant with a record of violence. Having released him and hidden him away in an East End flat, the Krays then found he was uncontrollable. Mitchell threatened to leave his hideaway to visit his mother. On Christmas Eve 1966, they arranged to have him shot dead in a van.

Their third murder was that of Jack McVitie. McVitie was another robber who had been in and out of the Firm. He had taken £1,500 to kill the twins' former financial adviser, and kept the money even though he had failed to carry out the contract. He was taken to a Stoke Newington flat, where Reggie attempted to shoot him twice with a gun that jammed. He then stabbed him to death in the presence of at least six other people.

In 1967, Nipper Read, who had always resisted invitations to join the Flying Squad, was appointed to take charge of a new investigation into the Krays. The inquiry was to be conducted in secret, and Nipper demanded that he be given an office away from the Yard and be allowed to select his own officers. He was well aware of the reluctance of any squad of detectives to pass information on to another department, but he was still shocked when he found that no one had added anything to the Kray files since the entries he had made himself two years earlier. Tommy Butler, with his obsession for secrecy, had not even registered his arrests and identification attempts.

Nipper succeeded in arresting the Krays and having them imprisoned by patience and inside knowledge. He first approached the Krays' formal financial adviser, secured limited immunity for him, and formed a dossier on all their commercial crime. He then arranged for mass simultaneous arrests of the Krays and their immediate associates to be carried out effectively with none of the suspects being tipped off in advance. The twins were arrested at their flat in Braithwaite Road, Shoreditch, in the early morning of 9 May 1968.

Next, with some willing press cooperation, he spread a rumour that further arrests were to be made. One of the men involved in the murder of Frank Mitchell surrendered. A member of the Firm turned on the Krays and offered to give evidence against them. The barmaid at The Blind Beggar, who had witnessed Cornell's murder, agreed, now that the Krays and most of their friends were in custody and unlikely to be bailed, to give evidence of what she had seen.

Nipper's investigations into the murders had to continue with the twins in custody, the committal proceedings looming, and the prospect of a trial within another three months. He succeeded in splitting the defendants, getting some to give evidence against the Krays, and maintaining the confidence of his principal witnesses. Ronnie and Reggie were sentenced to life imprisonment. Their elder brother, Charles, was given ten years. The Firm was wiped out without any help from the Flying Squad.

12
Robbery and Murder

The Criminal Justice Act of 1967, which introduced majority verdicts, had its roots in a Flying Squad operation in which only one of six defendants was convicted. John Swain, then the detective inspector leading that investigation, was so incensed at what he saw as jury manipulation that he composed a report on the trial which motivated the Commissioner and then the Home Secretary to seek legislation to overturn the requirement that a guilty verdict had to be delivered by all twelve members of the jury.

Early in 1965, John Swain was given vague information that a gang was planning a raid on a City bank on a Saturday morning. Later more information indicated that the bank was a branch of Lloyd's in Lombard Street, although the exact day was not known. 'There were immediate problems with surveillance,' said John. 'The City is quiet on a Saturday morning, and observation cars and vans would have stuck out a mile. We also had a problem in that our radios, which we thought were the most sophisticated possible, would not work among the City's high buildings. Luckily, the City of London Police had better equipment and helped us out. They also helped us to set up an observation post in another bank. So our job was getting there at six every Saturday morning and just waiting. But waiting for what? It seemed inconceivable that any team would try to force its way into a locked bank, even though there were people working inside. So there had to be an inside agent.

'Another of our team had a brainwave. Most bank staff working on Saturday morning would be young men who would leave at midday to play football or rugby. So on Saturdays there would be nothing strange about staff turning up with bags and holdalls. That way the guns, or cutting gear, could be introduced without suspicion. We also learned that early on Saturday mornings the confidential wastepaper was removed from bins left outside the bank. That particular piece of knowledge came in most useful.'

One Saturday morning in November, it became clear that the job was on. At 6.15 a.m. a member of the bank staff, Richard Barton, came out of the bank wearing overalls, went to the wastepaper bins, and then went back in. He did this three times. Half an hour later another man walked into the bank by a side entrance. Then a second member of staff, Frederick Williams, also in overalls, came out, went over to the waste bins, and went back inside.

A few hundred yards away a second squad team had seen three men leave two heavy sacks at the waste collection point. The men were arrested well away from the bank. At about 7.30 a.m. the two bank employees, Williams and Barton, came out, inspected the wastepaper bins, and took two heavy sacks left by the other three into the bank. A few moments later, Williams came out of a side door and looked up and down the street. Swain assumed that he was now looking for the three men who had dropped off the sacks, and had him arrested. The bank was a large building, and he could not risk Williams going back inside again. Williams took the officers back into the bank protesting that all he had taken from outside the bank was wastepaper. In his office they found Barton. Williams had three skeleton keys on him.

The two sacks were found hidden in a cupboard by Gwyn Waters. They contained a full set of cutting equipment. The skeleton keys opened all the doors leading to a grilled vault. There was plenty of evidence for a conspiracy. From then on it got harder.

The first trial at the Old Bailey was stopped when it was found that the wife of one defendant had attempted to speak to two of the jurors. At the second trial there were continuous objections to jurors, particularly to intelligent-looking or well-dressed jurors. Three days into the trial one of the jurors was discharged after he was seen in conversation with a well-known criminal. The following day, another juror reported that he had been offered £600 to stick out for a not guilty verdict. The judge refused an application to discharge the jury, and maintained his refusal the next day when a second juror was offered money. Then one of the defendants refused to come into the dock. The trial continued without him.

The trial ended and the jury retired. They returned to say that they could not agree. Directed to reconsider their verdict, they found four defendants not guilty, and only Williams guilty. When he appealed, one of the judges commented on the strength of the original prosecution case and added, 'One has the impression that the others got off because one of the bribery attempts succeeded.'

Within a year legislation had been introduced to allow a jury to bring in a majority verdict. Under the previous system, only one juror had to dissent from the findings for the verdict to be reversed, and it was not a difficult matter to bribe a single juror. The Flying Squad also began the practice of providing jury protection in trials involving professional criminals.

In 1966, three police officers in plain clothes were shot dead in Shepherd's Bush. The crew of Foxtrot 11 (11 was the number allocated to 'Q' cars, unmarked police cars carrying a team of three CID officers) had stopped a car near Wormwood Scrubs prison just after midday. It was one of those stops on a hunch: apparently the officers just did not like the look of the men in the Standard Vanguard. A minute later all three officers were dead, shot in cold blood by two of the men in the car. Flying Squad vehicles out on patrol rushed to the scene, and within an hour a joint investigation was underway with the squad working closely with divisional officers.

There was no information at all about any intended hold-up, or about local criminals who might be armed (armed robbers were still a comparative rarity in 1966, and anyone buying guns usually came to the squad's attention through informants). There was, however, one solid clue: the registration number of the Vanguard. It had been driven away at speed from the murder scene and had caused another car to swerve violently. The indignant driver had noted down the registration number, which he had given to police

139

with a complaint of dangerous driving. The registered owner of the car was a John Edward Witney, who was quickly pulled in and questioned by Dick Chitty, the detective superintendent in charge of the investigation.

'Sold it at lunchtime, yesterday' – the time of the killings – he told Dick Chitty. 'Bloke in a pub car park gave me twenty pounds for it.' It was a scarcely credible alibi, but unless it was disproved, it would put Witney out of the frame for the murders. There was a young witness who had seen the car being driven away and had described the driver as looking like Bobby Charlton; Witney certainly answered that description, but the boy was unlikely to make a definite identification.

Jack Slipper, who had worked in Acton, was then a detective inspector on the squad. He was given the job of testing Witney's alibi. After selling the car, Witney told police, he had gone to a particular betting shop in Acton. Jack Slipper knew the betting shop manager well enough to be aware that he was a friend of Witney's family, and was not therefore likely to say anything that would put Witney in trouble. So his interview with the manager was not conducted formally in a police station, but over a couple of pints in a pub near the betting shop. He soon established that Witney had not been in the betting shop. He had a reputation for trying to place bets on borrowed money, and the manager had warned his staff to let him know whenever Witney came in. He had not been in on the day of the murders. But would he put that in writing?

The manager had his local reputation and the Witney relatives to consider. There might be three policemen dead, but that would not weigh heavily against the knowledge that he had provided information to the Old Bill. Slipper took a chance. He knew that the manager would not make a statement immediately, so he let him go home to talk it over with his family, having arranged to meet him the following day. Slipper's approach worked. The manager came in and provided a statement blowing Witney's alibi, and also encouraged the counter staff to provide police with similar statements.

The next part of the investigation did not go as smoothly. The Vanguard had been traced to a garage in south London, from

140

which it seemed Witney had bought it. If the owner of the garage could identify Witney as the Vanguard owner, it was another step towards charging him. The alternative theory, that the man to whom Witney had sold the car had chosen the same garage to sell the car on to, was too far-fetched to consider. But the garage owner, clearly nervous, refused to identify Witney. He had been receiving stolen metal from Witney and two other men and was afraid that he would be prosecuted for this if he admitted he knew Witney.

'Not the man I sold it to,' he mumbled, unwilling to look either the police or Witney in the eye. Jack Slipper exercised yet more tact. He went back to the man's flat to take a statement from him, explained that he would have to give evidence in court, and left him alone with his family for two hours. When he returned, the room appeared to be crowded with relatives. The owner had changed his mind. 'It was Witney, Mr Slipper,' he said. 'I'll sign my name to it.'

Witney, seeing the case building against him, and against him alone, admitted that he was the driver and named John Duddy and Harry Roberts as the two killers.

Duddy was arrested in Glasgow and taken to London by Jack Slipper and Ginger Hensley. Slipper has always maintained that Duddy was treated so considerately on the flight from Glasgow that all the resistance went out of him and he admitted shooting one of the officers, and named Roberts as the killer of the other two. After a long search, Roberts himself was arrested hiding out in woods in Hertfordshire, having bought a complete set of camping equipment in Tottenham Court Road. The three men pleaded not guilty but were convicted and sentenced to thirty years each.

Tony Lundy, who joined the squad as a detective sergeant in 1969, was somewhat taken aback by the easy-going life style adopted by some members.

'Don't get me wrong,' he said, 'there were a lot of good coppers who would work like murder when there was a job to be done. But compared to the poor blokes on division who were working their bollocks off all the time, squad officers had it easy. And they didn't have as many informants as they used to. One or two to a unit if

141

they were lucky. They got a lot of their information from divisional detectives who just hadn't the time to pull in all the bodies they had evidence on.'

One of the jobs that came the squad's way in this manner was the shooting of a security guard at Earl's Court. Two youngsters, high on drugs, had shot the guard while he was collecting cash. Their names were given to the detective inspector on Tony's unit by a divisional detective.

'We put in a lot of hours tracing them, Joseph and Patrick Leigh, about seventeen and eighteen years old. We eventually nicked them, and they were convicted. Now, on division you'd just get on with the next job. But after a job like that, squad officers were inclined to rest on their laurels and go off for a bit of golf. It wasn't what I was used to at all. But a few months later when we went up to look for the gang that had shot a police superintendent in Blackpool, you couldn't have had a more committed squad of professionals. Even Ken Drury [later convicted of corruption] was busy kicking in doors with the best of them.'

But Tony Lundy, when he returned to division as a first-class detective sergeant in 1971, took advantage of his squad background in his work in Golders Green, and at the same time began a system which was to help him, the Metropolitan Police and the people of London enormously in later years. He turned a robber into an informant.

'There had been a shooting in East Finchley. I asked for help from the Flying Squad because we had some names but not enough officers to follow them through. We were able to nick the whole team, and one of them, Ronnie Clare, was persuaded to give evidence against the rest of them. We told the judge about this, and he got a much lighter sentence.'

At the beginning of the 1970s the Flying Squad found themselves investigating murders in Northern Ireland. Ernie Peyton, then Detective Chief Superintendent in charge of the Murder Squad, was already in Ulster investigating the killing of an RUC informant. Then three young Scottish soldiers, aged seventeen to nineteen, were killed in cold blood. They had attended a local bar and had been invited to a party by two girls they met there. They were taken to the supposed party in two cars, and on arrival at a house outside the town, they were shot dead by a waiting team of IRA assassins, who killed each of them with a single bullet fired into the head.

Ernie Peyton was asked to take over the investigation by the Army, who felt that the RUC, isolated from the community and hardly able to move outside their stations, were unable to do it properly. Peyton, in turn, asked for assistance from Scotland Yard, as he was clearly unable to investigate the killings on his own.

Detective Chief Inspector Peter Darke was one of the officers who were sent out to assist him. 'He asked for officers by name, and in turn you were asked if you would like to volunteer. Not a lot of option, really. About thirty of us went over including two WDCs. One of my first problems was that we were put into a hotel that had a divorced and singles disco. I had a hell of a job keeping my lads out of it. But we got on with the job. We had a lot of arrests for terrorist activities. It might seem impossible for the squad, which relied on informants, to have made any headway, but we were soon able to make contacts. Most of the Catholic population detested the IRA, so we had a lot of local sympathy, and the best possible cooperation from the RUC and the Army. We were able to identify most of the people responsible, but arresting them was another matter. Some of them lived over the border in Dundalk, and as there was no extradition treaty we could not touch them. We had a written confession from one man who had burned the jumpers that the killers were wearing. They were all blood-stained because they were standing close to the victims when they shot them.

'Anyway, he was detained but he escaped in one of those mass break-outs. A few weeks later he's appearing on Dublin television claiming that I had burned his legs with cigarettes. He showed the scars to the cameras. He had scars all right: when we arrested him he was already in poor health with ulcers on his legs for which we arranged medical treatment. It was these scars that he showed the cameras.

'Another of the team was shot dead by the Army on the day that detention was introduced. He came out, like a number of other

IRA men that day, wearing a black beret to signify he was a soldier. The bullet hit him above his eyes and just below the beret rim. We traced other people involved in the killings and were involved in about thirty terrorist-related prosecutions. But as soon as detention was introduced, we were brought back, because it had become just too dangerous to carry on inquiries in the normal way.'

13
Decline

Detective Chief Superintendent Herbert Sparks, who led the Flying Squad towards the end of the 1950s and who rejoiced in the nickname 'Iron Man', used to regale people with an anecdote which gave something of an insight into the methods of the squad detective of his day. It might also give a small clue to the reasons for the squad's rapid decline and near destruction in the 1970s. Theirs was not so much a fall from grace as a plummet, which resulted in a catalogue of dismissals, resignations on dubious medical grounds and the imprisonment of the squad's most senior officer for corruption.

Sparks once gave evidence at the Old Bailey against a professional villain he had arrested on robbery charges. He told the jury it had been a routine arrest carried out strictly by the book. He had called at the villain's home in the early morning while he was still in bed, woken him, identified himself, produced a warrant card, cautioned him and taken him quietly to the police station, where the suspect had admitted the offences with which he was subsequently charged.

As Sparks was completing his description of how he performed this model arrest, the defendant, who could restrain himself no longer, jumped to his feet in the dock and shouted: 'Lies! All lies! He came into the bedroom, he belted me, I belted him and all he said was, "Put your trousers on, Ginger, you're nicked!"' He also denied having made any confession. Of course, the court believed the policeman and the villain was safely convicted, but even Sparks would later admit that, although there was no doubt in his mind that the defendant was guilty, his evidence had not been entirely accurate and Ginger's version had been closer to the mark.

The story is a minor example of sharp practice compared to some of the refined corruption scams which came later, but it illustrates two points: first that squad detectives, and doubtless many other CID men, were not above giving fabricated evidence and 'gilding the lily' to convict those they believed to be guilty, and second that the courts, although they must have had some inkling of what was going on, were generally prepared to turn a blind eye to such corner-cutting, trusting that the detectives were putting the right men in the dock.

Even Tommy Butler, regarded as a paragon of diligence and integrity, appears not to have been immune from occasional embellishment of evidence. The train robber Ronnie Biggs, who admittedly may not be the most impartial witness, says that when Butler first interviewed him after his arrest in 1963, he advised him to make a full statement about his part in the crime and the roles of the other robbers. Biggs says that when he refused to cooperate Butler told him: 'It doesn't really matter, Ron. We've probably got enough on you and most of the others already, and what we haven't got we can make up.'

One of Butler's former police colleagues said that he would not have been remotely surprised if Biggs' story was true. 'Tommy Butler was a man of honour and would have died rather than dent the pride of the squad. But he also hated villains, especially violent ones, and did everything he could to get them off the streets. Sometimes he might not have done things completely by the letter but he always did them for the right reasons.

'Let me give you a hypothetical example. You are a detective who has been tapping the telephones of a gang of villains. You know they are about to rob a bank. They have collected their guns and put them in a bag but don't plan to load them until they are in their car outside the bank. You are waiting for them when they get there. When do you go in and hit them? If you do it before they load the guns, they could say they had found them dumped in the street and were just about to hand them in at the police station. At worst they would be convicted only of possession of firearms. Bearing in mind that the phone tap evidence would be inadmissible in court, you would really struggle to convict them on the more serious charge of possession of firearms with intent to rob. But if you wait for them to load up and enter the bank you put yourselves and the public at serious risk. There might be a temptation in those circumstances to go in and make your arrests before the guns are loaded but to tell the court later that they were loaded. It is risky legally, but can you honestly say it would not be for the benefit of the public?'

Such justifications were quite common among older CID officers interviewed for this book, and indeed may evoke some sympathy in broader sections of society, but there is no doubt that the culture of corner-cutting and 'verballing' – concocting confessions – in the interests of convicting hardened criminals contributed to the emergence of a more sinister and venal breed of squad officer.

There was no single incident or major Yard policy shift which could be pointed to as the start of the squad's moral decline. It was a gradual process which, paradoxically, stemmed from the very successes of their first four or five decades. As their fame grew, they became more convinced of their own invincibility and objected strongly to any outsiders questioning their methods. It is to the detriment of the Yard leadership of the 1960s that it allowed the squad to operate with virtually no supervision. Those chief officers who were not former squad men themselves did not ask too many questions as long as the arrest and detection rates remained high. Those who were naturally approved of the culture.

Caseloads increased sharply as the rate of serious crime continued to rise and the squad detectives were pushed to the limits. By the late 1960s, evidence and intelligence-gathering in some cases had become slapdash and defence lawyers were more frequently able to sow the seeds of doubt in the minds of juries. Professional criminals, seeing the start of a sea-change in attitudes to police integrity, became less inclined to plead guilty to offences they had committed and began routinely to allege fabrication of evidence.

The position of the squad men as undisputed champion thief-takers was also being challenged from inside Scotland Yard. *Ad hoc* serious crime squads had been set up to trap the Richardsons and later the Krays, both jobs that the Flying Squad might have been expected to be asked to take on, given their specific brief to infiltrate the underworld and attack organised crime. The regional crime squads, created as part of the 1966 structural reorganisation of the whole constabulary system, also began to encroach on traditional Flying Squad territory. These new squads were tasked to combat major travelling criminals who crossed force boundaries to commit their offences. Since many of these criminals were London-based, the Flying Squad men believed they fell within their domain and that the creation of the regional units impugned their effectiveness. Given this challenge, the pressure for results to maintain status was greater than ever.

Detective Chief Superintendent Brian Boyce, a tough, uncompromising officer who worked with Army intelligence in Cyprus before joining the police in 1959, was to have a profound effect on the squad in the 1970s and 1980s, even though he was never a member of it. A student of comparative religion and one-time professional jazz pianist, Boyce had worked on the Richardson inquiry as a sergeant protecting witnesses from possible interference and was part of the team led by Superintendent Nipper Read which arrested the Kray twins. Later in his career he served with distinction in the anti-terrorist squad and criminal intelligence branch and was offered the command of the Flying Squad, but turned it down to become the first head of the specialist operations task force, a unit made up jointly of Flying Squad and Fraud Squad officers, set up to establish what had happened to the £26 million-worth of gold bullion stolen in the Brinks-Mat robbery of 1983.

In 1971, as a first-class detective sergeant and later detective inspector, he was attached to a new 'gang-busting' serious crime squad, headed by Detective Chief Superintendent Albert Wickstead. Wickstead had already had some success against gangs in the East End but had little knowledge of the West End. It was Boyce and a number of other junior men who persuaded him to turn his attentions to Soho and in particular to the activities of a major pornographer and racketeer named Bernie Silver. What began as an attempt to clean up criminal elements in Soho was to end in the exposure of the biggest police corruption scandal in the history of Scotland Yard.

Boyce had a good idea of the murkiness of the waters he and his colleagues would be entering before the inquiry began. He had been alarmed for some time about the way the Flying Squad was developing. 'They had effectively claimed for themselves the policing of all serious crime and would take over a lot of the bigger jobs from divisional CID officers. They would only really touch the bigger criminals, so they were always chasing the same people and became closely involved with them,' he said. 'An exclusive culture was created around them with very little supervision from the Yard and very little questioning from the courts. In many respects it was a very good culture, because most of the squad detectives were honourable and hard-working, but they became very inbred in the job and thought they alone were the élite.

'In the fifties and sixties, the rough and tumble world they lived in led to short cuts which they saw as legitimate, but gradually the squad became infected by a breed of officer who was corrupt for reasons no one could justify. They sold their souls to criminals for money. By the mid-sixties the squad certainly had a major problem, and although people like Tommy Butler, who I think was an honourable detective, were not involved, I think they probably turned a blind eye to what was going on rather than bring down the reputation of the squad as a whole.

'The influence of these corrupt elements didn't affect only the squad itself. Squad officers would be posted to division every so often and would set up a sort of royal court there. Innocent young CID men with a simple view of what they should be doing would come into contact with them and be influenced by them. They wanted to become good detectives and to arrest the right people, and they might already have had an idea that there were some short cuts that could be taken for honourable reasons. But some of these middle-ranking Flying Squad officers would be asking them to do things which were obviously wrong, or to turn a blind eye when required.'

Insurance companies also played a part in corrupting the squad, according to John Weeks, Scotland Yard correspondent of the *Daily Telegraph* from the early 1960s to the late 1980s. 'It became a regular practice for some loss adjusters to sanction unofficial rewards to the squad teams for the recovery of stolen goods,' he said. 'Thefts of big lorries, containing anything from cigarettes to razor blades, were a real problem in the sixties and the insurance companies were taking a bit of a hammering, so they were happy to pay out a ten per cent reward to encourage the squad to concentrate their energies on these thefts.' The detectives were usually paid in kind rather than cash, and it was not unusual for the members of a squad team who had just recovered a stolen load to be seen wearing identical new overcoats, smoking the same brand of cigarettes, or sporting a row of similar new pens in the breast pockets of their identical suits.

Once the gravy-train was rolling, it was a short step for some of the more unscrupulous detectives operating in the West End to exact tributes from those running the booming Soho pornography trade in return for allowing them to pursue their seedy business unmolested. It was not that the Flying Squad officers were intrinsically corrupt, and indeed there were many officers who did not succumb. Neither was it only Flying Squad detectives who took bribes. One pornographer, Ronald Mason, who ran six book and magazine shops in Soho, claimed to have been paying regular protection money to divisional CID officers from as early as 1953.

But the Flying Squad and the Obscene Publications Squad, which contained a significant number of ex-Flying Squad men, simply had much more opportunity to be corrupt on a grand scale. They rubbed shoulders on a daily basis with some of the wealthiest criminals in London. The criminals wanted to keep on the right side of the police and were making such vast profits that they were happy to pay substantial bribes to keep their empires running smoothly. If a detective was going to be corrupt, the West End was the place to do it most lucratively, and the policing of the West End was largely controlled by the Flying Squad and the Obscene Publications Squad.

As more and more detectives compromised themselves (in the case of the Obscene Publications Squad the entire unit took on the mantle of a protection gang), it was inevitable that wholesale corruption would eventually be exposed. The exposure had its beginnings in a sensational news story published in *The Times* in November 1969. Although there was only an oblique Flying Squad connection, it is important to give some details of the affair because it gave the public its first real indication that there was something rotten in the underbelly of the Metropolitan CID.

Under the front-page headline 'London Policemen in Bribe Allegations. Tapes Reveal Planted Evidence', reporters Garry Lloyd and Julian Mounter bluntly accused three CID officers – Detective Inspector Bernard Robson and Detective Sergeant Gordon Harris of the Regional Crime Squad based at Scotland Yard and a divisional detective sergeant from south London named John Symonds – of planting evidence and accepting substantial bribes from a range of criminals 'in exchange for dropping charges, for being lenient with evidence in court and for allowing a criminal to work unhindered'. The newspaper made no bones about the fact that it believed these three to be merely the tip of the iceberg and called for 'the most stringent inquiry'.

Lloyd and Mounter had begun their investigations after *The Times* was contacted by a petty thief named Michael Roy Perry, who claimed he was being blackmailed by the police. Robson and Harris were threatening to 'frame' him for crimes he had not committed unless he paid them money and Symonds was offering assistance in escaping the prosecutions, also in return for cash. As far as the newspaper was concerned, these were not particularly unusual accusations, but the two reporters eventually became convinced that Perry was not just another convicted felon with an axe to grind. To carry their story further, however, they would need hard evidence. Perry agreed to be wired up with microphones and tape-recording equipment, both about his person and in his car, so that future conversations with the detectives could be recorded.

The resulting tapes made damning listening and formed the substance of the *Times* story. The two regional crime squad men had tricked Perry into leaving his fingerprints on a stick of gelignite which they had brought with them, and could be heard demanding £200 from Perry in return for not charging him with explosives offences. They also tried to cajole him into helping to fabricate evidence of receiving stolen goods against another man. Perry paid the £200 blackmail money in three instalments, handed over personally to the detectives at separate meetings in pub car parks in south-east London. On each occasion the tapes were running and the *Times* team, including a photographer, was observing from a discreet distance. Not all the recordings from these and several later encounters between Perry and his police contacts were fully audible, and on one occasion the equipment did not work at all, but there was enough material to confirm Perry's original allegations with interest.

Harris, who had served a substantial part of his CID career with the Flying Squad, and Robson came across as completely unprincipled extortionists, cynically squeezing Perry for what they could get and offering nothing in return. By contrast, Symonds, who had no prior connection with the other two, was offering Perry a genuine service, for a fee of course, which could be a great help to him in his criminal career. If Perry were to be arrested in the future, Symonds might well be able to see that the charges against him were dropped, or if he was planning a big job and gave advance notice of where and when it was to be carried out, Symonds could create false alarms to divert the attentions of the policemen who normally patrolled the area in question. In some cases, Symonds might even be willing to accompany Perry on burglaries to make sure nothing went wrong. He appeared to be offering a complete insurance package – a licence to commit crime.

The tape-recorded conversations between Symonds and Perry supplied the most memorable quotes in the *Times* story. In one such conversation, on 31 October, Symonds warned Perry to beware of detectives like Robson and Harris and said: 'We've got more villains in our game than you have in yours, you know . . . Don't forget to let me know straight away if you need anything because I know people everywhere. Because I'm a little firm in a firm. Don't matter where, anywhere in London, I can get on the phone to someone I can trust, that talks the same as me, and if he's not the right person that can do it, he'll know the person who can.'

It was the 'firm in a firm' allusion, which suggested a sub-culture of police corruption across London, that gave the story its main impetus. Coming from one of the down-market Sunday papers it might have had less of an impact. Plastered across the front page and leader columns of the most respected daily in Britain it could not be ignored. *The Times* passed over its dossier of evidence, including the tapes and a number of sworn statements, to Scotland

The Kray twins, Ronnie and Reggie, with their mother (*Hulton Deutsch*)

Frankie Fraser, left, with film star Stanley Baker, centre, and Eddie Richardson

Jean and Charles Richardson with brother Eddie, right

George and Rosie Davis celebrate his innocence (*Press Association*)

The Great Train Robbery of August
1963 caught the public's imagination.
The squad sought a number of men
. . . Ronnie Biggs (*Topham*)

. . . Bruce Reynolds . . . (*Topham*)

. . . and Charles
Wilson, seen here
flying back from
Canada where he
was captured. He
was shot dead in
Marbella in April
1990 (*Hulton
Deutsch*)

Detective Chief Superintendent Thomas Butler, head of the Flying Squad, at the trial of twenty people charged in connection with the Great Train Robbery (*Topham*)

Moment of arrest for William Tobin who was jailed for sixteen years for his part in the attempted armed robbery of a security van carrying £811,000 (*Daily Telegraph*)

Detective Chief Superintendent Albert Wickstead who led the investigation into the Humphreys/Silver affair (*Topham*)

James Humphreys and his wife, 'Rusty'

Soho pornographer
Bernard Silver, left

Commander Kenneth
Drury after his resignation
following a police
investigation into his
connections with James
Humphreys (*Topham*)

Detective Chief
Superintendent Brian Boyce
who headed the Brink's-Mat
investigations in 1985

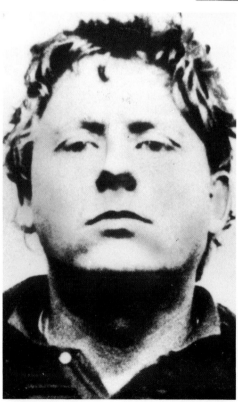

Michael McAvoy, the principal robber
in the Brink's-Mat bullion theft . . .

. . . Anthony Black, the inside man

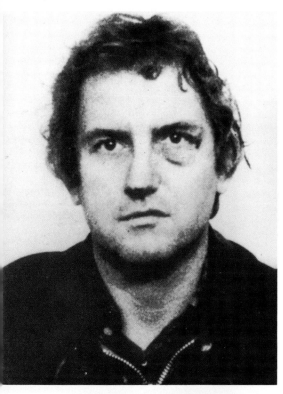

John Fleming, charged with
dishonest handling, brought back
from USA in handcuffs, had the
case against him dismissed by the
magistrate for lack of evidence
(*Press Association*)

In 1989 ITV cameras were given unique access to the squad to make a series of programmes that followed the squad's 45-strong team based at Tower Bridge (*Thames Television*)

Commander George Ness, current head of the Flying Squad (*Metropolitan Police*)

Yard the evening of the day it published the story, and Assistant Commissioner Peter Brodie, head of the Metropolitan CID, subsequently announced his intention to hold an inquiry.

The inquiry – and how and by whom it should be conducted – created a debate almost as intense as the corruption allegations themselves. The Metropolitan Police was unique among British forces in that it was not subject to the Police Act of 1964, under which the Home Secretary could insist that allegations of police corruption should be investigated by a team of officers from an outside force. In the Met, such allegations could only be investigated internally and where the allegations could lead to criminal charges against any serving officer, the investigators had to be drawn from the ranks of the CID rather than the uniformed branch.

This protocol posed a major problem where the *Times* allegations were concerned. If Symonds' boasts to Perry about the 'firm in a firm' were even partly true, then there was a core of corrupt officers within the CID. The last people anyone would logically choose to investigate the situation were the CID officers themselves. Even within Scotland Yard there was some dispute as to how the inquiry should be handled. As a matter of pride, Brodie, a self-possessed Old Harrovian, was anxious to ensure that it remained in-house. He did not believe there was any wider conspiracy of corruption and did not want an outside force poking around in Met business. Robert Mark, then Deputy Commissioner, took a different view. A provincial policeman who had come to London less than three years earlier, Mark still shared the suspicions of many provincial officers that the Met, particularly its CID, resented outside scrutiny because it had much to hide. He was in favour of the investigation being headed by a provincial officer but at that stage he did not have the power to override Brodie on CID matters. The Commissioner, Sir John Waldron, wavered between the two opinions and finally it was the Labour Home Secretary, James Callaghan, who cobbled together a compromise.

Callaghan, at one time parliamentary spokesman for the Police Federation, was generally pro-police and had no desire to throw the good name of Scotland Yard to the wolves. At the same time he appreciated the need for an independent arbiter to be associated with the forthcoming inquiry. He achieved what he saw as the necessary balance by allowing the Metropolitan CID to carry out the investigation but appointed an HM Inspector of Constabulary to 'advise and oversee' it. He would not have absolute power to dictate terms to the inquiry team but he would have direct access to the Commissioner and the Home Secretary if he felt they were following the wrong course. A halfway house it may have been, but it was the first time a provincial officer had been given any power to investigate allegations of wrongdoing in the Met.

The Yard team was headed by Chief Superintendent Fred Lambert, a former Flying Squad man then attached to C1, the central pool of detectives based at headquarters. Lambert had served on the Flying Squad with Harris, one of the three detectives under investigation, and was on friendly personal terms with him and his family. The HMI selected to advise was Frank Williamson, a former chief constable of Cumberland and Westmorland, who had never served as a policeman within 100 miles of London. Williamson was given offices at Scotland Yard for the duration of the inquiry and immediately set about forming his own team of provincial officers he knew and trusted.

Deep suspicion existed between the two teams from the outset and quickly developed into open conflict. The Met CID was determined to see off the country bumpkins and the provincial men were equally set on nailing down what they saw as a deep seam of corruption at Scotland Yard. The first exchanges all went the way of the home side. Williamson's officers were prevented from interviewing any Metropolitan detective in the course of their work and concerted efforts were made to keep them on the fringes of the main inquiry. On one occasion the provincial team's diary and work schedule was stolen from their office, never to be returned. But perhaps the most blatant example of subterfuge came five months into the inquiry when Lambert, the head of the Yard team, was summarily removed.

As the investigation progressed, Williamson and Lambert had developed a growing rapport which alarmed the chauvinistic old guard within the Met. The bumpkins were being given far too much freedom of movement. Four more detectives had been suspended and the inquiry was beginning to touch on police activity in Soho, where a real can of worms lay waiting to be opened. Swift and decisive action was necessary to retrieve the situation.

On 13 May, Lambert was visited by Deputy Assistant Commissioner Dick Chitty and berated for the way he was conducting the inquiry. A short time later he was called in to see Commander Wallace Virgo, head of C1 and Lambert's immediate boss, to be told he was being transferred to a backwater administrative job. It was made clear to him that this was a punishment for disloyalty and he was told that a more reliable officer would replace him as head of the *Times* inquiry. That officer was Detective Chief Superintendent Bill Moody, head of the Obscene Publications Squad. With hindsight, it is hardly surprising that Virgo regarded Moody as a safe pair of hands. At the time Lambert was sacked the two senior detectives were partners in a Soho corruption racket which dwarfed the modest ambitions of Robson, Harris and Symonds. Within four months, the demoralised Lambert went on sick leave and resigned from the police without ever returning to duty. Under Moody's careful leadership, the *Times* inquiry never went beyond the original allegations made by the newspaper against Robson, Harris and Symonds. No new evidence of any moment was produced by the Yard inquiry team and Symonds' claims of the existence of a 'firm in a firm' were dismissed as rubbish.

Williamson was angry and depressed about the outcome of the year-long inquiry, which he believed should have led to charges being laid against a dozen or more detectives. As it turned out, only the three named in the *Times* story were committed for trial and one of them – Symonds – jumped bail and fled abroad with apparent ease. Williamson had tried but ultimately failed to bring the corrupt elements within Scotland Yard to book and blamed the Home Office for not giving him enough support. On New Year's Eve 1971, just days before the trial of Robson and Harris began at the Old Bailey, he resigned at the peak of his career, eleven years before compulsory retirement age.

One man who sympathised deeply with Williamson's feelings was Robert Mark, soon to become Commissioner of the Met. Mark, who had served with Williamson years before in Manchester, was angry about the way the HMI had been treated but also saw a positive side to the saga. In *In the Office of Constable* he wrote:

> It had disclosed to the world that there was widespread and, as events proved, justified lack of confidence in the way allegations of crime by Metropolitan detectives were investigated. . . . I was convinced that the Home Office had at last realised that all was not well and I was in the happy position of knowing that any kind of inquiry could only rebound to my advantage and [bring about] the exposure of a situation which had already lasted far too long.

Robson and Harris were convicted in early March 1972 after a seven-week trial, thanks largely to the investigative work of *The Times* rather than that of the Metropolitan Police, and sentenced to seven and six years respectively (Symonds returned to Britain in 1980 and received a sentence of eighteen months). As the two regional crime squad men were being accompanied to the Old Bailey cells, the Yard was already well enmeshed in a fresh crisis, centred this time on the running of its central drugs squad and the activities of two ex-Flying Squad detectives who had recently been transferred to the drug unit

Vic Kelaher was one of the most dynamic officers the Flying Squad had had in recent years. He was the son of a policeman, and had been brought up for part of his childhood in a police orphanage, joining the Met as a civilian clerk at the age of fifteen before graduating into the police ranks. He was keen, bright and dedicated, and in 1968 became the youngest detective chief inspector in the history of the CID. During his two tours in the Flying Squad he had specialised in cultivating informants in an area where information was notoriously difficult to come by: the tight-knit West Indian community. Through these contacts he developed a sound knowledge of the London drugs trade, especially soft drugs like cannabis, which were used and dealt freely in black districts long before they became commonplace elsewhere.

It was natural, therefore, that when the Yard hierarchy was looking for a new man to raise the profile of the Drugs Squad,

Kelaher should be one of the first to be considered. The Met had been slow to appreciate the scale of the threat posed by drugs and their specialist unit had never been above twenty for the whole of London. A little cocaine and a few amphetamines among the champagne set and in showbusiness circles, some opiates in the Asian areas and cannabis and home-grown marijuana in Notting Hill and Brixton had hardly seemed worth getting excited about.

But by 1968, the picture was changing rapidly. The young middle classes were increasingly experimenting with cannabis, which was widely seen as a relatively harmless thrill, and many American rock music heroes of the day were associated with psychedelic drugs like LSD, amphetamine sulphate (speed) and, in the more suicidal cases, heroin. The fashion for these harder substances drifted gradually across the Atlantic, and although they never really took the same hold in Britain as they had in major US cities, they became a genuine cause for concern. In addition to the drug usage, there was also the problem of the violence associated with drug trafficking.

Scotland Yard wanted a more effective Drugs Squad, not least because the Customs and Excise, who were (and still are) responsible for drug policing at British ports of entry and conducted their work with publicly acknowledged efficiency, were beginning to make the police look rather incompetent and ignorant in the drug field. Kelaher was seen as the ideal leader of a revamped squad and took over in May 1968. His methods were often unorthodox but he knew the terrain and he got results. He favoured the American policing style, which involved a lot of work under deep cover and could include 'sting' operations, whereby agents would actually set up drug deals in order to identify those genuinely involved in the drug trade.

Sting operations were officially frowned on in Britain because they could involve the police acting as *agents provocateurs* and lead to extremely messy court cases. They also normally required the participation of at least one genuine drug dealer working on the side of the police, usually for payment and immunity from prosecution. Such informants had to be protected, even though they were still involved in the criminal underworld, and in effect became 'licensed' by the police to deal drugs.

157

Kelaher and his top lieutenant, an old Flying Squad colleague named Detective Sergeant 'Nobby' Pilcher, had no ethical reservations about sting operations or licensing of informants, and they set about breaking up the main LSD- and cannabis-importing networks in London. They quickly scored several good successes and by early 1970, the Met had reclaimed its image as the premier drug policing agency in the country.

But some of Kelaher's methods had drawn criticism, in some cases disbelief, from policemen in the provinces and from some customs investigators. An informant referred to Kelaher by Oxford CID claimed to have been paid for his information and help in drugs; another told Hampshire CID officers when arrested for possession of LSD that he had been supplied with the drugs by Metropolitan officers; a third told Lancashire detectives he had been robbed of a consignment of amphetamine tablets by five Flying Squad detectives, who had then gone on to use the drugs for their own purposes; a fourth told customs he had been involved in operations where the police had both bought and sold drugs without declaring the transactions to higher authority.

The situation came to a head on 5 March 1971, when Kelaher was arrested by customs officers investigating a conspiracy to import heroin and cannabis from Beirut to London. The exporters were two Lebanese Arabs named Karim and Omar and the receivers included a West Indian club owner called Basil Sands, who was a significant drug dealer in his own right and also a regular informant for the Met Drugs Squad.

Customs identified one particular consignment of 24 lb of cannabis, shipped into Heathrow in a cargo of 'oriental goods', and mounted full surveillance on it. The drugs were taken from the airport to a hotel in Earl's Court, where they were met by none other than Chief Superintendent Vic Kelaher. Customs had had several acrimonious disputes with Kelaher in the past and were not entirely displeased with the predicament he now found himself in. He was one of six people they arrested that night on suspicion of drug trafficking. Wisely, Kelaher said absolutely nothing on his arrest and was released a few hours later without charge while customs, the Home Office and the police decided what they should do. There was strong circumstantial evidence that Kelaher had been involved in an illegal drug deal but no hard proof. Within two weeks he had been removed from the Drugs Squad.

At the trial of Sands and the other four conspirators in June and July 1971, Kelaher told the court he had become involved with the cannabis shipment with the intention of identifying and arresting the group of international traffickers behind it. Sands had been his chief informant on the job, he said, and three other Drugs Squad officers, including Kelaher's old Flying Squad colleague Nobby Pilcher, gave evidence on Sands' behalf. One of the other defendants testified however that Sands was in fact the prime mover in the conspiracy and said the others would never have become involved had it not been for him and his claims to be immune from the possibility of police harassment. The jury believed this version of events. To the intense embarrassment of Scotland Yard, Sands was convicted and jailed for seven years and the credibility of the four detectives who testified on his behalf was torn to shreds.

The whiff of corruption was strong, and coming so soon after the Robson-Harris inquiry (although before the two regional crime squad men came to trial), Assistant Commissioner Brodie felt he had little option this time but to invite an outside force to investigate. On 20 July, Harold Prescott, Assistant Chief Constable of Lancashire, was invited to look into the allegations against Drugs Squad officers and related matters, the first provincial officer to have full control over an inquiry into the Met CID. The edifice had fallen and further developments occurred quickly. By December, five Flying Squad officers, who had also been involved with drugs policing, had been charged with trying to extort money from a south-east London drug dealer named Soltz and stealing part of his stash of amphetamine tablets, and in the autumn of 1972, after minute scrutiny of Drugs Squad affairs over the previous three years, Kelaher, Pilcher and four other detectives were arrested and charged with a variety of offences ranging from perjury to conspiring to pervert the course of justice.

During their trial, it was never suggested that they were selling drugs or setting up deals for their own profit, and there was some recognition that their unorthodox methods were pursued for reasons the men themselves believed to be honourable. Kelaher and two others were acquitted of all charges but Pilcher and two constables were found guilty of perjury. The specific allegations were that the officers had been unable to gather hard evidence to match details of a drug deal they knew about from tapped telephone conversations, so they had simply invented some. The judge was the draconian Melford Stevenson, and he gave short shrift to a recommendation for leniency from the jury.

'You poisoned the wells of criminal justice and set about it deliberately,' he told the convicted men at the end of the trial. 'What is equally bad is that you have betrayed your comrades in the Metropolitan Police force which enjoys the respect of the civilised world – what remains of it – and not the least grave aspect of what you have done is to provide material for the crooks, cranks and do-gooders who unite to attack the police whenever the opportunity occurs.' Pilcher was sentenced to four years and the two constables to eighteen months each.

The case came as another unwelcome illustration to the public that police methods had become cavalier and in some instances corrupt. The Flying Squad had had at least one dishonourable mention in every one of the cases but it was not until later in 1972 that they would command the full spotlight.

14
Fall

On 17 April 1972, Robert Mark took over as Commissioner of the Metropolis. As Assistant Commissioner and then Deputy for the previous five years he had struggled to find his feet. A provincial officer thrust into a hostile atmosphere at Scotland Yard, he had had a particularly frosty reception from the CID, who regarded everyone from outside forces as 'carrot-crunchers'. Many of those CID officers would have cause to regret their unkindness.

In his five-year reign as Commissioner, Mark single-handedly destroyed the supremacy of the CID over the uniformed branch in the Met and jettisoned hundreds of detectives on the way, some on mere suspicion of corruption. Like a manic surgeon, he hacked and slashed at what he saw as the diseased parts of the CID until he was down to the bare bone. From there he felt he could make a fresh start. His stated aim was to 'make virtue fashionable again' in the Met and no one was going to stand in his way. The phrase with which he became most closely associated perhaps summed up his philosophy: 'A good police force is one which catches more criminals than it employs.' It showed Mark's ironic sense of humour but was not intended entirely as a joke.

Mark had always been highly critical of the way the CID investigated complaints against its own members and he was committed to radical change. The *Times* inquiry, Drugs Squad investigations and Flying Squad arrests had given him the cause he needed and he set about the job of cleaning up the CID from his first day in the Commissioner's chair. As Deputy, he had already set up a uniformed squad known as A10, a dedicated anti-corruption unit, and this was to be the main instrument of his wrath.

In *In the Office of Constable*, Mark described the problems he faced on taking over command of the Met.

There was not only a lack of adequate coordination between police and civilian departments, there was longstanding and traditional ill-feeling between the CID and the uniformed branch to an extent unknown in any other British force. The uniformed policeman in London bears the brunt of violence, whether political, industrial, criminal or from hooliganism, and he had long resented the airs and graces of the CID, generally known as 'the department'. The CID regarded itself as an élite body, higher paid by way of allowances and factually, fictionally and journalistically more glamorous. It also, unlike its provincial counterpart, enjoyed an immunity from external supervision and investigation.

This facilitated for many decades three kinds of wrong-doing. The first, institutional corruption, of a comparatively minor kind but affecting a significant minority of detectives, such as 'charging' for bail, suppressing additional and sometimes more serious charges and failing to bring previous convictions to notice. Very often, the dubious cover for this kind of malpractice was 'the need to cultivate informers'. The second, more spectacular corruption affecting fewer but more specialised or senior officers, such as those concerned with major crimes like bank robbery, illegal drugs and obscene publications. The third, quite different, a widespread general acceptance that in London at least, the system of justice is weighted so heavily in favour of the criminal and the defence lawyer that it can only be made to work by bending the rules.'

Mark's aim was to put the Met's house in order with speed (he was fond of quoting Macbeth's dark soliloquy before the assassination of Duncan: 'If it were done, when 'tis done, then t'were well it were done quickly') and ruthlessness but without destroying the morale and motivation of honest detectives in the force. It was also crucial that the public should see the reforms in action and that there were no secrets about disciplinary strategies.

On 23 April, less than a week after his accession, Mark took the first major steps towards debunking the CID by placing all divisional detectives under the specific control of uniformed commanders, making the four previously all-powerful area detective commanders at Scotland Yard answerable to uniformed deputy assistant commissioners who comprised the newly beefed up force inspectorate. He followed up by taking responsibility for complaints completely out of CID control, putting the policing of pornography and vice in Soho in the hands of the uniformed branch and ordering that in future there would be regular and routine interchange of officers between uniformed and detective branches. Perhaps the most significant change was in the choice of the new Assistant Commissioner (Crime) to replace the retiring Peter Brodie. Since time immemorial the job had gone to a career CID man who could be relied on to protect the detective branch against attempted interference from outsiders. Mark's choice for the job was Colin Woods, a career uniformed officer with no Met CID experience, whose main expertise was in traffic policing.

If the CID stalwarts thought Mark simply wanted to teach them a sharp lesson in humility and hoped that everything would return to normal once he had made his point, they were in for a nasty shock. Two weeks after these new structures and appointments were announced, he called a meeting of senior detectives. They expected a steadying, soothing note to be struck. They were wrong.

'I told them simply that they represented what had long been the most routinely corrupt organisation in London, that nothing and no one would prevent me from putting an end to it and that if necessary I would put the whole of the CID back into uniform and make a fresh start,' Mark said some years later. 'I also made it plain that I was not witch-hunting. Anyone who henceforth did his duty honestly and efficiently had nothing to fear so long as evidence of past wrongdoing was not forthcoming. But woe betide anyone found doing wrong in the future. I left them in no doubt that I thought bent detectives were a cancer in society, worse even than the criminals and some of the lawyers with whom we had to deal. I did not ask for questions . . . The message got over loud and clear. The century-old autonomy of the CID had ended.'

Mark's swiftness of action impressed the cabinet, who had been hoping desperately that the new Commissioner would give an early public demonstration of his determination to put the Met's house in order. On 3 May 1972, Mark received the following note from the Home Secretary, Jim Callaghan: 'Dear Commissioner, Quick, Decisive and Right! All I hoped you would do. Congratulations!'

Having put the new structures in place, Mark now began to look in detail at individual units and to root out bad practice. His logical starting-point was the Flying Squad – that most aloof, most élitist and most hostile to change of all CID units. The squad had a proud history but at the time was on the ropes and ripe for investigation and reform. One former officer had just been jailed in connection with the *Times* inquiry; Kelaher and Pilcher were well on the way to the Old Bailey on corruption charges and five serving officers were under suspension, having been charged with attempted extortion in connection with the Soltz case. But even these serious setbacks were to pale into insignificance when placed alongside the emerging scandal of Commander Kenneth Drury.

On 27 February 1972, the *Sunday People* revealed that Drury, the man in overall charge of the Flying Squad, had recently returned from a luxurious holiday in Cyprus and the Lebanon, arranged, booked and paid for by a notorious Soho pornographer named James Humphreys, a man with nine criminal convictions and three terms of imprisonment behind him. Humphreys and his wife, Rusty, a former stripper, had accompanied Drury and his wife and they had met some rather dubious friends of Humphreys' while in Cyprus. Drury tried to bluster his way out of trouble, saying that Humphreys was one of his top informants, that he went to Cyprus hoping to obtain information about the Train Robber Ronnie Biggs and that he and his wife had paid their own way. The Commander was immediately suspended and on 1 May, two weeks after Mark took over, he left the police force never to return.

It had been an impressive scoop for the *People*. Drury was one of the most important detectives in the country and had been made up to the rank of commander less than a year earlier. He had had little formal schooling and began his working life as a post office messenger at the age of fourteen before joining the Army in 1938 (some of his disillusioned colleagues now said this was the job to which he was best suited). He fought in Belgium and France in the early part of the war and was evacuated from Dunkirk. He then joined the special investigations division of the Military Police. He left the Army with the rank of sergeant-major and went straight into the police. After divisional duties, he served in C1, the central CID pool, the Murder Squad and on special secondment in Ulster. He became second in command of the Flying Squad in 1970 and Commander on 12 April 1971. Most of his colleagues believed he had been over-promoted and even his own lawyer said he had been promoted 'for his guts rather than his intellect', but he was certainly brave, and received twenty-three commendations in a twenty-six-year career. He had a habit of standing up and shouting down the telephone which earned him the nickname 'Trumpet' among his fellow squad detectives.

Humphreys was a horse of a rather different colour. A dyed-in-the-wool south London boy, his early criminal career bore all the hallmarks of the inveterate loser. He was forever being caught and a series of convictions for theft, house-breaking, handling stolen goods and finally a postal order robbery meant that he was in prison more than out of it through his late teens and twenties. In 1962, however, on release from Dartmoor after serving his sentence for the postal order robbery, he moved into the West End and his career took a marked change for the better. He formed a company called Humphreys Entertainments Limited and opened a strip club behind Shaftesbury Avenue. With the help of Rusty, an old girlfriend whom he married in 1963, business boomed. Over the next few years Humphreys opened new clubs in Macclesfield Street, Walker's Court and Berwick Street. He treated his girls well and the business was more or less legitimate. Jimmy organised the books while Rusty organised the strippers, in between doing a little erotic dancing herself.

Humphreys bought two Rolls-Royces, a country farmhouse near the Kent-Sussex border, a holiday villa in the Balearic Islands, gave liberally to charity, became director of an amateur football club and now directed his London operations from a fancy apartment-cum-office in Dean Street. The sleaziness of Soho was becoming quite fashionable with the media cult of the late 1960s and Humphreys even acted as adviser to the popular television

165

drama series *Budgie*, which starred Adam Faith as a chirpy West End hustler.

It was all a far cry from Humphreys' earlier abortive enterprises and could have continued indefinitely had he not succumbed to greed. Profits from the clubs were excellent by any normal business standards but were dwarfed by the money being made by others in Soho from harder pornography. In 1969 Humphreys decided to take a cut of this action himself.

The big profits were being made from renting flats to prostitutes and buying and distributing magazines and blue films, mainly imported from continental Europe and the US. Most of the material could nowadays be openly displayed on the shelves of the average newsagent but at that time the obscenity laws were more enthusiastically enforced. Humphreys quickly realised that to be able to work in the pornography market, he needed police contacts, particularly within the Obscene Publications and Flying Squads, the two units which controlled the policing of Soho. The OPS, appropriately nicknamed 'the Dirty Squad', was run by Detective Superintendent Bill Moody, who was nominally supervised from the Yard by Commander Wally Virgo, operational head of C1. These were the two officers who had seen to it that the *Times* inquiry did not probe too deeply into the broader workings of the Metropolitan CID.

Moody ran Soho's pornography vice trade like a feudal baron. Anyone who wanted to open new premises had to pay him a lump sum and those with existing businesses paid a weekly or monthly fee. If they chose not to pay, they would be raided by the OPS and eventually closed down. There were thirteen detectives on the squad by 1971. Seven took a share of the money and were later convicted. Those who didn't were quickly frozen out by their colleagues and forced to transfer. The squad became the most efficient blackmail gang in London, and because Virgo was also on the payroll, there was no danger of interference from the higher echelons of Scotland Yard.

In a *Daily Telegraph* feature in 1977, Tom Sandrock and John Weeks wrote:

The total amount of hush money paid by the porn merchants

will never be known but it is estimated to have reached hundreds of thousands of pounds. It was paid for licences to trade, for tip-offs in advance of raids, so that shops could be cleared of the bulk of obscene books leaving only a few to be seized. Further payments secured an 'adjustment' of evidence and acceptance of a substitute [defendant] to face charges if a prosecution could not be avoided.

Friday night was payout night at Scotland Yard for the Dirty Squad officers. The weekly bribes ranged from £10 or £20 for a new detective constable to up to £250 for the top men. Some of the lower ranks, especially newcomers, began to have consciences about the bribes and a few refused to accept the money, but envelopes containing the appropriate amount of cash were left in their desk drawers anyway.

The only potential nuisance to Humphreys once the OPS had been paid off was the Flying Squad. Although the squad did not police pornography with the same intimate concentration as the OPS, they were active in Soho and could easily feel they had reason to raid the premises of people on the fringes of criminality like Humphreys. It was therefore important to bribe some squad detectives as further insurance against police intervention.

Humphreys' first close Flying Squad contact was Detective Inspector Alistair Ingram, who introduced him to a number of other junior and middle-ranked officers. Humphreys met Drury in March 1971 at a promotion party thrown by Ingram at a Wardour Street restaurant. At the end of the evening, Humphreys paid a £70 bill for food and drinks for himself, Drury and three other Scotland Yard detectives. 'The bill came and I picked it up and just paid it,' Humphreys said. 'It was as simple as that. There was no discussion about it at all.' He maintained contact with Drury and a number of other Flying Squad men, entertaining them at West End restaurants and hotels, throwing parties and always paying the bill. In a twelve-month period from March 1971 Humphreys paid Drury £5,000 in cash and £5,000 in kind – more in total than he earned as a Metropolitan Police commander. In return the police officers ensured that

Scotland Yard did not interfere with Humphreys' illegal business activities.

By his own estimate Humphreys was making £2,000 per week from nine pornographic bookshops, about £6,000 per week from the flats he rented out at inflated rates to prostitutes and up to £1,000 per week from his strip clubs at the time of the *Sunday People* exposé in February 1972. Humphreys' partner in many of these enterprises was Bernie Silver, viewed by those police officers who were still remotely interested in the detection of crime in Soho as a more dangerous and powerful character than Humphreys.

The *People* story signalled ruin for Humphreys, Silver and Drury, although initially the Commander could be shown only to have been guilty of a serious lack of judgement in taking a free holiday with a pornographer. It was enough to have him drummed out of the police but not enough for him to be brought up on criminal charges. Likewise Humphreys and Silver were suspected by Mark and others of having had corrupt relationships with many detectives but as yet there was no concrete proof. It took a Serious Crimes Squad investigation to uncover the full extent of Soho corruption.

The inquiry was launched at the beginning of 1972 and actually pre-dated the *Sunday People* revelations. Detective Chief Superintendent Bert Wickstead, head of the squad, had been persuaded that Silver and Humphreys should be targeted and had let loose some of his more enthusiastic young detectives on the job. Detective Inspector Boyce was a natural choice, having made many shadowy contacts while playing the piano around the West End clubs before he joined the police. For the first few months, the inquiry team quietly gathered information against Humphreys and Silver but as they proceeded it became increasingly clear that the whole of the OPS and a substantial part of the Flying Squad were institutionally corrupt. 'We hadn't set out specifically to expose police corruption but once we got into Silver and Humphreys we could see it was all around us,' said Boyce. 'We had to take it all the way.'

The inquiry really began to gather momentum in October when a man named Peter Garfath, a former lover of Rusty Humphreys, was attacked in the gents' toilet of the Dauphin Club, Marylebone by four men and badly slashed with razors. One of Boyce's informants, a brothel-keeper, told him that Humphreys had been behind the attack and that he should put pressure on Garfath to make a statement. Garfath was quickly traced and interviewed and named Humphreys as one of his assailants (an allegation Humphreys always denied). Although Humphreys had by this time fled to Holland, the Serious Crimes Squad now had enough material evidence against him to issue a warrant for his arrest and launch a series of punitive raids on his premises and those of his competitors in the pornography trade.

Humphreys was picked up at a hotel near Amsterdam and extradited back to England, where he was tried in April 1974, convicted of the attack on Garfath and sentenced to eight years' imprisonment. Bernie Silver was arrested a few months later, having also spent some time abroad hoping the heat would die down. He was sentenced in December 1974 to six years and fined £30,000 for living off immoral earnings over an eighteen-year period. Six of his associates also went to prison on a variety of vice-related charges. The war against London's leading pornographers was effectively over. The weeding out of corrupt detectives had only just begun.

After Drury's resignation and Garfath's statement, Commissioner Mark had set up an independent inquiry into all allegations of police corruption arising from the Humphreys-Silver inquiry. It was headed by Deputy Assistant Commissioner Gilbert Kelland using officers from A10, the Serious Crimes Squad and West End Central, and was to last almost four years. Personal diaries kept by Humphreys in 1971 and 1972 and subsequent statements made by him in Wandsworth prison, detailing compromising meetings with thirty-eight named detectives, provided the backbone of the investigation and gradually dozens of pimps, prostitutes, pornographers and Soho hustlers came out of the woodwork to give corroborating evidence and to point the finger at the Flying Squad and OPS. Humphreys cooperated fully with the inquiry, feeling he had been let down on two fronts by his erstwhile friends in the police. Not only had they failed to protect him against prosecution but they had actually named him as an informant against other criminals, an allegation which put his life in considerable danger.

Once Humphreys began to name names, Mark saw the scale of the problem and completely disbanded the OPS, replacing the plain clothes men with uniformed officers selected for their zeal and honesty. Virgo, Moody and many other officers were suspended or joined Drury in premature retirement, hoping to avoid prosecution. Most were caught up with in the end and brought to book. On 28 February 1976, almost four years to the day since Drury's Cyprus holiday with Humphreys had been exposed in the *Sunday People*, Virgo, Moody, Drury, two other Flying Squad detectives and seven other OPS men were arrested. The OPS men were tried first, receiving sentences ranging from twelve years for Virgo and Moody to three years for the lesser fry, and were followed in June 1977 by the three Flying Squad men – Drury, Ingram and Detective Inspector John Legge.

In their book *The Fall of Scotland Yard*, the authors Barry Cox, John Shirley and Martin Short describe the difference in tone between the trials of the OPS men and those of their Flying Squad colleagues.

> The OPS had been a humourless, miserable crew, singularly concerned with taking all the money that they could from the dirty book trade. Their attitude seemed consistent with pornography itself: it somehow lacked a sense of fun. The Drury-Ingram trial was altogether different. As Flying Squad officers they prided themselves on a flamboyant image and the court was awash with tales of hand-made cufflinks, silver goblets and epic drinking sessions in expensive restaurants and clubs. So well had Drury lived in those hard-drinking days that Humphreys had actually felt obliged to supply him with a course of slimming tablets and a rowing machine to work off excess flab.

Legge, who admitted having spent a holiday at Humphreys' villa on Ibiza, was acquitted early in the trial on the grounds that he had always paid his own way. Humphreys said of him in evidence: 'He was the only policeman who ever took me out to lunch and paid the bill.' The other two were not so lucky. Both tried to persuade the court they had used Humphreys as an informant in the best traditions of the Flying Squad. Said Drury: 'You can't just go to an informant when you need something from him. You have to socialise with him, befriend him. That is how the Flying Squad gets most of its tip-offs and that is what makes the squad so successful.' The jury was unimpressed and found Drury and Ingram guilty on all counts. Drury was sentenced to eight years' imprisonment, reduced to five on appeal, and Ingram to four years. Drury served just two years in open prisons before being released on parole but his spirit was crushed and he died, aged sixty-two, in February 1984.

The *Daily Telegraph* editorial on the day after his conviction voiced the deep public contempt for the way some elements of Scotland Yard had betrayed the trust placed in them.

> This newspaper is not slow to draw attention to the qualities of the police . . . but we make no attempt to disguise the fact that yesterday's sentences and similar ones recently reveal a fearful decline of standards in the most admired police force in the world. The Metropolitan Police have not proved immune to the general decline which has afflicted other areas in our society. We would like to be able to say that this latest trial has resolved the problem of corruption . . . but we fear that this may not be so.

As a postscript to the story, two men who had been sentenced to life imprisonment for the murder of a sub-postmaster in the course of a robbery at Luton in 1970 were released by the Home Secretary, William Whitelaw, because of doubts over their convictions. It had been a Flying Squad prosecution led personally by Drury, and the principal witness had been a squad informant named Alfred Matthews, who received a £2,000 reward for his cooperation. Matthews had actually been part of the robbery team but had been offered immunity from prosecution. He was described by one appeal court judge as 'an habitual liar', but the convictions had been allowed to stand. However, once Drury had himself been exposed as a liar and a corrupt officer, Whitelaw became increasingly uneasy about the Luton convictions. Ordering that the men be freed, he said: 'I have concluded that in view of my responsibility for the maintenance of public confidence in our system of criminal justice, the matter should now be resolved.'

The Flying Squad was in a shambles. Resignations, dismissals, enforced transfers and suspensions were running at an average of forty to fifty a month across the whole of the Met CID by 1974 and the squad was one of the hardest-hit units. They were necessary, but in some cases indiscriminate. One compulsory transfer ended particularly tragically when a forty-three-year-old Flying Squad constable with an exemplary record committed suicide the day before he was due to be returned to uniformed duties. His wife said: 'He felt he had been thrown on to the scrapheap after twenty years' loyal service. He was very proud of being in the Flying Squad and he was so dispirited about being put back on the beat.'

The squad had lost its direction. Its remaining men had become confused about their role and insecure about how they were viewed by the Yard leadership. The squad no longer had jurisdiction over the West End, its use of informants – its stock-in-trade from the earliest days – had been thrown into disrepute, most of its experienced officers had gone or were on their way out and it seemed more than likely that there were further corruption allegations yet to come. If the expertise and dedication of honest squad officers were to be preserved, a clear message was required from the Commissioner that he was not bent on their destruction.

15
Up From the Ashes

Although the Flying Squad would not fully regain its confidence and self-esteem until the 1980s, the seeds of recovery were sown within a year of Commander Drury's resignation. Despite his evangelical pursuit of reform and his contempt for the worst excesses of the CID, Robert (soon to be Sir Robert) Mark recognised that uniformed officers alone could not combat the incessant annual rise in serious crime. Good intelligence and inside underworld information were needed and the most skilful information gatherers were, by and large, to be found in Scotland Yard's specialist detective units.

As with its creation in 1918, the rehabilitation and redirection of the Flying Squad in the 1970s was prompted by a public perception that the police were beginning to lose the battle against violent crime. In 1918 the specific problems were from mobile house-breakers, organised gangs and smash and grab raiders. In 1972 they were bank robbery and the routine use of firearms.

Some older squad detectives still believe that the systematic break-up of the old CID by Mark and others from 1969 fostered the impression that the Metropolitan Police was in terminal decline. This, they argue, gave the career criminal an added bravura and a belief that he was unlikely to be caught whatever he did. Even if he was unlucky enough to be caught, so much mud could be slung at police witnesses because of the ongoing corruption inquiries that he would have a fair chance of acquittal at the crown court. The conclusion of the argument is that Mark was partly to blame for the growth of armed crime in the early 1970s. If he had left the CID old guard more or less intact, they would, for all their faults, have identified and cracked down hard on the worst of the gunmen from an early stage, discouraging others from following in their footsteps.

However, some of the 'professional' robbers interviewed for this book, while agreeing that the police had contributed to their increasing boldness in that era, had a very different view of how they did so. Bobby King, an armed robber who was active through the 1960s and early 1970s before being jailed for fifteen years in 1974 for his part in a £296,000 raid on Ralli Bros Bank in the London jewellers' ghetto of Hatton Garden, said it was the corruption itself within the CID, especially the Flying Squad, rather than the corruption inquiries that inspired many armed robbers with new confidence. 'There probably was a time when if a robbery team heard that the Flying Squad was on their case they would have been more worried than usual, but that was not the case in my day. If you had been doing a bit of work and you got caught, especially out of town, and you learned the Flying Squad were involved with the police investigation, you started to feel a bit better. You knew you could always do business with them for cash.'

There is probably some truth in both these viewpoints but neither is the main reason for the proliferation of armed bank robbery. The fact is that it became fashionable among the most adventurous and daring members of the underworld because it was brash, lucrative and glamorous. It was generally carried out by criminals who fifty years earlier would have been smash and grab raiders and country house burglars. Bank robbery normally required careful, intelligent planning, access to weapons, enough muscle and implied violence to subdue the tellers instantly and – most important of all – a steely nerve. It was not a crime for the faint-hearted and within the underworld armed robbers were regarded as the aristocracy. The respect they were afforded by their peers was a potent incentive to aim for ever greater heights of daring.

The image of the armed robber had been much enhanced by the Great Train Robbery of 1963. Although it involved the use of coshes and pick-axe handles rather than guns and most of the

174

robbery team were picked up by the Flying Squad within a few weeks, it was a crime that captured the public imagination. The gang had shown an impressive knowledge of the railway signalling system in stopping a Royal Mail train with consummate ease and the amount of money involved – £2.6 million in untraceable banknotes – was unprecedented. The robbers had shown cunning, audacity and an irreverence for one of the more visible symbols of the British establishment. These antics were widely admired in the early years of a decade in which irreverence became the height of fashion. The fact that three or four of the principal train robbers escaped the clutches of the police and lived famously self-indulgent lifestyles in exotic foreign countries until the money ran out reinforced their impudent, free-wheeling image.

Those criminals who wanted to emulate the spirit of Ronnie Biggs, Bruce Reynolds, Buster Edwards and the rest did however have to find a new vehicle for doing it. Robbing a train full of money was a tremendous one-off achievement but hardly something which could be done with any regularity. There simply were not many opportunities like that around and to know which train to hit and where and how to hit it would need an enormous amount of inside knowledge which most robbers did not have the wit or the inclination to acquire. Their thoughts turned naturally to another symbol of the establishment, but one which at least had the decency to remain stationary while being robbed – the high street bank.

Bank robbery was by no means a new phenomenon but the standard tactics used by the robbers changed radically after 1963. The traditional method had been one of stealth – breaking into the bank under cover of darkness and cracking open the safe or vault, either by springing the locks, blowing off the doors with an explosive charge, or cutting into them with an oxy-acetylene burner or thermic lance. Improvements in safe and lock manufacture made all these methods increasingly difficult, unpredictable and time-consuming. The longer it took to get into the safe, the higher the chance of detection, and this gradually deterred the conventional safe-crackers, known in the criminal vernacular as 'petermen', and the blowers and cutters.

But as one metaphorical door appeared to be closing for the bank robber another was opening. The banks were trying to project a more welcoming, less austere front to their customers and part of their way of doing this was to make their branches more inviting and sociable. This meant the replacement of the old floor-to-ceiling walls and imposing steel grilles or hatches between cashier and client with a more open-plan design, comparatively low glass screens replacing the old hatches. The new designs succeeded in tempting more genuine customers into the banks. They also encouraged the patronage of those who wanted to make withdrawals by force.

Open plan design and glass screens were a great boon to the bank robber, but the advantage they offered could not be fully exploited with traditional weapons like the iron bar, the knife and the cosh. To terrorise a cashier into handing over money in a hurry and to discourage any potential 'have-a-go heroes' among the spectating customers, it was necessary to put a gun to the glass screen. Guns were easy enough to come by and since the Train Robbery there was very little disincentive to use them. The prime movers in the train robbery had received thirty years' imprisonment, the equivalent of a life sentence, for a crime which did not involve the use of a single firearm, so why not carry maximum firepower? Capital punishment had been abolished in 1965, so even if something did go wrong and someone were shot or killed, the sentence could not be much longer.

A clutch of gangs, usually three or four strong but sometimes more, had emerged by the late 1960s, all using similar strategies. The personnel of each gang was fairly fluid, with one or two constant members and a pool of less regular freelance operators. They would enter the bank at a dash, do a lot of shouting, possibly fire warning shots into the ceiling to show they meant business, and level guns at the most vulnerable-looking cashiers while demanding money. Some carried squeezy bottles filled with ammonia, to blind temporarily anyone who offered resistance or cashiers who were slow to cooperate, and others brought step ladders to enable them to clamber quickly over low-level grilles or glass partitions. Sledgehammers to smash the locks on doors which gave counter staff access to the tills were also often carried.

Police intelligence on these new gangs was limited, partly because of the debilitation of the Met CID and partly because these young Turks did not tend to come from the traditional family-dominated criminal stamping-grounds. This was a fresh breed of young, mobile crooks, streetwise, discreet, well armed and interested only in the most profitable forms of crime.

The most active team appeared to be operating mostly in north and north-west London and, following a string of successful jobs which betrayed no clues to their identity, they became known to the north London CID as the 'Crash Bang Gang'. They had begun operations in the spring of 1969 and had steadily increased their level of activity. Between July 1971 and July 1972 they were believed to have carried out eleven bank robberies, almost one a month, netting a total haul of around £250,000. Detectives could not be certain that all the incidents were the work of the same gang, but there were striking common characteristics. On each occasion a group of between four and six men used shotguns and handguns, wore woollen balaclava masks, were well equipped with sledge-hammers and ladders and worked at speed as a cohesive team. They struck in daylight, displayed remarkable self-assurance and invariably made a clean getaway with a large amount of cash.

At 9.40 a.m. on 10 August 1972, the gang reached the high point of its career with a textbook raid on the Wembley branch of Barclays. Six armed masked men burst into the bank as a team of Security Express guards was delivering a consignment of new bank notes and collecting a larger quantity of old ones for storage in the bank's central vaults. One of the men fired a warning shot into the ceiling and yelled to the staff and customers at large: 'Lie down or we shoot.' Another, wielding a sledgehammer smashed through two doors, allowing his partners to slip behind the counters to where the money was. A further shot was fired through a glass partition as an extra warning to the shell-shocked audience. The robbers ignored the tills and the new notes, taking only the old money which was being collected by Security Express, conveniently already bagged up and entirely made up of untrace-able used notes. One gunman provided cover while the other five carried the money through the main doors to a waiting builder's van, and with one more wave of a sawn-off shotgun and a few final threats the gang made off. The entire operation had taken less than two minutes and the haul was £138,111. It had been so quick, terrifying and unbelievable that none of the staff or customers could clearly describe a single one of the raiders. The raiders had, in the words of one analyst, 'created a gap in comprehension and rushed through it, like a military task force taking a pass'.

The police investigation of the robbery was led by two highly experienced former Flying Squad men, Detective Inspector Victor Wilding and Detective Sergeant Michael McAdam, both then working on divisional CID duties at Wembley. One suspect whose name was thrown up early in the inquiry was Derek Creighton Smalls, an overweight north Londoner in his mid-thirties with a Mexican-style moustache and a weakness for alcohol and gambling, who was known to his friends as 'Bertie'. Although Smalls' previous criminal record was fairly unremarkable, he had been suspected of involvement in another bank robbery in Palmers Green, just a few miles from Wembley, three months earlier, but the evidence had been regarded as insufficient to hold him. He also approximately fitted the description given by one of the Wembley witnesses of the man who fired the shotgun into the ceiling. His name was logged for future consideration but he was not visited immediately. Instead, Wilding decided to harass a few of the known robbers and handlers on the local patch to see if any further information could be gleaned. Search warrants were obtained and a dozen addresses raided.

At one house detectives uncovered a cache of stolen goods. They were nothing to do with the Wembley raid but the man in whose possession they were found instantly became anxious to curry favour with the police. Hoping his own indiscretions would be overlooked as a quid pro quo, he gave them the names of five men he claimed had been behind the Wembley robbery: Bertie Smalls, Bruce Brown, Bryan Turner, Danny Allpress and Phil Morris. Brown and Turner had also been named by another informant to Detective Constable Joan Angell, who had passed the information on to the Wembley inquiry team. Wilding was sure he was making real headway.

Brown, an outwardly respectable businessman who owned a

smart house in a north-west London suburb and was captain of his local golf club, was placed under surveillance and eventually arrested on 30 August, twenty days after the robbery. The officers who entered his house with a search warrant eventually found him hiding in the loft dressed only in his underpants. He admitted he had been expecting their call. Allpress was also arrested but released after questioning. Smalls and Turner were said by acquaintances questioned by the police to be sunning themselves in Torremolinos and Morris was also missing from his home.

Tangible evidence soon emerged against Brown and Turner in the form of large wads of banknotes found in safe deposit boxes they held in central London. Some of the notes were found to bear initials and other marks made by tellers at Barclays' Wembley branch in the course of their normal business. There was also some forensic evidence such as fragments of plaster and glass from the bank found on Brown's clothing and a few fairly positive identifications by witnesses.

Scotland Yard, prompted by Deputy Assistant Commissioner Trevor Williams, the man in overall charge of policing north London, decided to widen the inquiry. They realised they had an expert gang on their hands and believed it might hold the key to the worrying spate of north London bank jobs over the previous year. A specialist robbery squad of twenty-five officers was set up, still under the control of divisional CID but numerically dominated by detectives drafted in from the Flying Squad and the Regional Crime Squad. They were given a list of thirty-six armed robberies to examine and asked to search for any common links.

As an opening shot to fire up the new squad, Brown was charged with armed robbery in connection with the Wembley raid. However, he had never made any admissions or implicated anyone else. The case against him was looking promising but there was still nowhere near enough against Turner to put before a jury, so the newly strengthened team initially focused on him. They quickly scored two successes. At the home of an Islington builder friend of Turner's named Fred Haig they found a briefcase which the builder admitted belonged to Turner. When they forced it open they found a .45 revolver and two shotguns. A visit to Turner's girlfriend in Wembley also proved fruitful. She admitted that

Turner and others had come to her flat on the Chalk Hill estate immediately after the robbery. It was not incontrovertible evidence of involvement but the case was building all the time. The big break came a few days later, just before Christmas.

Wilding and another detective now turned their attention to Bertie Smalls and visited his home (by now he had moved south to Croydon) to make sure he had not returned surreptitiously from Spain. There they found the family au pair, who was employed mainly to look after Mr and Mrs Smalls' three children. She initially claimed that Bertie was still abroad but under more intensive questioning broke down and admitted he was back in Britain, staying with family in the Northamptonshire market town of Rushden. Early on the morning of 23 December, the robbery squad, backed by reinforcements from the Regional Crime Squad, raided the house. Some had gone armed but in the event Smalls, confronted at 7.00 a.m. while still in his underpants, put up no resistance.

It was obvious from an early stage that Smalls was keen to make some sort of deal with the police. It was he who had put together the Wembley team and without him Brown, Turner, Morris and Allpress would not have become involved. He had also discharged a gun during the raid and felt that when the whole story unfolded he would be facing a prison sentence of anything up to twenty-five years.

In March 1973 he offered to betray all his past criminal associates and testify against them in exchange for complete immunity from prosecution himself. He told Wilding he could serve up every major robber then active in north and west London. The detectives had little doubt that Smalls could deliver top-grade information which could, temporarily at least, turn back the tide of armed robbery in London. Operationally and politically, it would be a shrewd move to do business with him. A few days later, after detailed discussions between Bertie's lawyers, the Director of Public Prosecutions and a number of senior Scotland Yard officers, the deal was struck. Bertie Smalls became Britain's first 'supergrass'.

Officials at the DPP's office set down an eight-point agreement, which was sent to Smalls' solicitors for approval. By today's standards it was an incredible *carte blanche*, excusing Smalls for all his past misdemeanours. Provided he had not committed murder or treason he would not be prosecuted for any offence, and would be held in police custody rather than prison cells until the end of all the trials in which he was to testify. This would lessen the chance of his being killed or injured by fellow members of the underworld who hated nothing more than one of their own who turned Queen's evidence. No statement made by Smalls could be used against him in the future, his wife, Diana, was not to be implicated in any past offence and Diana and the children should be moved to a safe place under the protection of the police pending all court proceedings. Once all proceedings were finished, the Smalls family, Bertie included, would be provided with new identities and a new home at a secret location of their choosing. No attempt would be made to get Smalls to pay back the proceeds of any past robberies he admitted to having been involved with.

In return for this comprehensive insurance package, Bertie would give a full account of his recent criminal career, naming every associate and being prepared to give evidence against any or all of them at subsequent trials. If he should deliberately miss anything out or decline to answer any reasonable questions, the agreement would become null and void and he would have to take his chances in court with the rest of the Wembley gang. The same would be true if his statements were not regarded by the police and the DPP as strong enough to secure a significant number of convictions against habitual criminals.

For forty-eight hours Smalls dictated a comprehensive state-ment to Wilding, his boss, Commander Roy Yorke, and a detective sergeant. Bertie's memory was remarkable and by the time he had finished he had described more than twenty robberies committed between 1968 and mid-1972 and outlined the roles played by more than thirty named individuals. He made no secret of his own part in these crimes, secure in the knowledge that he would not have to answer to the courts. The total cash sum involved was approaching £1.5 million.

The next task for the police was to start rounding up the suspects. It was essential that as many as possible should be rounded up simultaneously so that word would not get around the criminal fraternity that a big trawl was underway. The Flying Squad was a natural choice to coordinate the round-up and the squad's number two, Detective Chief Superintendent Jack Slipper, was placed in charge. The raids took place in locations as far apart as Hertfordshire and Devon and at the end of the day of the operation the police were satisfied they had pulled in most of the principal targets and that the rest would not be far behind.

In the ensuing months, remand hearings at which Smalls gave evidence against the men he had sold out had the flavour of farce, with the defendants veering between outward shows of non-chalance and explosions of anger. They developed a habit of singing songs while prosecution witnesses were testifying and the two with which they usually serenaded their old friend Bertie were 'Whispering Grass' – the song from which the slang term 'grass' for a police informer derives – and 'We'll Meet Again'. The latter carried a particularly sinister undertone of implied retribution which was far removed from the sentiments of the original songwriter.

From the magistrates court, the Smalls cases went finally to the Old Bailey, where all but a handful of the accused were convicted and given long terms of imprisonment. Twenty-seven defendants were jailed for an aggregate total of 322 years, an average of twelve years each. Despite their protestations of innocence and frame-ups, it soon became clear that Smalls had offered up the right men from the immediate dip in robbery statistics. In 1972 there had been sixty-five armed bank robberies in the London area, compared with twenty-six in 1973. This sixty per cent reduction in a single year had never been seen before and has not been seen since. The immunity deal, unorthodox as it may have seemed, had been monumentally successful.

It was, however, strongly criticised in the Court of Appeal by Lord Justice Lawton, who heard the appeals against conviction of sixteen of Smalls' associates in early 1975. While allowing the convictions to stand, he criticised what had earlier been described by defence counsel as an 'unholy bargain' between a villain of Bertie's pedigree and the DPP and said he felt it should never happen again. When the same appeals were taken further to the House of Lords, Lord Dilhorne, the presiding judge, said it was essentially none of Lawton's business what deals were made between the DPP and prospective court defendants. But the criticism had been registered both at Scotland Yard and at Queen Anne's Gate – the office of the Director. They agreed that while supergrasses should continue to be encouraged to 'do a Bertie' with the promise of substantial reductions in their own sentences, total immunity would not be given in the future.

After the trials, the Smalls family went off to a new life in the affluent hinterland to the north of London but Bertie just couldn't settle. He had already squandered all his criminal profits – estimated by him at around £250,000 – on gambling, booze and loose women and had little intention of engaging in any form of legitimate work. Within a week of the Lawton appeals, he had negotiated a deal with the *Daily Express* to tell his life story for £10,000. Perhaps the most incredible aspect of the story was that, after the police had gone to such lengths to preserve his new identity, he allowed himself to be photographed in a newspaper which was read each day by well over three million people.

James Davies, the journalist who interviewed Bertie in a London 'safe house', remembers him as rather nervous but also enjoying the intrigue of the situation. He kept saying he was putting his life on the line but still agreed to give a candid sketch of his recent past, further infuriating those who might have wanted to do him harm. Davies had the impression that perhaps he was taking the risk of talking to and being photographed in the popular press partly to alleviate the boredom of his new life and partly as a challenge to underworld 'hit men', who had reputedly been offered £50,000 bounty if they could locate and murder him. 'There are definitely people out to get me,' he told Davies. 'If they ring my bell then good luck to them but it is my job to see they don't.'

In between tales of checking his car for bombs every morning and never going out to the same place twice for fear of recognition, Smalls gave an amusing insight into how close he had become to his bodyguards during the two years he and his family were under police protection. Describing one day when he, two armed policemen and a policewoman decided to go for a run in the country, he said: 'It was a hot summer day and we was by the

183

Thames. I said I fancied a dip but we didn't have no costumes. I went in anyway, in the skin . . . One of the lads followed me, then the girl said she fancied a swim. Finally we were all in happily splashing about in the river with pleasure boats going past, until one of the lads said "What about the guns?" and went back and sat on the bank with the hardware.' A picture was published of Smalls at a party in his cell, wearing a policeman's helmet, a stunt which horrified Assistant Commissioner Gilbert Kelland, then head of the whole Metropolitan CID.

'This glamorising of and over-identification with a notorious criminal was something that I was determined would not happen again,' he said. 'It had to be faced that these criminals were totally amoral people with very little regard for anyone other than themselves . . . An important responsibility of senior supervisory officers engaged on such inquiries was to be alert to the pressures on the officers handling the informant and not to hesitate quietly to change them if this seemed necessary.' Kelland was also concerned about the public relations implications of newspaper photographs showing a professional and dangerous armed robber, who was out of jail only because he sneaked on his fellows, being fêted by the police. To use him reluctantly as a weapon in the war against crime was one thing, to count him as a pal was quite another.

Smalls, by now a father of four and seriously overweight owing to his sedentary lifestyle, also gave James Davies a vivid description of his feelings before a bank robbery and his general philosophy on the carrying of guns. He claimed to have been one of the first London bank robbers routinely to use a sawn-off shotgun and justified it by saying: 'I reckoned it was really safer for everybody. If you are only carrying axe-handles you have to use 'em, haven't you, and people get hurt, plus they fight back and maybe hurt some of your mob. If you pull a gun they are terrified. The bank clerks don't feel they have got to be heroes in front of the birds, do they?'

All armed robbers were tense and nervy before a job, he said, and he himself was no exception. 'This nervous tension I used to feel didn't stay with me all the time, only till I got started. Once I start I feel completely calm, one hundred per cent, everything comes brilliant to me. I might be fogged up a minute or two before but the minute it's on, it's like the sun coming out from behind a cloud.'

Two years later, even more inexplicably since little or no money would have been involved, Smalls again spoke on the record for a London Weekend Television documentary. Again he bleated about how hard-up he was but this time expressed some sympathy for those he had informed on: 'It's not very nice but it's a thing I'd made my mind up to do and I had to do it. I feel sorry for them now.'

Bobby King, one of those convicted solely on Smalls' evidence, actually saw him shortly after being released from his own fifteen-year sentence. 'He was in a car driving up through Crouch End and I pulled my car in behind him. I didn't really feel anything towards him after all that time. I could never forgive him for what he did but I couldn't really say I hated him. Besides, if I had done something to him, the list of suspects would have been pretty short. So I just drove off and left him.'

For the Flying Squad, the Smalls saga proved to be a watershed. The special robbery squad created in the wake of the Wembley bank raid had proved such a success that by 1976 it had been doubled in strength, most of the supplementary officers being transferred from the Flying Squad. During the following two years, the robbery squad was gradually beefed up and the main Flying Squad run down in numbers until, in June 1978, the two units were officially combined under the leadership of the head of the Flying Squad, Commander Donald Neesham. Two thirds of the 150 squad men were now engaged full-time on robbery investigations and the proportion was increasing almost by the day. Officially, the squad was re-christened the Central Robbery Squad but the name did not stick, largely because of the sentimental attachment of squad detectives to the Flying Squad name and its famous swooping eagle crest. Within three years the new name had been dropped but robbery investigation became the sole purpose of the squad.

The reorganisation, executed by Assistant Commissioner Gilbert Kelland and Deputy Assistant Commissioner David Powis, was not without opposition among the older squad officers. For many years, the main work of the squad had been generated by its own informants and the detectives had been able, with a few exceptions on really major crimes, to pick and choose their work. As a robbery squad, much of the work would now be imposed from outside. Powis, a portly, immaculately dressed man with little CID experience, was not popular within the squad and he knew it. He played up to his critics by developing a slightly eccentric image, wearing a tweed angling hat with his dark pinstriped suits around the Yard and speaking in the florid and antiquated language of the music hall barker. The least insulting of several nicknames he was given by his men was 'Crazy Horse'.

'They were not lazy and they were not incompetent. In fact they were among the best officers in the force,' Powis said of the squad detectives. 'But they were just not being used properly. They were still choosing their own work while divisional officers were being swamped with crime, particularly with armed robberies. We introduced a policy which required the squad to investigate specified crimes. Most of them approved of the changes but there was considerable opposition from the old guard, who thought they were entitled to carry on in the way to which they had become accustomed.'

Most reactionary of all was the small team of squad officers who specialised in pickpockets. The 'dip squad' was something of a hangover from the pre-war days when pickpockets had been a serious problem. By the late 1970s, if the detectives involved were not at race meetings or other public events, they spent their time hanging around the busier areas of the West End. Powis was determined to put them to more important work but the inspector in charge simply ignored his instructions.

'It may be desirable to have a special squad or some sort of campaign against organised foreign gangs of thieves when they are about but the squad was spending an inordinate amount of time catching comparatively unskilled teenagers,' said Powis. 'I told the inspector in charge that the squad had to be diverted to more serious crime but the next day he took his men back to Oxford Street. I gave him one more warning, he persisted, so I transferred him back to uniform. Unfortunately the poor man died soon after from a heart attack and I was pilloried in some papers as a hard-hearted supervisor who had caused him enormous stress. But on the whole, the squad relished their change of role.'

The 'supergrass' system was also being refined all the time, so that by the end of the 1970s, a firm set of ground rules was in place for the recruitment, handling and housing of 'resident informants', as they were known in official police parlance. There was still unease in legal circles about the large sentence reductions being given to some extremely nasty armed robbers in exchange for information, but to the police, the supergrass deals were an exciting development. Almost without exception, they were handled by the Flying Squad and robbery squad.

After Bertie Smalls came Maurice O'Mahoney. Arrested in June 1974 in connection with a £17,000 armed robbery near Heathrow Airport, O'Mahoney was as dangerous if not a more dangerous and violent criminal than Bertie Smalls. In the course of his confessions, the west London robber admitted his part in 102 crimes involving the total theft of almost £200,000. These included thirteen robberies in which firearms were carried. The DPP made it clear as soon as O'Mahoney offered information in return for a shortened sentence that no deal in the Bertie Smalls mould was possible. The most appropriate place for a man of O'Mahoney's pedigree was in jail, and any sentence reduction would have to be decided by his trial judge.

O'Mahoney decided to take a chance that the trial judge would be lenient, and while in custody at Chiswick police station he made a total of fifty-nine statements naming ninety-two men whom he said were responsible for crimes ranging from lorry theft and robbery to attempted murder and involving the aggregate theft of more than £2 million. In return, he was offered a new identity when his own sentence had been served. His trial was to be held before he gave evidence against those he betrayed, giving him the option of not testifying in the subsequent trials if he was not given a light sentence himself.

In the event his trial judge, Sir Carl Aarvold, accepted that O'Mahoney deserved recognition for his willingness to turn Queen's evidence and sentenced him to just five years' imprisonment. Sir Carl told the court that if he had not cooperated with the police, the defendant would have received twenty years for the 'grave and terrible crimes' to which he had pleaded guilty, but he recognised that to inform on his associates took courage and determination and was greatly in the public interest.

After O'Mahoney came a crop of supergrasses attracted by the reduced sentences and the sincere police attempts to protect their resident informants from retribution. A significant factor here was the prospect of serving almost an entire sentence in police cells rather than the potentially more hostile environment of prison, and the promise of a new life on release.

Five years became the unofficial sentence tariff for the supergrasses who came after O'Mahoney, confirmed in the Court of Appeal in 1977 by Lord Justice Roskill, who was hearing the appeal of a supergrass named Charlie Lowe. Despite the considerable help Lowe had given to the police after his arrest, the judge at Chelmsford crown court had been unimpressed and sentenced him to eleven and a half years for various offences of armed robbery. Lowe appealed and Lord Roskill cut his sentence to five years, saying: 'It must be in the public interest that persons who have become involved in gang activities of this kind should be encouraged to give information to the police . . . Unless credit is given in such cases there is no encouragement for others to come forward . . . in these circumstances we think justice will be done if we reduce the sentence to five years.'

In an authoritative and highly readable thesis on the supergrass phenomenon, written for a command course at Bramshill police staff college, Flying Squad Superintendent Bob Robinson sets out some of the pros and cons of such controversial deals with hardened criminals. Although a strong supporter of the system, Robinson saw it as a short-term measure to take out the new crop of armed robbery gangs who were terrorising London at the time. He was aware of the longer-term dangers of the police being seen to be too close to their natural opponents:

There is a grave danger of police completely losing their credibility should they decide to put all their eggs in the criminal's basket, while ignoring the need to establish their credibility.

But he stressed the need to look after top-level informants,

188

attending to their needs and making sure they were psychologically strong enough to go through with their court testimony. In some cases this involved the building of strong friendships between informants and police handlers. Robinson concludes his thesis with the following quote from a High Court judge: 'It is not in the public interest that there should be honour among thieves.'

Paradoxically, one of the most striking crimes investigated by the squad in this period involved neither firearms nor supergrasses. The robbery was one of the rare old-fashioned kind, a break-in at a bank when it was closed, and an immediate attack on a specific target. This robbery had added glamour because the newspapers could describe it as being 'in the heart of Mayfair'. Such robberies were becoming old-fashioned because of the peculiar risks attached to them. Professional criminals had realised that there were fewer risks, albeit with a lesser reward, in a quick armed raid, either on the bank itself, or on a consignment of money in those vulnerable seconds in which it is being transferred from a security van to the bank.

When the Bank of America in London's West End was robbed in 1975, no one knew, and no one will ever know, just how much was stolen. The first newspaper reports spoke of £300,000; as the extent of the robbery became known, the estimates went as high as £12 million. At the subsequent trial of the principal robbers, bank officials could not, or would not, give an estimate of just how much had been stolen. The team of six had taken the contents of over eighty security boxes, the owners of some of which have never been traced, while other known owners were shy of revealing the specific contents of their own box.

The problem, of course, with safe deposit boxes is that there is no record of what is in them. A similar robbery in the 1960s caused serious problems for a well-known bankrupt. His safe deposit box in a Baker Street bank had contained over £1 million in jewellery and shares, but because he had earlier stated in court that he was virtually penniless, he had been unable to tell the police just how much he had lost. Underworld gossip was that he was then blackmailed by the thief, who, having stolen the box, appreciated the businessman's problem had the contents of his box become public knowledge. One of the popular rumours about the Bank of America robbery was that one safe deposit box contained £50,000 of Mafia money earmarked for buying drugs.

Less than £1 million of the money and jewellery stolen from the Bank of America was ever recovered, At the eventual trial the judge's long sentences (twenty-three years, seventeen and sixteen years) were calculated to prevent the robbers from enjoying the wealth they were thought to have salted away.

So the Bank of America was an old-fashioned robbery. The robbers' target was the bank's safe deposit store in which there were hundreds of private security boxes, each of which could be holding anything from a worthless will to a fortune in jewellery. The bank was entered on a Friday night, and the doors to the vault opened. The doors were almost like something out of a Hollywood epic: large, bronze, each with a separate combination lock. The only damage done was to a metal strip that locked across the two combinations to prevent their being turned by accident. The strip was forced off and the doors opened, clearly by someone who knew the combinations. The safe deposit room was then torn apart, the security boxes forced open, and worthless documents scattered over the floor. The robbery was cut short by the appearance of three computer staff working upstairs in the bank. They were threatened with guns, and tied up. The robbers left prematurely.

The first officers to arrive on the scene were detectives from West End Central, followed very quickly by the Flying Squad. Bob Robinson recalled: 'As soon as the squad got there, they had a pretty good idea who had been involved. We'd heard that there was a big bank job coming off, and knew most of the team that were planning it. The only thing that we didn't know was which bank it would be. In fact, some of the squad had been keeping "obo" on the team for so long, that they'd given it up as a bad job, and put most of the blokes on to other possibles.'

About forty squad officers were briefed on the movements of the known suspects. Only one was at home, a James O'Loughlin, who was stopped coming out of the block of flats where he lived carrying a new suitcase, containing £250,000 in cash and jewellery. At first he denied that he lived in the building but changed his story when his flat was searched and three matching suitcases were found with a receipt from Harrods showing that he had bought the luggage for cash the day after the robbery. Luckily, the owners of the property found in O'Loughlin's possession were not as shy about their possessions as a number of other depositors, and the property was quickly identified as coming from the Bank of America.

The informant system turned up another suspect, Colin Buckley, who had been seen with other members of the team. He was a self-employed electrician with no criminal record. Further discreet inquiries by the squad revealed that Buckley had been working at the Bank of America. He had been helping to install a new alarm system after an earlier attempt at a break-in by the same team had failed; a break-in that Buckley had also set up. There were enough reasons for Buckley to help police with their inquiries. He was a first-timer unused to withstanding interrogation, and did not have the security of professional criminals, who knew that if they were sent away there would be good friends to look after their families. As an outsider, he also had no knowledge of the culture which would prevent a professional from talking unless he was offered a deal.

Although Buckley was unable to help with the names of those who had taken part in the raid, he was able to explain how the gang obtained the two combinations to the vault. The vault could be opened only by two employees, each of whom knew half of the combination number, and Buckley had found a way of reading the combination by sheer accident. He was a very small man, only five-foot-three and of a very thin build. Because of his size he was able to work in the ceiling of the bank, in the concealed ducts carrying lighting and phone wires. While he was working there one morning, he had dropped his screwdriver, which had made a hole in a plastic ceiling tile. As he bent to recover it, he found he was looking directly down at the two bank clerks operating the combination to the vault doors below him.

He then discovered that, with the aid of a powerful mini-telescope, he could see which numbers were being turned. Buckley had been able to watch the routine a number of times and was shrewd enough to realise that the combination was changed regularly. He let his good luck become known to the gang who had failed in the previous attempt, and very quickly he was approached by members of the eventual robbery team. It was a simple proposition. Find the combination on the day that it was needed, tell the team, and he would get part of the proceeds without having to participate in the robbery.

Buckley spent seventeen hours in the ceiling waiting for the safe to be opened on the Friday before he could reassure the gang that they had the current combination. He had already shown several of the team round the bank, identifying them as temporary assistant electricians. The gang then came in through a side door using Buckley's keys.

Bob Robinson and his colleagues found Buckley's story hard to believe, until he volunteered to demonstrate how he did it. 'Funny little bloke,' Bob remembers. 'Seemed a bit shocked that we didn't believe him, and screwed this little telescope thing into his eye to show us how it worked. We took him back to the bank. They were a bit lairy when we said he was going to get back into the roof and do a run-through of what had happened. They'd changed the combination, of course, and didn't fancy putting on a demonstration to show off the new one, so we arranged for a dummy run, with the two clerks dialling any old set of numbers, and Buckley in the roof watching them. He was right. He got the numbers spot-on, first time.'

The major suspect was a greengrocer called Len Wilde or 'John the Boche'. He was known as a planner rather than a doer, a man who could pick any lock on the market. Wilde (who also used the name Minchington) was arrested but refused to say anything about his part in the robbery although it had been confirmed by some of the lesser lights, including Buckley, who had been sentenced before the rest of the team was tried. One of the others, Billy Gear, pleaded guilty after the squad had confronted him with a parking ticket that had been put on his car which he had parked on a double yellow line outside the bank. He had been late on the scene because he had had to take his son to the dentist. He had drawn attention to himself not because of the parking ticket itself, but because he had paid the fine the very next day, an almost unique occurrence at the central ticket office. Gear had thought that if he paid up quickly there would be less chance of his car being associated with the robbery.

Another four men were arrested as a result of the surveillance that had been kept on them earlier. One of them, Mickey Gervaise, later became a supergrass instrumental in convicting the 1982 silver bullion robbers described in Chapter 17.

Squad officers then discovered that one of the problems for the team after the robbery was the amount of jewellery and gold found in the safe deposit boxes. The cash had been shared out in a flat in Lambeth (whose owner was to serve eighteen months for helping the gang), and after the money had been divided they turned to the jewellery, which none of the gang was competent enough to value. It was therefore divided into equal piles, each of which was assigned a number, for which the gang drew lots. One of the unconfirmed stories about the robbery has it that one of the team decided to use his cash share to buy gold and jewellery from the others, and ended up with so much that he had difficulty walking down the stairs from the flat.

During one of the many remand hearings, O'Loughlin escaped from Marlborough Street court. He was leaving the courtroom in a long procession of prisoners and escorts who had become used to the routine of weekly appearances and must have relaxed. O'Loughlin stepped back into an alcove, waited for them all to pass, and then, carrying a sheaf of papers he had picked up from a ledge outside the court, walked through the jailer's office as if he was a solicitor's clerk and left the court by the front door.

He was finally found in his girlfriend's flat after it had been searched several times. Jack Slipper, who had been running part of the investigation, had been trying to persuade the girlfriend to get O'Loughlin to give himself up. 'Talking to her like a Dutch Uncle,' as one of his colleagues described it, 'telling her what a terrible time she'd have with a boyfriend on the run, never being able to settle down, and the girl giving him a complete blank.' Again, the Flying Squad system worked An informant had told Mick O'Leary, then a Chief Inspector in C8, where to find O'Loughlin. He was in his girlfriend's flat all right, but living in a secret compartment built below a staircase, the entrance to which was hidden by brushes, mops and other cleaning materials. The hiding place was well enough equipped to allow him to stay out of sight for two days at a time.

Eventually five men all arrested by the Flying Squad through their informants were convicted of the robbery, with Wilde receiving the longest sentence, twenty-three years. Buckley, who had earlier been sentenced to seven years, appeared as a prosecution witness and gave evidence against all of them.

One man, Frank Maple, suspected of being involved, had fled to Spain and could not be extradited. Before arrangements could be made for his extradition, the Spaniards themselves deported him to Morocco. He next appeared in Austria charged with robbery at a hotel. He was sentenced to nine years' imprisonment and then deported to England in the belief that he would receive a longer sentence for the Bank of America robbery. Unfortunately, by then Buckley, the principal witness, had been released from prison, and had been provided with a new identity. He refused to attend court to give evidence against Maple unless he was paid. The squad officers then dealing with the case naturally could not agree to this, and Maple was released without even the inconvenience of a court appearance.

16
Closing Ranks

The squad was now showing good aptitude for its more streamlined role but it continued to be dogged throughout the 1970s and into the early 1980s by accusations of corruption. The whole of the Met CID was on the rack in that period and it was in the interests of the criminal fraternity to keep them there with an avalanche of complaints about sharp and illegal practices.

Some of these complaints proved to be genuine and well founded but a large proportion were simply mischievous or the desperate claims of men trying to avoid conviction for crimes they had committed. In his annual report for 1974, Robert Mark said that the average number of complaints being investigated by the Met against its officers on any given day was around 1,300. That year, at the height of the anti-corruption drive, 106 officers were made to leave the force, some of whom were later prosecuted.

The Drury-Humphreys-porn squad saga rumbled on through the courts until 1977 – a full five years after Drury's enforced resignation – casting a continuing dark cloud over the squad, and a number of new allegations were given full consideration by A10, Mark's internal anti-corruption unit. One of the more intriguing examples came out of the Bertie Smalls investigation and, unusually, originated from a serving police officer. The affair rather took the gilt off what was otherwise regarded as a wholly satisfactory operation.

The complaint was made against Detective Inspector Wilding two years after the Wembley bank raid by one of the very few woman detective constables attached to the Flying Squad, Joan Angell. Angell maintained that within three days of the robbery one of her informants, codenamed 'Mary Frazer', had contacted her and told her that Bruce Brown and Bryan Turner had been among the robbers involved. The tip was passed on to the robbery squad and when Turner was charged, Angell put in a formal request for the payment of a reward to Mary Frazer for her help. Not only was this request refused but she discovered that rewards for the information about Brown and Turner totalling £2,175 had been paid on the authority of Wilding and his immediate boss, Detective Chief Superintendent Dick Saxby, to another informant codenamed 'William Wise'.

After making an official complaint through A10, Angell further discovered that her original claim on Mary Frazer's behalf had disappeared from Flying Squad files and all record of her even having registered it had been deleted. Fortunately, she had kept a photocopy of her claim form and the clerk who typed the original application made a statement verifying that it had been submitted through the correct channels.

Wilding and Saxby told A10 that while Mary Frazer may have proffered the names of Brown and Turner before William Wise, Wise had given specific information about the London safe deposit boxes held by the two men which contained tens of thousands of pounds in proceeds from the robbery. Wilding also produced William Wise for A10 to interview and Angell produced Mary Frazer. A10 eventually concluded that there was no evidence of impropriety. Their final report suggested that there was a moral responsibility to give some of the reward money to Mary Frazer, who had given her information in good faith and had been badly treated. A year later, following personal representations by Angell to Sir Robert Mark and banking representatives, Barclays Bank paid Mary Frazer £1,000. As soon as the affair was over the embittered Angell, a model detective with fourteen years' experience, resigned from the police.

A second mini-scandal also emerged from the Smalls case when, some months after his conviction for armed robbery, Bruce Brown accused Chief Superintendent Saxby of having stolen £25,000 from his safe deposit box when searching it. This type of allegation was extremely common but this claim was taken more seriously than usual because of a set of taped telephone conversations between Saxby's wife, Eunice, and Brown's wife, Glenys. Saxby and Brown had belonged to the same golf club and had socialised together for some time before the robbery and their wives had become fairly good friends. Eunice Saxby and Glenys Brown spoke frequently on the telephone and Glenys hit on the idea of taping their conversations over a period of about three months in the hope of gathering solid evidence to back up her husband's claims.

Eunice spoke on the telephone of her husband's anxiety at Brown's allegations and said she thought he might be engaged in an attempted cover-up of impropriety. She also mentioned a mysterious package of money she saw her husband with but was unclear about how much it contained and what had been done with it. The tapes created a stir and raised some doubts about the integrity of certain members of the robbery squad, but they did not constitute strong enough evidence of corruption for prosecution, or even disciplinary action. Saxby was cleared by A10 but then went on the sick list. A few months later he left his wife and retired to Florida.

This was also the era of George Davis, whose slogan 'George Davis is Innocent OK' was painted on countless railway and road bridges and walls across London by his supporters as part of a campaign to have his conviction for armed robbery quashed. Davis had been given a seventeen-year sentence in March 1975 for his part in the robbery of the London Electricity Board offices in Ilford. He claimed he had been wrongfully arrested and that evidence against him had been fabricated by robbery squad and Flying Squad detectives. The subsequent campaign, orchestrated by his formidable wife, Rose, to have his case reviewed reached the nation's living-rooms in the summer of 1975 when the campaigners broke into the Headingley cricket ground in Leeds late at night and dug up the pitch, causing a crucial Test Match due to be completed the next day to be abandoned. (It rained for the whole of the day so there would have been little prospect of play anyway, but the message was brought home and the campaign began to gain some degree of popular support.)

An independent inquiry into the case was set up by the Home

Secretary, Roy (now Lord) Jenkins, but before it was completed Jenkins declared that there was sufficient doubt about the conviction to justify Davis' release. He was freed in May 1976, to the chagrin of the Flying Squad. The release was a tribute to the dynamism of Rose Davis and the influence of the pressure group on certain politicians. Jenkins did not detail the exact reasons for quashing the conviction and no policeman was ever charged with having 'fitted up' Davis, leaving the whole issue in the air and an implied smear on the squad.

But the squad detectives had the last laugh. On 23 September 1977, just over a year after his release, they pounced on Davis and five other men in the act of robbing a security van as it made a cash delivery to the Bank of Cyprus in Holloway. As they waved shotguns at the security guards a robbery squad team, which had received advance information about the raid, ambushed them. Davis and his confederates – who included Michael Ishmael, who had been tried for armed robbery with Davis after the Ilford LEB job but acquitted – received sentences of between twelve and sixteen years and the argument over whether George Davis was innocent ceased to be relevant.

But the squad was not always in a position to be quite so self-righteous. Two other Flying Squad officers, Detective Superintendent John Keane and Detective Sergeant Terence Lynch, were charged with criminal offences in separate incidents in 1979 and both were subsequently convicted. Keane was sentenced to three years for offering £10,000 to a fellow officer – Detective Inspector Bernie Gent – as a bribe to drop charges against a third man accused of large-scale theft. Gent told A10 (in itself a sign of the times), who kitted him out with a secret tape recorder, which he wore for his next meeting with Keane. A good recording was obtained of Keane repeating the bribe offer and he was arrested. It was unclear how much the thief was to have paid Keane for getting him off the hook but the judge, John Leonard QC, was quite certain that 'a large sum of money' would have been involved.

The Lynch case was a much more commonplace story of graft, which had distinct shades of the *Times* inquiry. Lynch, who had been in the Met fifteen years, was convicted of asking a garage proprietor caught in possession of stolen goods for a £1,000 bribe 'to smooth things over' for him. Predictably, Lynch claimed in his defence that he was merely using the man as an informant to identify and track down top-grade car thieves and had had no intention of taking money for himself. The jury did not believe him and he was jailed for eighteen months. Sir James Miskin QC, the Recorder of London, told Lynch: 'I know of nothing which damages society more than corruption and no corruption is more serious than when a member of our splendid police force is involved. That dents justice.' After the batterings of the previous few years, it was at least reassuring that one of the most eminent members of the judiciary was still describing the Met in general as 'splendid'.

Corruption cases like these against squad members continued to trickle through the system but their scale and importance was to be dwarfed by a much more concerted investigation into alleged Met impropriety by an outside force. It was an inquiry which began with information supplied by the Flying Squad and which was later to be used as a stick with which to beat the squad itself.

In August 1978, Assistant Commissioner Kelland was contacted by the Commander of the Flying Squad, Donald Neesham, and told of a series of corruption allegations made by a robber turned resident informant, then housed at Finchley police station. They related particularly to bribery and conspiracy involving City of London police officers in connection with recent armed robberies at the offices of the *Daily Express* and the *Daily Mirror* at Fleet Street and Holborn Circus respectively, and Williams and Glyn's bank in the City. On the *Mirror* raid a security guard had been shot dead by the robbers.

The general allegation was that certain City detectives had been paid by the robbery gangs not to investigate the crimes too fully and also to arrange bail for any of the robbers unfortunate enough to be caught. Peter Marshall, Commissioner of the City force, immediately asked Mr Leonard Burt, Assistant Chief Constable of Dorset, to investigate the allegations and there began one of the most acrimonious inquiries in the history of the modern police service. It was called Operation Countryman.

The operation, run for the first twenty-two months by a team of

199

provincial officers from the West Country before being handed over to the Chief Constable of Surrey and finally to Scotland Yard, went on for more than four years, cost in the region of £3 million and led eventually to the conviction of just two City detectives. Although the inquiry looked at allegations against many Met officers, not one was convicted of criminal impropriety.

The Dorset team claimed that this was because they were obstructed at every turn by Met and City officers and the Director of Public Prosecutions. They implied that numerous guilty detectives were allowed to escape justice because evidence against them was suppressed. The Met hierarchy hit back by accusing the Countryman team of being driven by prejudice against both London forces and said that they had believed the unsubstantiated lies of dozens of career criminals in their unhealthy desire to gain convictions.

Predictably, the wags among Scotland Yard's rank and file chose a cruel nickname for their country cousins and as ever it contained a vegetable allusion. Whereas the glamorous Flying Squad had become universally recognised as 'the Sweeney', the Countryman team became known around the Yard as 'the Swedey'.

Allegations – many against Flying Squad detectives – flooded into the provincial investigators from criminals all over London and a dozen serving and former squad officers were suspended pending further interviews. The Countryman officers were warned by their Metropolitan colleagues to treat the claims with some circumspection since they were being made by the very people who had most to gain from the Flying Squad and other specialist units being forced on to the back foot. Among the quickest to accuse the police were those who had been arrested or convicted on the evidence of supergrasses. If they could bring down the reputation of their accusers they might yet walk free.

'The Countryman team was set up to look at allegations against City of London detectives but it was obvious from the start that what they really wanted was to have a go at the Flying Squad and show them up as an academy of scoundrels,' said John O'Connor, who was a squad chief inspector up to 1978 and became its Commander in 1987. 'It was one of my informants who started the inquiry but once it got going they were taking allegations from all sorts of villains. I was suspended for twenty months on the word of an armed robber I had never met. He claimed he bribed me to steal some incriminating statements against him from the safe of Whetstone police station and said he had handed over money to me somewhere in the West End – he couldn't remember where. That was it, no evidence. There was nothing to it and the charge was eventually dropped with no further action but it nearly finished my career.'

While the provincial officers of Operation Countryman could justifiably claim that the Met was obstructing their inquiries, Met officers also had complaints about the naive manner in which some of those inquiries were conducted.

One of the first criminals to give evidence to Countryman was David Smith, who was being held by the Finchley robbery squad as a supergrass. There was already suspicion about the armed robberies that were taking place in the City, an area notorious for being difficult to escape from in a car at speed, and for the ease with which major criminals were bailed there. Several of the first supergrasses to be turned by the Finchley robbery squad provided information about corruption in the Met and the City to Countryman.

The first disagreement between Countryman and the Flying Squad came when Countryman made it clear that they would be present in court while a Keith Warne gave evidence against Berkeley and Williams for a particular robbery (see Chapter 17). Detective Chief Inspector Tony Lundy, who was in charge of the case, saw that the known presence of Countryman officers at the trial would have an unwelcome effect. Warne, with Lundy's full cooperation, had already spoken to Countryman about corruption. If he saw Countryman detectives in court, he might well mention this in evidence, and a jury, hearing daily media stories about Countryman and police corruption, might then decide that they were being asked to judge a case involving corrupt officers and dismiss it. Lundy was able to arrange through the DPP for the Countryman officers to be told not to attend court. Countryman saw this as deliberate obstruction by the Flying Squad.

Even worse interference by Countryman came with the arrest of Joey Maybur for an armed robbery. In 1979 the Finchley robbery squad had been keeping surveillance on the Sheraton Park Hotel in Knightsbridge. They had some information that a security van was going to be robbed outside. On the day the raid came off, however, the team of three villains turned out to be after the takings of the casino at the hotel. They arrived just as the money had been taken from the safe for delivery to the bank. The three robbers took the squad by surprise. They had been set up for an attack on the van, and when the team walked into the hotel, plans had to be changed rapidly.

Inside the hotel the team produced guns and took £16,000 from a table. A quick-thinking cashier slammed the safe door shut on £100,000 that had not yet been taken out. He was smashed across the face with an iron bar for his trouble before the gang ran out, with the squad officers still on their way to the hotel. The robbers' getaway car, driven by a freelance journalist working for the *Sun*, was rammed by a squad taxi and delayed long enough for other officers to arrive and arrest those inside. The man wielding the iron bar turned out to be Joey Maybur, an active criminal who had already served eleven years for armed robbery.

While they were waiting for trial, Countryman interviewed Maybur, who was on weekly remands, and proposed that he be given bail because he had promised to assist them. The squad naturally objected to bail. When he finally appeared for trial, Maybur pleaded guilty and the rest of the team pleaded not guilty. 'We couldn't work out what was going on,' said Tony Lundy, who was also in charge of this case. 'They'd been caught bang to rights, no way of getting away with it. Then we found out what the plot was. Defence lawyers asked that Maybur be sentenced immediately instead of following the usual practice and waiting until the end of the trial. For some reason the judge agreed, and a Countryman detective got in the box and said that he was giving them valuable assistance. So the judge gave him eleven years instead of the expected twenty. After that the others changed their pleas. Now, as the leader had only been given eleven years, they had to receive lesser sentences of seven and eight instead of the sixteens and eighteens that they might have got. To top it all, when Countryman came round to see Maybur to get their half of the deal, he told them to get stuffed. So effectively Countryman's lack of sophistication earned a reduced sentence for an active robbery team. I think that at first the squad were only too willing to help Countryman, but they made so many mistakes that we started to be careful with them.'

After almost ten years of voluntarily placing itself under the microscope and undergoing a painful process of self-cleansing, Scotland Yard had had enough. There was a general feeling in the Met that some of the Countryman allegations probably had substance, but the Yard leadership decided there was a danger of a large number of innocent policemen being destroyed to satisfy the prejudice and vanity of the provincial team. Their reaction was to close ranks. Said Assistant Commissioner Kelland: 'In my position as AC (Crime) I was committed to getting rid of any detective who behaved criminally or unethically and I continued to demonstrate this. But I also had a duty to support the great majority who were honest and hard-working. Detectives are men of the world, not shrinking violets, and as long as they have the confidence that their own senior officers are being fair, they are not deterred from doing their job.'

The uniformed men put in by Sir Robert Mark to clean up the CID were now siding with the CID against outsiders from the provinces, as their predecessors had done in the late 1960s and early 1970s. Their decision to stand firm against what they saw as largely false innuendo was strongly supported by Sir David McNee, the combative Scotsman who had taken over as Commissioner on the retirement of Sir Robert Mark in 1977. The Director of Public Prosecutions was also privately critical of what he saw as the weakness of some criminal cases prepared by the Countryman officers against London detectives.

The dispute came to a head in February 1980 when Arthur Hambleton, Burt's Chief Constable in Dorset, gave a television interview on the eve of his retirement which included the assertion that up to twenty Met and City detectives would be charged with corruption as a result of Countryman. As the inquiry was still in midstream and no prosecutions had yet been finalised, the Yard, the DPP and the Home Office were furious at Hambleton's pre-emptive comments. Three months later, Countryman was placed under the control of the Chief Constable of Surrey, assisted by Met

Deputy Assistant Commissioner Ron Steventon, until its conclusion in 1982. A total of eight Metropolitan detectives, several of them past or present members of the Flying Squad, were tried for various corruption-related offences and all were acquitted before juries. Three of the eight were subsequently dismissed from the police following disciplinary inquiries, one resigned and the other four returned to duty.

John O'Connor, not one of those charged, was brought straight back into the fold and it is an indication of how Kelland and the others viewed the flimsiness of the Countryman allegations that he was posted soon after to a public sector anti-corruption unit. 'I decided to go for a quiet life and they couldn't stop promoting me,' he said.

The Countryman officers complained bitterly that their exposure of corrupt policemen had been deliberately suppressed. One newspaper report of the time summed up their feelings:

> They believe London has the most corrupt detective force in the country and that the system is oiled by a handful of 'brokers' who link criminals with corrupt policemen and in return receive money and a licence to commit crime. They can prove in court only a fraction of what they believe.

After the last of the Countryman trials, a group of Liberal MPs pressed in Parliament for further action against detectives believed by the Dorset officers to be guilty of corruption but they were quickly seen off by Scotland Yard assisted by the Home Secretary, Sir William (now Viscount) Whitelaw. Whitelaw wrote to David Steel, the Liberal leader, saying he thought another independent inquiry would be pointless and an insult to the Met, which had amply demonstrated its own commitment to rooting out corruption. He gave the force a final vote of confidence in the House of Commons in November 1982, when he said: 'I have concluded it would be wrong to have an inquiry. It is right to back the new Commissioner [McNee], Deputy Commissioner and Assistant Commissioner for Crime. A great deal has been done in recent years to root out corruption in the Metropolitan Police. They have my full confidence in doing so. I want them to get on with the job.'

204

17
Supergrass Master

If one man epitomised the changes in the Flying Squad in the late 1970s it was Tony Lundy, a workaholic who was unwilling to stand fools of any rank and unsympathetic to officers who put the job second to anything else. His relationship with one of his informants, Roy Garner, has been the subject of internal and media investigations (including three television documentaries and one book) for several years but his record of leading a robbery squad which recovered millions of pounds' worth of property and put scores of armed robbers in prison is undeniable.

Lundy, who had first joined the squad in 1969 as a detective sergeant, had not been impressed with its work-rate, and when he returned to it in 1977 as a detective chief inspector he found little improvement. Morale was naturally low because of the recent conviction of Commander Drury. 'There were still old salts about living on past reputations,' he said. 'Good detectives, hard workers, but with no objectives set they went round waiting for someone to give them work.' Lundy had no doubt been lured back to the squad by rumours of imminent change, and also by a feeling that a policing policy which required officers to limit their investigations to within artificial geographical boundaries was not an effective policy.

'I'd been at Willesden,' he said, 'when a couple of informants began putting in some local prostitutes as part of a hotel burglary team. We found a really sophisticated set-up. The whole organisation was run by a pimp, Jubi Taylor. His girls would go back to the hotels with wealthy clients and tell Jubi which rooms were worth turning over. Jubi used a couple of young pale-skinned West Indians who dressed well and looked very much like young Saudis. They were able to walk into hotels without question and screw the rooms that the girls had located for them. We found that they were even using the plastic information notices from the hotel phones to slip the catches.

'We ended up recovering a million pounds' worth of property and arresting twenty-seven people, but none of it was to do with Willesden, and I was getting the same sort of thing that happened ten years later on the Brinks-Mat inquiries. "Why are you getting mixed up in this? Shouldn't someone else be investigating these jobs?"'

More than anything else, it was the attraction of freedom of movement that brought Lundy back to the Flying Squad.

'There were two superintendents and four chief inspectors each running two inspectors. Each inspector had a unit of about eight detective sergeants and detective constables. There were still no set objectives, and my first change was to stop lunchtime drinking. It made me unpopular for a while, but those who didn't like it had a clear choice. They could go back to division where there was no time for lunch-hour drinking. When Powis and Kelland introduced the expected changes the next year, they weren't popular either. There was a great deal of resentment from people who felt entitled to rest on their laurels, but those who saw that the villains were having things too much their own way were desperate for leadership.'

Within a year of his return, the expected changes had been put in place. The squad was divided into four robbery squads with separate area offices and given the direct responsibility of investigating all armed robberies and organised robberies involving more than three criminals. Lundy had always believed that the squad should be investigating crime rather than nominally investigating criminals, work which was now passed to C11, the Criminal Intelligence Branch. (The squad is now SO8 and C11 is SO11.) During the following twelve months, a concentration on armourers who supplied firearms to robbers brought in sixty-four weapons which had been used, or were about to be used, in armed robberies.

One of Tony Lundy's first operations set the pattern for his next four years on the squad. It was the arrest of a robbery team and the turning of one of its members to give evidence of all the crimes in which he had been involved.

In 1977, before Lundy rejoined the squad, an informant had told him of a team of three category A men who were plotting the robbery of a Security Express van at Colindale. Lundy passed the information to the Regional Crime Squad, and then joined up with them when he came back to C8. Surveillance had been thorough enough to pinpoint the scene and date of the robbery, and Lundy had his mixed team of Flying Squad and Regional Crime Squad officers ready for an ambush. They knew the café at which the gang met up, and had identified the stolen getaway vehicles left in place round the 'plot'. But just before the security van was due to arrive, two of the robbers drove through the plot in their own car, clearly did not like what they saw, drove back to the café, and then went home.

There had been intercepts on all their phones, and men who had been discussing details daily suddenly stopped phoning each other. Someone on the police side had clearly blown the job. Lundy's style had never been to wait for something better to turn up, but to act on the evidence available. This 'go in and get them' attitude never endeared him to senior officers who had a more cautious approach. There was sufficient evidence already to justify arrests for conspiracy. So, a week later, arrest teams were assembled at 4.00 a.m., given sealed envelopes, the contents of which were known only to Lundy and his detective inspector, and told to drive to specific locations. Then, at a radio signal from Lundy, the envelopes were opened and the teams arrested the person named in them. They also took possession of a specially equipped surveillance van which the gang had used to watch the deliveries by the Security Express van.

Three men were arrested: David Smith, Alf Berkeley, and 'Fat' George Williams. Smith became Lundy's first major supergrass. 'It wasn't just a matter of him agreeing to provide information,' says Lundy. 'He had to be put under the right sort of pressure.' And the right sort of pressure in this case was knowledge of another crime in which Smith had been involved, and about which he suspected the police knew nothing.

This was the Thatched Barn robbery, named after the site of the attack in Borehamwood in Hertfordshire. Two elderly men collecting company wages were ambushed by a robbery team which smashed their car windows and threatened them with sawn-off shotguns. The men handed over the money. Before they left the scene, one robber pulled off the glasses of one of the men and squirted ammonia directly into his eyes.

Lundy knew of a similar robbery in Kent and had information that a man called Keith Warne had provided a flop (a safe house) for the robbers immediately afterwards. He also knew that Warne and Smith were friends. There was enough there in the Lundy way of working to bring in Warne for a chat, and Warne, seeing himself mixed up in armed robberies – he was a con-man, unused to violence – started to talk, almost immediately admitting to sheltering Smith and Williams after the Kent robbery. The third man in the team, George Williams, also weakened in the face of Lundy's hints that Smith and Berkeley were talking and told Lundy where he had hidden a stolen car. In the car were the crash helmets that would link the three men to the Thatched Barn robbery. Smith added to the store of information by revealing that Williams had guns used in other robberies hidden under the floorboards in his house.

Lundy was now able to approach Smith with what was to become a classic persuader: 'You're bang to rights for the ammonia robbery, and the team is certain to go down for the conspiracy. The others are beginning to talk [the robbers had all been kept at separate stations]. If you don't roll, and one of the others does, you won't be out for twenty years.'

There was another pressure. Smith's wife had been called in to persuade him to talk, and she was anxious to help Lundy because he knew about the affair she had been conducting with one of Smith's friends. Smith started to talk. The bargain was that if Smith told everything about every job in which he'd been involved, the courts might be persuaded to reduce his probable twenty-year sentence to five. (One current supergrass, Charlie Lowe, had just been given five years instead of an expected eleven, which the judge indicated would have been the proper penalty.)

Over the next weeks Smith confessed to seventy-nine robberies, naming all those who had taken part in them and agreeing to give evidence against them in court. To Lundy's dismay, Smith also confessed to a murder.

He had struck a jeweller in an East End robbery – 'I only gave him a little tap on the head,' said Smith – and then saw in the next morning's paper that the victim had died. The jeweller was found to have had an abnormally thin skull, and the DPP was satisfied with a charge of manslaughter. Lundy's fear had been that if Smith were charged with murder he would face life imprisonment and would therefore not profit from any supergrass arrangement, and consequently would stop providing information.

Lundy was also able to arrange a strange bail for Smith, who was making two appearances a week at Highgate court to confront the robbers that he had named. He was clearly in danger of attack if not of being murdered. So the court agreed to bail him to Finchley police station, where two of the traditional police cells were furnished with extra lights, chairs and a television set. He was taken out regularly by police officers to identify the scenes of admitted robberies, and to point out the homes of accomplices. In fact he was having a more comfortable time than his wife, who one evening brought her two young daughters to Tony Lundy and told him she was fed up and it was about time that Lundy, who had caused all this trouble anyway, looked after them.

Sixty-one of the sixty-nine people arrested for robbery, conspiracy or receiving as a result of Smith's information pleaded guilty. Another six were found guilty in court. Almost a million pounds' worth of property was recovered, and one seemingly respectable couple were found out by their sins. They had collected £29,000 in insurance money after hiring Smith and Berkeley to carry out a bogus burglary at their house. As a result of Smith's information the burglary was solved, insurers reclaimed their money and the couple were sentenced to five years each. Smith also provided information about a more serious burglary carried out by a team which included a man called Mickey Morris, who, years before, had been acquitted of shooting the doorman of a club who had refused to admit him.

Smith told Lundy that Morris was part of a team that had carried out a number of 'tie-up' burglaries, in which the criminals got into a house, tied up the occupants, and then threatened them with violence if money was not produced. The particular robbery that Smith put Morris in had involved the stripping of a sixteen-year-old girl and a threat to rape her in front of her parents. There was plenty of evidence against Morris but he was living in Benidorm, and could not be extradited.

Lundy asked permission to go to Spain to find Morris to see whether he could get him to come back. He was initially accused of trying to finance a cheap holiday and let his feelings be known forcibly. Deputy Assistant Commissioner Wyn Jones, who had refused his request, eventually allowed him to go.

'All I had was the name of a Spanish officer in Benidorm. I couldn't speak Spanish. We arrived at Alicante at about ten p.m., hired a car and set out to find Vincente. We kept being directed to the headquarters of the Guardia Civil, but Vincente was in their national police. When we finally met up it was two in the morning. He had only broken English, but his lieutenant, Felipe, spoke perfect English. I thought we'd just say hello and meet the next morning, but I'd met two people who were willing to work harder than we were. We spent two hours talking about Mickey, showing them photographs, and feeling each other out. In the end they seemed as keen to capture Mickey as we were.'

Within six hours of talking to Lundy, the Spanish police had found Morris, seen his passport and discovered the address he was using. A check with Lundy through London showed that the passport was stolen. A later check at Morris' address when he was out turned up a marriage certificate in his true name. The Spaniards arrested Morris on a spurious murder charge. The night before, a German man had committed suicide by feeding exhaust fumes into his car. Vincente, in broken Spanish, showed Morris the car, and demonstrated how the body had been found. Felipe hid his knowledge of English and nodded understandingly in support of Vincente. Morris tried to hold his patience and explained that this was a common form of suicide.

'Suicide?' asked Vincente, as if the possibility had never occurred to him.

'Yes, suicide!' yelled Morris, getting into the car and demonstrating how it had been done. Finally, the Spaniards admitted their stupid mistake. There was still this matter of the passport and marriage certificate which had been seized when Morris was arrested. Could Señor Morris explain why they did not match?

Señor Morris quickly thought up a story of a row with his wife, a dash to Spain, a reconciliation, and now this embarrassment of giving a false name to obtain a passport. He had his real passport in London. Perhaps things could be put right if he went back to London and returned immediately on his real passport?

'We must speak to your wife about this,' said the Spaniards, and Mrs Morris was summoned to the police station. Vincente left them in the care of Felipe, whom Morris believed could not speak a word of English.

'Couple of right wallies here,' Morris told his wife. 'Haven't checked nothing with Scotland Yard. Just concerned with some red tape about passports. You book me a flight. Get your mum to meet me at Heathrow with my own passport, and I'll come back straight away. The Old Bill won't ever know I've been in the country.'

Vincente returned and agreed that all could be put right if Morris came back into Spain on his proper passport. Then they could dispose of the false one as if it had never existed. Mrs Morris booked the flight. Could Morris do a favour for Vincente? There was a certain young lady in London . . . Would he perhaps take her a present from Vincente?

'No problem,' said Morris, always sensing an advantage in doing a favour for the police. Documents were signed. Property was handed back. They set off for the airport.

'Stop!' shouted Vincente. 'We have forgotten the present.'

'We'll miss the flight,' said a worried Morris. 'Look, I'll buy her something in London. You tell me what to get. We can fix up paying when I get back.' A smile of relief from Vincente, a confident grin from Morris, and he was safely on his flight back to Heathrow – where members of Lundy's unit were waiting to arrest him. He got fourteen years, and Lundy had captured him without speaking a word to him, or even being seen by him.

Lundy had another trip abroad at the start of this second spell: to Rome to arrest 'Joe the Greek'.

'There had been a series of robberies at cinema box offices. Two men, one very tall, one very short. Both carrying guns. The short one was a maniac. He fired when there was no need. He shot at one woman cashier in a bank. Luckily the bullet lodged in her hair. He shot a supermarket manager three times in the stomach. He used dumdum bullets. We had no ideas until an informant named the tall man as George Wilkinson, and the short one as Joe Vratsides, or Joe the Greek.'

The informant told them that Wilkinson would be going to The Crown in Cricklewood, a huge pub which enabled the officers Lundy had recalled to duty to be in place before Wilkinson came in. But the sheer size of the place also allowed Vratsides, who was coming to the pub to meet Wilkinson, to see him being arrested by squad officers. Vratsides immediately returned to a nearby flat where he had stored his guns and an escape bag, and left there one step ahead of the squad, who made it their next call.

Vratsides' unprovoked use of a firearm and his choice of dumdum bullets were strong enough grounds for his picture to be circulated to all newspapers as England's top criminal. He was arrested in Rome under another name for possession of a gun and ammunition when his luggage was searched at the airport. A diplomat called in to check his passport recognised Vratsides from the English newspapers. Lundy rushed out to Rome, proved to the Italian authorities that the man they were holding was using a false passport and had previous serious convictions, and persuaded them to let him fire the gun for a ballistic test.

'It took over a week to get permission,' he recalled. 'But they had one or two other things on their mind. Aldo Moro had just been assassinated and that was taking up all their time.' Vratsides got two years in Italy, and was then extradited and, on the strength of the ballistic test matching the victims to his gun, was given twenty years in Britain. He got another life sentence inside for the attempted murder of a fellow prisoner.

But once Smith had started rolling as a supergrass, Lundy had little time to act on tips from his normal informants. Keith Warne, who had provided the first information about Smith and Berkeley, escaped from Regional Crime Squad custody, and was eventually arrested in Kilburn, where he had made sufficient IRA contacts to become a Special Branch informant. Smith also named a man known as 'Bob the Dog' as being 'at it' without being able to provide any firm information linking him to a particular job.

Bob the Dog was tall, dark, very fit and walked with a distinct limp. He was left alone until there were two almost identical robberies at Wembley tube station separated by only a fortnight. On each occasion a tall, dark man held up the same security guard with a sawn-off shotgun, grabbed the money he was carrying and ran off to a waiting car. On the second occasion the guard ran into an office, and a clerk closing the door against the robber was fired at. As the robber ran off, he was clearly limping. The Finchley squad arrested Bob the Dog, who denied having anything to do with either robbery, but he was identified by witnesses, and could give no explanation for the £5,000 paid into a bank account the day after the first robbery, in which £5,000 had been stolen.

Bob the Dog was charged and remanded in custody for trial. While he was in custody, the Finchley squad arrested a Jimmy Gallant and a Sammy Samuels for conspiracy to rob Sainsbury's in Edgware. Gallant turned supergrass and named Samuels as the Wembley robber. Samuels admitted both robberies, and added that the reason for his limp at the second robbery was that when he had fired the shotgun, some of the pellets had hit him in the thigh. Lundy immediately had Bob the Dog brought to the Old Bailey, where he produced the two confessions and had him released.

As the result of information from another robbery team, Lundy had to give a team of contract murderers to other detectives to deal with. 'This greengrocer who'd been nicked told me he could put me on to a team who had carried out four or more contract killings,' Lundy explained. He was disbelieving at first, but when the robber told him that the team were planning to kill two police officers who had once given evidence against them, he realised that he was being given genuine information. 'But my squad had so much work on hand that we just could not spare the time to deal with this new stuff. So I went to see Powis. Powis put Frank Cater

213

on it. Cater eventually nicked them. He got made commander on the strength of the job. No one ever said thank you to the squad, who'd put the job up first.'

The contract team had been Bruce Childs and 'Big H', Henry McKenny, who had murdered George Brett and his ten-year-old son, Robert Andrews, and three other people, who were all killed in a teddy bear factory before being dismembered, put through a mincing machine and burned. If Tony and his squad had not probed beyond the original robbery for which the informant had been arrested, it is likely that the contract killings would have gone on. (Big H had found killing to be more profitable than armed robbery, for which his height always made him an easily identifiable suspect.)

Tony Lundy's five years on the Flying Squad ran on two batteries. One was his network of informants, of whom Roy Garner was the most important but by no means the only one. The other was the ladder of supergrasses leading from one robbery to another. One man, Colin Francis, confessed to forty post office robberies. In the course of his grassing he implicated a man named Paddy Flanagan, a convicted armed robber, for possession of a gun. Flanagan in turn put away a robbery team which included a man called Chrissy Wren.

'Who'd ever heard of Chrissy Wren?' said Lundy. 'But he turned, and he gave us sixty villains who were nicked within three weeks. But he didn't just give us burglars and robbers. He gave us cutters [safe-breakers], which we'd never had before.'

But with Chrissy Wren came the seeds of Tony Lundy's transfer from the Flying Squad. For Wren denounced Mickey Gervaise as a burglar. Mickey Gervaise took part in a huge silver bullion robbery, and with the silver bullion robbery came the whispering campaign that caused the Yard to abandon Lundy. To understand the sequence, it is necessary to understand Tony Lundy's relationship with Roy Garner.

Garner, now serving sixteen years for a conspiracy to import cocaine, was, in the late 1970s, a successful north London businessman with a large house, a small farm, a club and a pub. He had a few early convictions and in the 1980s was the subject of a two-year police operation which failed to unearth any evidence to prosecute him, in spite of rumours that he was an active receiver of stolen property, and responsible for at least one murder. He, like many major criminals, was also a police informant, and his main contact was Tony Lundy.

'The situation was crystal clear,' Lundy maintains. 'He provided me with information and if there was a reward I recommended him for it. I did the same for a number of informants. Garner and the others knew the rules. There was no protection. There was no point in bringing my name up if they were nicked. You get involved in villainy, that's down to you. Do it on my patch and I'll have you, and all the help you've been in the past won't make the slightest difference. Of course, most of the best informants are villains themselves. You don't get Sunday School teachers passing on anything of use about armed robbers.'

On at least one job, which involved a massive conspiracy to forge five-pound notes, Lundy told Garner to ring David Powis direct and supply the information to him. In fact the Deputy Assistant Commissioner, who had adopted the habit of paying informants in person, paid more than one reward to Garner under his police alias of Dave Granger. At least one national journalist believed that Garner was Powis' informant rather than Lundy's.

'He was a useful informant,' claimed Lundy. 'He got paid out by the insurance company for the forged fivers – that was nothing to do with me. He got £37,000 for a faked jewellery robbery in Hatton Garden.' It is on record that Lundy worked hard to ensure that Garner received the £180,000 reward paid out for the silver bullion robbery after the Yard had suddenly introduced a policy, against the wishes of the insurance companies, of recommending a maximum payment of £5,000.

The silver bullion robbery took place in March 1980. A lorry carrying £3.5 million in silver bullion belonging to the East German government was hijacked on the A13. A bogus police officer (his uniform provided by a real but dishonest police sergeant) waved the lorry into a coned-off layby. Seven other robbers, two of whom have never been identified, dressed as Ministry of Transport officials, produced guns, forced the three-man crew into the back of a waiting van and dumped them in a garage. The silver, of course, disappeared, and nothing was heard of it for ten weeks. The four robbery squads put their informants to work, the insurers advertised the usual ten per cent reward, which shrank as the price of silver shrank, intercepts were put on likely phones, but nothing came back. The silver had disappeared and the robbers had successfully covered their tracks.

But one of them panicked. Mickey Sewell wanted to get out of the country. One of his closest friends, Mickey Gervaise, had been arrested because of Chrissy Wren's information. Mickey Gervaise had been in custody for ten days, and was known to have turned supergrass, and he had been another member of the silver bullion team. Even now, on this Friday night, Sewell told Garner, Mickey Gervaise might name him and there could be a tap on his door at any time. Could Garner help him to get out of the country. Spain, perhaps?

'Come back tomorrow,' Garner told him. 'I'll think of something.'

The next morning Garner rang Lundy. At first Tony's wife, Vi, refused to wake him. He had been working without a break for three weeks on the Wren information and had not been to bed for seventy-two hours.

'This is very important,' Garner told her. 'Just say silver bullion to him.' The two words brought Lundy out of a deep sleep and to the phone. Within an hour he was talking to Garner in an East Finchley pub, and two hours later he was at Enfield police station talking to Mickey Gervaise. Garner, who was acutely conscious of the value of his information, had supplied Lundy only with the name of Mickey Gervaise, although Sewell had named everyone except the two unknowns.

'I was furious,' said Lundy. 'Mickey had been there almost ten days, and the rule is that you tell everything. Every detective in London wanted to know about the bullion job, and here was Gervaise, pretending to be a supergrass, telling me about other jobs and keeping the most important stuff back.'

Lundy called out the officer in overall charge of the Gervaise investigation, Detective Superintendent Reg Dixon, and they saw Gervaise together. Gervaise thought that his questioning was over for the week, so when the two senior officers turned up on a Saturday afternoon, he knew something unusual had happened.

He asked to speak to Lundy alone, a suggestion that Dixon had no trouble accommodating. Lundy, after all, was the supergrass master, and it would not be surprising if any supergrass saw him as being more reliable than other, less connected officers.

Gervaise was clearly embarrassed by what he was about to tell Lundy, because of the strong connections there were between the Metropolitan CID and freemasonry. Many aspiring detectives had apparently found that their paths were made smoother if they became masons; yet it is fair to say that other officers saw sport as another promotion ladder. Both options were based on the theory that a senior officer given a choice of selecting an officer he did not know or one with whom he drank and ate socially was more likely to choose the latter. Gervaise believed that being on the squad was synonymous with being on the square, and that Lundy was a freemason.

'Bit awkward this, Mr Lundy. It's about Lennie Gibson. Isn't he in the same lodge as you?'

Lundy certainly knew Gibson through a boxing club they both supported, but made it clear that he was not a mason and that he owed Gibson no allegiance. So what was the problem with Gibson?

'He was on the silver bullion job with me,' said Gervaise, who went on to name Dolph and Renato Aguda, Bob Deanus and Mickey Sewell as other team members, with a man called Bolster Parker as an inside man in the security firm. Lundy and Dixon then went to the home of the then head of the squad, Detective Chief Superintendent Mike Taylor, to tell him what had happened and to discuss the next moves. Lundy went back to Garner to make sure that the names supplied by Gervaise matched those supplied by Sewell. More importantly, Lundy wanted to know where the silver was. Garner did not know this, but he emphasised that as Gibson and Dolph Aguda were close friends, it was essential that they were arrested together. If they were arrested separately, neither would say anything.

Detective Superintendent Dave Little, in charge of the silver bullion investigation, was now brought in, and other squad officers were called back from Saturday leave to form surveillance units to track down the named men while C11 got authority for the routine phone intercepts. It was essential that Gibson was arrested before anyone else. Sewell had indicated that Gibson alone knew where the bullion was hidden, and if he was alerted by other arrests he might dispose of the silver.

It was two days before Gibson and Dolph Aguda were located and arrested. All the other robbers except Sewell had already been found and were then also arrested. Dave Little took over the interrogation of Aguda, while Lundy took Gibson. He was aware from the outset that neither Gibson nor Aguda (members of the same masonic lodge) would speak without knowing what the other was saying. He had been warned of this by Garner, who was also a member of the lodge. Gibson was clearly willing to confess, but wouldn't say anything without Aguda's agreement. Lundy was able to arrange for the two to meet in his presence, where Aguda finally agreed with Gibson's view and decided to tell the detectives where the silver was hidden.

All the bullion, save for twelve bars, which Mickey Sewell is alleged to have taken as his share, was recovered from a garage in Southgate.

In January 1981, Gibson, the two Agudas and Parker pleaded guilty. The three principals received ten-year sentences, and Parker seven years. Sewell was still missing and Gervaise had his admission counted in with the rest of his supergrass confessions. Deanus, the only robber not to have been interviewed by Lundy, was found not guilty. Two other men who took part in the robbery have never been identified. When Sewell was eventually arrested he was not charged with the bullion robbery because by then Gervaise had been discredited as a supergrass.

When it came to paying the ten per cent reward offered by the insurers, Tony Lundy recommended that it be paid to Garner. Garner had provided the original information, had assisted in tracing Gibson, and had correctly assessed that Gibson and Aguda would each say nothing without consulting the other. David Powis and Gilbert Kelland, who were trying to limit insurance payouts to £5,000, were reluctant to agree to the payment, but after many protests Garner eventually received £180,000, and shortly afterwards Lundy, who had already been recommended for promotion to superintendent, was transferred back to division.

'Ron Steventon, the DAC who made the transfer, would not tell me the reason for it. It would have been standard practice for me to stay on the squad until the time came for me to be made up. Sending me back to division was pointless, as I had so many cases running at the Bailey that I'd never be available for duty on division. I found out later that an anonymous letter had come in accusing me and two other officers of corruption over the insurance reward. I was the only one transferred.'

Lundy also became a victim of his own supergrass syndrome. Number 5 Regional Crime Squad had arrested an active criminal called Billy Young, whom they wanted to turn. At the time of his arrest Lundy was on sick leave with his foot in plaster, One of the RCS detectives rang him to ask for all the information he had on Young, and as a result of that information Young turned. But when he learned that the information had been supplied by Lundy, he decided to kill two birds with one stone by working off his grudges against the detective and Dave Spicer, a bookmaker associate of Lundy's. He named Spicer as supplying him with locations for burglaries. Spicer was charged with conspiracy and later cleared after serving three years' imprisonment. During the time he was detained he was asked by RCS officers to give evidence against Lundy with the implication that he would not face charges if he could implicate Lundy in criminal charges. He could not and so went to prison.

But the allegations that would lead to ten years' investigation of Lundy had taken root at the Yard and in the media. Controversy over his methods and ethics continue to this day but despite relentless scrutiny by highly experienced investigators, no allegation of criminal misconduct has ever been proved.

18
Back to Business

With Countryman finally completed and, for the first time in a decade, no large-scale corruption investigations on the horizon, the Flying Squad was able once again to concentrate its full attentions on the problem of armed robbery. It had been a decade in which the professional armed robber had taken the high ground and the police were now desperately scrambling to get back on terms.

Before Bertie Smalls' arrest in 1972, the annual total of armed robberies in the Metropolitan Police district was 380. For the next two years or so, the initial impact of Smalls' confessions enabled the Flying Squad and the Regional Crime Squad to hold down the rate of increase but by 1978 it had risen to 734. By 1982 it had more than doubled again to 1,772. This represented an increase over the ten years to 1982 of 366 per cent, easily outstripping the ninety per cent increase in the general crime rate over the same period. The proceeds of armed robbery in the capital in 1982 amounted to some £12 million and the use of firearms was now *de rigueur* in all major robberies. The squad was struggling against the most casually violent, sophisticated criminals in the country.

Scotland Yard research suggested that of all serious armed robberies in Britain, sixty per cent were committed in London and its immediate environs and three quarters of the rest were carried out by gangs that contained at least one London-based robber. Robbery teams, normally loose federations of around twenty criminals who would come together in varying sub-groups for specific outings, existed all over London. A considerable number – men like George Davis, Michael Ishmael and the Krays' former henchman Freddie Foreman – operated out of east London and others congregated around Islington and Holloway in north London. West London also had its contenders but the most important spawning ground by far for the career armed robber was a relatively small part of south-east London encompassing Bermondsey, Rotherhithe and Walworth. The domain fanned out for a radius of three or four miles but here, within shouting distance of the Old Kent Road, was the epicentre.

Mainly contained within the London borough of Southwark, the area houses a highly traditional working-class community in warrens of tough terraced streets interspersed with imposing tower block estates. It is similar to the East End in that many of its inhabitants owed their livelihoods in days gone by to the London docks, where graft and pilfering operated on a grand scale and there was a general indifference to the rule of law. Unlike the East end, however, the area was left relatively intact after the wartime bombing raids.

The Elephant and Castle in particular had been known as a den of pickpockets, street robbers and commercial burglars since the 1920s and with the steady decline of the docks and other core industries in the 1960s and the consequent widespread unemployment, theft and robbery came to be regarded in some quarters of south-east London as a perfectly legitimate career. It was a short step from pushing things from the backs of lorries to taking them by force, and a plethora of street markets and second-hand shops in the area offered useful outlets for stolen goods. From this base of criminality the epic robber evolved. It was the home of many of the Great Train Robbers and is an area where successful armed robbers are still seen as important role models by younger generations of criminals.

After the Train Robbers came the Richardson brothers, who, while not primarily involved in robbery, were violent criminals of immense power on their own 'manor'. After the Richardsons came men like the Arifs, the Brinks-Mat robbers and their ilk – hard, successful and comparatively wealthy. They were not only capable of robbery on an epic scale: many were also beginning to see the virtue of putting some of their profits into the burgeoning drugs trade.

Once eschewed by traditional London villains as 'unclean', drug trafficking became such a profitable and relatively low-risk enterprise that no major criminal could afford to ignore it. As one squad detective put it: 'What's the point of going over the pavement with a shotgun to rob a hundred thousand pounds when you can make ten times that from one consignment of drugs? The only sensible reason to commit armed robbery now is to finance a drug deal. You'll get anything up to twenty years for armed robbery – life if someone is killed – whereas the average serious drug conviction might get you six or seven.'

Another development which worried Scotland Yard was the growth and increasing determination of jury-nobbling attempts. Although not a new phenomenon, jury-nobbling seemed to grow markedly from the mid-1970s and armed robbery trials were seen as particularly susceptible. Members of the same gang or friends of the defendants were known to have followed some jurors home from court, or to have found out their identities from court lists and then tried to corrupt or intimidate them. This problem has now been tempered, though not wholly overcome, by the expensive measure of twenty-four-hour jury protection by police and telephone intercepts in sensitive cases.

One of the most satisfying convictions secured by the Flying Squad in the early 1980s was that of Billy Tobin, a south-east London robber with an impressive criminal pedigree and some very unpleasant friends. According to Assistant Commissioner Gilbert Kelland, Tobin used to boast about his ability to 'fix' juries and was acquitted on robbery and firearms charges four times between 1976 and 1980. He was also reputed to be a leading 'armourer' who rented weapons out to other criminals for specific jobs and earned the nickname in Flying Squad circles of 'Moss Bros'.

In November 1980, the squad received information from one of its informants that Tobin and five other men intended to attack a security van containing about a million pounds as it drove past a large comprehensive school in Dulwich on a regular cash run. It was a fairly intricate plan, which involved the hiring of a mobile crane, the jib of which would be used to smash open the doors of the van. The raid was to be carried out at about 1.00 p.m. on 16 December and the informant said that if anything went wrong, the gang would be prepared to take schoolchildren hostage to ensure their escape.

Because they suspected that there might be an inside man, the squad did not want to alert the security company but warned the headmaster of Kingsdale Comprehensive School to make sure his pupils were nowhere near the firing line that lunchtime. They then prepared an ambush.

At 1.10 p.m. on the appointed day the gang rammed the security van, which was carrying £811,000 in cash, right outside the school gates. Tobin was observed driving the crane and smashing the jib through the rear door. At this point the trap was sprung. Tobin and one of his five accomplices tried to make a run for it and a squad sergeant fired three shots at them. One bullet went straight through the collar of Tobin's coat but miraculously neither robber was hurt. Both men fell to the ground and surrendered.

The proceedings were recorded by police photographers and seven loaded weapons and ammunition recovered. The evidence looked watertight but all six defendants pleaded not guilty at their Old Bailey trial. Their barristers exercised their right to object to a maximum of three potential jurors each as the jury was being sworn in, a total of eighteen objections. They dismissed as many as they could of those who looked remotely middle-class. The final twelve on the original jury included ten from Tobin's stamping-grounds of Bermondsey, Rotherhithe and Greenwich. However, they were all discharged after three days of evidence when it was discovered that the son of a female juror was a friend of one of the defendants.

A new jury was sworn in (which included, according to Kelland, a man with a spent conviction for robbery) and sat through an acrimonious five-week trial, during which all jurors were given twenty-four-hour armed protection.

Tobin vehemently maintained that he had been the victim of a sustained Flying Squad vendetta because he had slipped through their fingers so many times and claimed to have been lured to the scene of the Dulwich robbery by the squad informant. The weapon he was carrying had, he said, been placed in his hand. To illustrate his constant 'harassment' at the hands of the police, an itinerary was then produced of his arrest record over the previous six years.

In 1974, shortly after coming out of prison, he was accused of committing a £60,000 gin robbery but the charges were dropped before the case came to crown court. In October 1975 he was charged with a £50,000 television warehouse robbery. Despite having been identified by police officers eight times, he was acquitted by a jury. A year later he was acquitted again of an armed lorry hijack. In March 1977 he was arrested with others for a £115,000 robbery at the Express Dairy depot, Wembley, but was again acquitted and in 1978 he was charged on ten counts of conspiracy to rob and possession of firearms with intent in connection with the £197,000 robbery at the *Daily Mirror*, in which a security guard was murdered. Again he was acquitted after a four-week trial. This was one of the cases which sparked Operation Countryman, and Tobin was alleged to have been one of the major criminals who paid City of London police officers to arrange bail and dilute evidence.

After more than sixteen hours' deliberation, the jurors found four of the gang guilty and one not guilty but were unable to reach a verdict on Tobin. Given the evidence against him and his track record the police smelled a rat but had no proof of impropriety. A retrial was ordered and the whole process began again. Halfway through the second trial two women jurors complained of receiving threatening telephone calls warning them of the dire consequences of arguing for a guilty verdict. Tobin, who presented himself as an honest company director, claimed they had been made by police officers trying to blacken his name still further. A new eye-witness also popped up – almost a year after the robbery – to testify that he had seen the crane driver at Dulwich and that it definitely had not been Billy Tobin.

This time, however, Tobin's luck ran out. The jury displayed what Mr Justice Leonard described as 'conspicuous cheerfulness and courage despite the threats' and convicted Tobin by unanimous verdict. He was sentenced to sixteen years in prison.

The surprise witness also had cause to rue his involvement in the trial. Police inquiries proved that he had been paid to lie on Tobin's behalf and he was given a three-year jail sentence some months later after pleading guilty to perjury.

It was to be a group of Tobin's friends and acquaintances from south-east London who, two years after his own conviction for the Dulwich raid, would carry out the robbery of the decade, the most significant, in fact, since the Great Train Robbery twenty years earlier.

There were other contenders for the title, such as the Security Express raid at Shoreditch on the Easter weekend of 1983. Apart from being the largest cash robbery ever carried out in Britain (the proceeds were £6.25 million) it created the legend of the Costa del Crime, 'that little piece of Spain which fell off the back off an English lorry'. All five main suspects, including Freddie Foreman and Ronnie Knight, both friends of the Krays and the latter the ex-husband of the actress Barbara Windsor, emigrated to Spain rather than face police questions. Their subsequent antics and attempts to get them back have provided untold entertainment for the dedicated student of criminal anthropology.

Then there was the Knightsbridge safety deposit box robbery, the haul from which was valued at a minimum of £20 million and by some estimates could have been twice that amount. This one was a bit of a cheat, since the manager of the deposit centre, Parvez Latif, was in on the job, but the amount stolen and the flamboyance of the main robber, the self-styled 'Italian Stallion' Valerio Viccei, made it a significant Flying Squad milestone.

Yet for drama, intrigue and sheer scale neither of these investigations can compare with the Brinks-Mat inquiry.

At 6.30 a.m. on 26 November 1983, six security guards arrived for work at an anonymous industrial unit on an equally anonymous factory estate near Heathrow Airport. The bare brick and corrugated steel of the walls acts merely as cladding for the vaults of the Brinks-Mat security company, one of Britain's strongest safes. Brinks-Mat is responsible for protecting some of the most valuable cargoes to arrive at and depart from London

Airport and it is here they are usually lodged between journeys.

On this particular Saturday the principal cargo was gold bullion for shipment from Gatwick Airport to the Middle and Far East via Cathay Pacific. The owners, Johnson Matthey Bank, had packed it into shoebox-sized cardboard parcels and delivered it to the Heathrow unit the previous day. It was the job of the security team to see that it arrived safely at Gatwick before 8 a.m. At 6.40 a.m., five men wearing balaclavas and trilby hats and armed with shotguns and semi-automatic pistols burst into the control- and rest-rooms of the unit where the guards were chatting before beginning their morning shift.

'Get on the floor or you're fucking dead!' yelled the leader of the gang, who then proceeded to terrorise each guard in turn. Two had their trousers cut open with a Stanley knife and petrol poured on their crotches. The leader threatened first to set fire to them and then to cut their penises off if they did not cooperate. A third guard was battered to the ground with a pistol and all six were at some stage handcuffed and had hoods placed over their heads.

No resistance was put up by the guards and the robbers quickly gained entry to the main vaults, which contained three safes. One of the safes, which they were unable to open because one of the guards was so petrified he could not remember his part of the combination, contained several hundred thousand pounds, although they had no way of knowing this. The others, to which the gang did gain access, held travellers' cheques to the value of about £150,000, uncut diamonds worth just over £110,000 and 20 kilos of platinum worth £160,000. If they had stopped at that point they could not have complained too much about making £420,000 from a morning's work.

But the real prize was in the boxes scattered around the floor of the vault outside the safes. They contained 6,800 bars of the purest gold. In all it weighed three tons and was valued then at £26 million. Unable to believe the size of their haul, the gang loaded the bullion on to trolleys and transferred it to two waiting vans before heading off into the early morning gloom, leaving the guards bound and handcuffed but otherwise unharmed.

It was not until almost two hours after the raid began that the

227

guards managed to free themselves and the police were alerted. The Flying Squad was called in and its head, Commander Frank Cater, took personal charge of the investigation. The total stolen was valued at £26,369,778 – the biggest robbery ever in Britain.

Cater's first step was naturally to interview the six guards and make searching inquiries into their backgrounds, a step which produced rapid results. One, Anthony John Black, was found to be the brother-in-law of Brian Robinson, a robber of some repute whose career was well known to the squad. He was known among his criminal associates as 'the Colonel' because of his organising ability and leadership qualities. Robinson was a close friend of another career robber named Michael McAvoy, who fitted the general description of the aggressive leader of the Brinks-Mat raiders. Both men moved in the same circles as Billy Tobin and the Arif brothers.

Under intensive questioning Black caved in and nine days after the robbery made a full statement admitting that he was the inside man and had made impressions of keys to the outer doors of the Heathrow vaults for the other members of the gang. Duplicate keys were made up and it was because of these that the gang was able so easily and so stealthily to gain entry to the factory unit. He had also provided information about combination locks and security routines. Black identified the robbers he had dealt with as Robinson, McAvoy and a third man named Tony White, who had been charged with Billy Tobin five years earlier in connection with the *Daily Mirror* robbery but acquitted. All three denied involvement but Robinson and McAvoy were also later picked out of identity parades by some of the other security guards.

Black's was the first case to go before the courts, in February 1984, less than three months after the robbery. As the star witness against a gang with £26 million at their disposal, he was in considerable danger and could not be housed in a normal prison. There were whispers that a £50,000 contract had been placed on his head and with so much at stake the police had no reason to doubt them. If anything they felt the figure might be a little low. Black was therefore held in a cell at Paddington Green police station, the most secure station in the country and one normally used to detain IRA terrorists. Being of good previous character and having made a full confession, Black was given six years' imprisonment. The words of Judge David Tudor-Price on delivering his sentence must still ring in Black's ears. 'Never again will your life be safe. You will be segregated at all times and you and your family will forever be fugitives from those you so stupidly and so wickedly helped.'

In late October, Black gave his performance at the Old Bailey trial of Robinson, McAvoy and White but the result was far from a foregone conclusion. White in particular had reason for hope, not having been picked out in any of the identity parades. It was essentially his word against Black's with a few disputed admissions thrown in. The other two looked to have a tougher job on their hands but both provided outwardly sound alibis and constantly denied any involvement in the robbery. It took almost four days of consideration before the jury came back with their verdicts. White was acquitted, Robinson and McAvoy convicted, but on only a 10-2 majority. They had expected long and punitive sentences if convicted and they got them – twenty-five years each.

At this stage, the Brinks-Mat robbery was unique only because of the size of the haul. The planning and execution were slick and ruthless but by no means incredible considering the involvement of an inside man. Similarly, the sentences were severe but not as severe as those of the Great Train Robbers. In the ensuing nine years, however, Brinks-Mat would become one of the most important, wide-ranging investigations in the history of Scotland Yard.

The robbers had been surprised, even shocked, by the amount of gold they had snatched and moving it was going to cause some problems. After storing it, probably underground, for a few months the robbers decided to enlist some help in converting it into cash. Through their extensive south London contacts the gang quickly selected a team of advisers. The linchpin was Kenneth Noye, a haulier and property developer who had progressed through his own efforts from his childhood home in the drab suburbs of south-east London to the village of West Kingsdown, Kent.

The plan Noye put to the robbers and their agents was that the gold should be melted down to remove its identifying marks, adulterated with base metals to disguise its high purity and resold as 'scrap' gold on the legitimate precious metals markets of Sheffield and Birmingham. Noye had obtained a legitimate receipt from a Jersey bullion dealer for eleven gold bars worth £100,000, which would travel with the gold in case of police intervention. As long as the gold was moved in consignments of eleven bars, the receipt would cover the carrier. The melting down was to be done on a private smelter and the resale would be handled by Garth Chappell, who was a director of a bullion company called Scadlynn. The robbers would realise the full value of the gold, with Noye and his associates taking the fifteen per cent VAT charged to the buyer on its resale after smelting.

It seemed a perfect plan, to which the robbers, as represented by their middle-man Brian Perry, a south London mini-cab company proprietor, readily agreed. In the six months from July 1984, almost half the three tons of bullion was transported, eleven bars at a time, from its hiding place in London to Noye's house in Kent and then on to the smelter. It was sold in the markets – much of it to the original owners Johnson Matthey, who needed to replenish stocks after the robbery – and the proceeds were banked in the Scadlynn account at a small branch of Barclays Bank at Bedminster, Bristol.

Between September 1984 and January 1985 more than £10 million went through the Bedminster account, most of it withdrawn in cash by Chappell for distribution to the rest of the robbers and handlers. So many fifty-pound notes were required to finance the transactions that the Bedminster branch had to apply to the Bank of England for a special batch. The serial numbers of the notes they supplied all began with the prefix A24, a fact which was to provide crucial evidence in court cases to come. It was, according to one prosecution lawyer, 'a river of cash which turned into a torrent'.

January 1985 proved to be the watershed in the Brinks-Mat inquiry. But for the events of that month the robbers still at liberty – now seriously wealthy – and the receivers who helped them might have had a fair chance of salting away their ill-gotten gains and quietly disappearing from the scene. But after what happened in the garden of Noye's home on 25 January the police were determined to give them no respite.

In December 1984, with the retirement of Commander Cater imminent, a new man was put in charge of the Brinks-Mat inquiry. Detective Chief Superintendent Brian Boyce was appointed with a specific brief to galvanise the twenty detectives still working on the case and to find out what had happened to the bullion even if the bullion itself could not be recovered. From the outset he concentrated on Noye and his right-hand man Brian Reader, who was suspected of being the main courier for the criminal conspiracy, ferrying gold from Noye to Scadlynn and cash from Scadlynn to Noye. Using the techniques he had learned in C11, Scotland Yard's criminal intelligence branch, he placed Noye's neo-Georgian mansion under twenty-four-hour watch. Part of this surveillance involved two C11 officers camping out in the grounds of the house. They wore black outfits and black balaclavas, the type of kit more associated with officers of the Special Air Service.

On the night of 25 January, almost three weeks after the surveillance began, one of the C11 men, Detective Constable John Fordham, was flushed out of his hiding place by Noye's three Rottweiler dogs. Noye came out into the darkness to see what had caused the commotion armed with a kitchen knife and a torch. The lead-up to the confrontation between the two men is something only Noye could describe in detail but the end result was that Fordham was stabbed ten times with a seven-inch blade – five times in the chest, three in the back, one in the head and one in the armpit. He died before reaching hospital.

At the subsequent murder trial, the prosecution alleged that Reader had also been on the scene and had held Fordham's arms while Noye plunged the knife into his chest. The most compelling evidence for this hypothesis was that Fordham had not sustained any wounds on his hands and arms, which would have been suspected if he had tried to fend off the blows.

Noye's defence was that Fordham, dressed all in black and prowling around in the gardens, could have been anyone. Noye said he had thought him a violent intruder and claimed to have been in fear of his life, which was why he lashed out so frantically.

The jury took Noye's part and both defendants were acquitted on the grounds that Noye had acted in self-defence and Reader's involvement was not proven.

But the killing of Fordham took the Brinks-Mat inquiry on to a different plane as far as Scotland Yard was concerned and Boyce turned down the leadership of the Flying Squad to set up a special task force, made up of Flying Squad and Fraud Squad detectives, which would be dedicated to running down all the Brinks-Mat receivers and finding the routes through which the money had been laundered. 'After Noye had been acquitted, John Fordham's father came up to me and said he held me personally responsible for his son's death. In my position as head of that operation he had every right to do so,' Boyce said. 'As far as I was concerned, after John Fordham was killed it became a matter of honour that none of these people should profit from his death.'

McAvoy and Robinson were horrified by Fordham's death. Their appeal against sentence was imminent and they now knew they had no prospect of a reduction. In desperation they tried to make a deal with Deputy Assistant Commissioner Brian Worth, operational head of CID at Scotland Yard. In return for a reduction in sentence from twenty-five to ten years, they would give their half of the bullion back. The deal had been that they would share half the haul, while the other half would be split between the other three original robbers, the handlers and anyone else who needed paying. Worth was interested. He could make no guarantees but if the gold was given back he would put in a good word with the Court of Appeal.

Unfortunately for the two robbers, their associates on the outside were unwilling to part with the gold over which they now had complete control. They were prepared to stump up a million or two in cash as a gesture of good faith but the message went back to McAvoy and Robinson in prison that no gold would be surrendered.

In January 1986, McAvoy smuggled a letter out of Leicester prison to a friend on the outside asking what was going on and voicing his growing suspicion that he was being betrayed. The letter, intercepted by the police, suggested that McAvoy was threatening to inform on the rest of the gang if his gold was not given back. He said he was not going to be 'fucked for my money and still do the sentence'. In the long run, however, he was, but old habits die hard and even *in extremis* he could not bring himself to 'grass' on his faithless friends.

As Boyce said: 'At the time McAvoy tried to make the deal, I am sure he believed he had control of the missing gold, but by that stage the domestic side of the robbery, which is to say the ordinary south London criminals who stole the gold, had given way to the corporate side. The corporation was not about to hand over all its assets and McAvoy was, in their view, trying to hand back proceeds on which they all had a claim.'

That corporation, set up to launder and reinvest the profits of the robbery, now included men like John Gordon Parry, the shady son of a south London bookmaker, who had served a prison sentence for drug smuggling. Parry and his corrupt solicitor Michael Relton set up 'a vast international money-go-round with millions of pounds being lodged in coded bank accounts in London, Switzerland, Liechtenstein, Jersey and the Isle of Man'. Almost all deposits were made personally in cash. With the help of several dubious financial advisers recruited by Parry and Relton, shelf companies were set up in London, Panama, the Cayman Islands, Spain and a number of British dependencies in the Caribbean and millions of pounds of Brinks-Mat money was transferred between them in a mass of bogus transactions, so that when it finally returned to London to be invested in a property company called Selective Estates, its origin was virtually impossible to trace.

From an initial £7.5 million laundered in this way an impressive property portfolio was composed. At the height of the boom it was worth £18 million pounds and included three wharf sites in London docklands and prime residential buildings in Cheltenham. The funds were also used to finance extravagant lifestyles for the families and friends of the robbers and receivers, with the purchase of luxury homes in Kent, at least two hotels and several villas in Spain. McAvoy's first wife Jacqueline, whom he divorced while in prison, moved from a drab flat in Herne Hill, south London, to a substantial mock-Tudor house in Bickley, and his mistress Kathy Meacock, whom he married after his divorce from Jacqueline, was whisked from her council flat in Walworth to a sumptuous farmhouse near Bromley. Parry moved from a cottage in Greenwich to a house in Westerham, Kent which in 1987 was worth £400,000.

From January 1985 until early 1993 the task force hounded the Brinks-Mat suspects. Noye, Reader, Chappell, Parry, Relton, Perry, the second Mrs McAvoy and at least a dozen others were convicted in a series of Old Bailey trials and jailed for periods of up to fourteen years. An operation codenamed Cougar and headed by Boyce and Detective Superintendent Tony Lundy delved into money-laundering activities in the Caribbean and came up with some startling results. Much of the Brinks-Mat money had been laundered through the same channels as those used by the US mafia and various international drug syndicates. It proved a significant degree of collusion between British organised criminals and their counterparts overseas.

There were also disappointments for the police. A prime suspect, John Fleming, had gone to Spain shortly after the robbery and was eventually shipped back to Britain – via South America and Florida – in the late summer of 1986. He was suspected by the squad of having been one of the original robbers, charged with dishonestly handling around a million pounds and freed before his case even reached crown court by the Horseferry Road magistrate, who said the case against him was non-existent.

It is also a fact that, ten years and twelve trials after the robbery only eleven of the 6,800 gold bars stolen have been recovered. Some £20 million in laundered profits has been traced, but the only gold found was eleven bars seized from Noye's house on the night of John Fordham's death. And even with those there was considerable doubt that they all came from the original haul.

It is still quite conceivable that half the bullion – 1.5 tons – may not yet have been melted down and converted into cash and one man suspected of the original robbery, a friend of Michael McAvoy and Billy Tobin named John Lloyd, is still wanted for questioning, so the Brinks-Mat saga may not yet be over. Loss adjusters for the insurers of the Johnson Matthey gold are also

234

anxious to get their money back. Next year they are expected to begin a series of civil actions against everyone who has ever been suspected of handling money from the robbery. In those actions, the appellants will not have to prove their cases beyond reasonable doubt as in criminal cases but merely on the balance of probabilities. Acquittals at crown court do not preclude civil litigation so it is certain that Fleming and others have not heard the last of Brinks-Mat.

EPILOGUE
Future Prospects

Seventy-five years after the realisation of Frederick Porter Wensley's vision of a roving detective unit unfettered by divisional borders or local accountability, the fortunes of the Flying Squad have come virtually full circle. It has been a roller-coaster ride that has generated unparalleled variations in levels of public esteem. At the height of its reputation the squad could reasonably boast of being the most highly acclaimed police unit in Britain and one that had won a considerable degree of international fame. At its nadir in the mid-1970s it was seen by many as a major contributor – if not the major contributor – to the infection of corruption which helped destroy for ever the Utopian 'Dixon of Dock Green' image of the police in this country.

There is little doubt that Sir Robert Mark's memorable tongue-in-cheek definition of a good police force as being one that arrests more criminals than it employs was directed largely at the squad and it is as a result of the misdemeanours of earlier decades that the activities of the squad are now so tightly structured.

In their heyday squad detectives dealt with whichever classes of criminals took their fancy, from Soho pimps to Oxford Street pickpockets, from south and east London extortionists to dockland lorry thieves. They certainly worked long hours and made impressive numbers of arrests but their work had no external direction and no definable focus apart from 'getting to the roots of crime'.

Today, they deal almost exclusively with armed robberies of banks, building societies, betting shops, post offices, jewellers and security vans. In 1992 the 170 squad officers carried out around 700

237

armed operations and arrested 247 criminals, most of them habitual carriers of firearms. In none of those operations, against the most desperate and dangerous of men, did a squad officer have to shoot a robber.

The squad has four bases in London at Barnes, Lea Bridge Road, Finchley and Tower Bridge and while it is theoretically restricted to investigating robberies in the London area, it also deals with some robbers who also operate in other parts of the country. With a clear-up rate of about thirty-four per cent, it is one of the most effective of all specialised units and to be entitled to wear the Flying Squad tie, complete with swooping eagle motif, remains the ambition of many thrusting young detectives in the Metropolitan Police.

But because of the way policing philosophy has developed over the past decade, the need for the Flying Squad is now being seriously questioned by those who dictate policy at Scotland Yard. The trend is away from centralised units and towards local policing for local communities. The buzz words are 'public ownership' and 'community direction'. Senior policemen no longer talk of a police 'force', preferring the term 'police service' lest they should appear to be authoritarian rather than 'caring'. Quality of service should be seen to be delivered in a spirit of partnership and any hint of sharp or excessively robust practice eliminated. Victim support has become as important as catching criminals – some would say more important.

The motives for this sea change in police thinking are understandable and in some respects laudable but for the Flying Squad it could have damaging consequences. They are a professionally confrontational crew who are rarely seen in public in anything other than an aggressive posture. To try to categorise them as part of some smiling, avuncular service is a ludicrous notion. They cannot easily be defined in the management newspeak of the modern police service. They also form one of the very few police squads and certainly the largest one which does not perform a truly national function yet is able to cross all boundaries within the Metropolitan Police district without prior reference to local commanders.

To some among the police leadership, especially those with little or no CID experience the squad is seen as an unnecessary anachronism. Why, they argue, should it not be disbanded and its constituent detectives divided between the eight areas of the Met to form the basis of a series of more localised squads under the control and direction of local police chiefs? Furthermore, a reorganisation of the force is under way which would reduce the eight areas to four new semi-autonomous 'super-areas' plus a fifth covering the centre, arguably making the case for dismantling the squad more compelling. If they are to be more autonomous, why should they not investigate their own armed robberies? The face of national policing is also changing and the newly restructured Regional Crime Squads, backed by the embryonic National Criminal Intelligence Service could easily be 'tasked' to take over much of the work currently handled by the Flying Squad.

Ironically, the arguments for keeping the squad intact are much the same as those put forward for its creation by Frederick Wensley seventy-five years ago. Its supporters say London needs a unified team to fight 'project robbers' – the 1990s equivalent of the 'motor-bandits' and suburban house-breakers regarded as major threats to social stability in 1918. Squad detectives need to be able to cultivate informants all over London and not to have to ask local commanders every time they need to cross divisional frontiers. If they are keeping surveillance they can hardly abandon their target because he travels, say, from Victoria to King's Cross or from Waterloo to Paddington.

Career armed robbers are still among the most sophisticated and artful of criminals and without a centralised intelligence collection plan they would inevitably be more difficult to catch. They are no longer simply groups of men who 'go across the pavement' to rob cash and then retire to an agreeable hideaway until it is all spent. Most are heavily into the drug trade and have access to covert money-laundering routes. A significant proportion of armed robberies are carried out to finance other crimes and investments. It is perhaps the most dangerous of criminal occupations but the gains are high and the wages are in cash.

At the time of writing it is not clear how the new Met Commissioner, Paul Condon, will place the future of the squad in his wider game plan but the early signs are that he regards it as a necessary part of the central CID and does not intend to break it up.

The present head of the squad, Commander George Ness, who also leads the serious, international and organised crime branch (SO1), believes that any move to disband the Flying Squad would be a gross error of judgement. Although he may not exactly be an independent judge, his rationale for the continued survival of the squad would win support from many less partisan observers of law enforcement policy in this country. 'The Metropolitan Police is about the pursuit of excellence and nowhere is excellence better demonstrated than in the Flying Squad.'

Bibliography

Ascoli, David, *The Queen's Peace*, Hamilton, 1979.

Ball, John *et al.*, *Cops and Robbers*, Book Club Associates, 1978.

Browne, Douglas G., *The Rise of Scotland Yard*, Harrap, 1956.

Campbell, Duncan, *That was Business, This is Personal*, Martin, Secker & Warburg, 1990.

Capstick, John, *Given in Evidence*, Long, 1960.

Cox, Barry *et al.*, *The Fall of Scotland Yard*, Penguin, 1977.

Fabian, Robert, *Fabian of the Yard*, British Book Centre, 1953.

Firmin, Stanley, *Crime Man*, Hutchinson, 1950.

Firmin, Stanley, *Scotland Yard, The Inside Story*, Hutchinson, 1951.

Frost, George, *Flying Squad*, Rockliff, 1948.

Gosling, John, *The Ghost Squad*, W. H. Allen, 1959.

Grant, D., *A Fragmented History of the Flying Squad and its Drivers*, Boxing Programme Notes, 1976.

Greeno, Edward, *War on the Underworld*, Hutchinson, 1960.

Hambrook, Walter, *Hambrook of the Yard*, Hale, 1937.

Harrison, Richard, *Whitehall 1212*, Jarrolds, 1947.

Hobbs, Dick, *Doing the Business*, Clarendon, 1988.

Hogg, Andrew *et al.*, *Bullion*, Penguin, 1988.

Jackson, Sir Richard, *Occupied with Crime*, Harrap, 1967.

Jennings, Andrew *et al.*, *Scotland Yard's Cocaine Connection*, Arrow, 1990.

Kelland, Gilbert, *Crime in London*, Bodley Head, 1986.

Laurie, Peter, *Scotland Yard*, Bodley Head, 1970.

Lucas, Norman and Scarlett, Bernard, *Flying Squad*, Barker, 1968.

Mark, Sir Robert, *In the Office of Constable*, Collins, 1978.

Morton, James, *Nipper*, Macdonald, 1991.

O'Mahony, Maurice, *King Squealer*, W. H. Allen, 1978.

Pearson, John, *The Profession of Violence*, Weidenfeld and Nicolson, 1972.

Read, Piers Paul, *The Great Train Robbery*, W. H. Allen, 1978.

Richardson, Charles, *My Manor*, Pan, 1991.

Robinson, R. T., *Queen's Evidence: A Study of the Supergrass Phenomenon*, Bramshill, 1976.

Scott, Sir Harold, *Scotland Yard*, Deutsch, 1954.

Sharpe, F. D., *Sharpe of the Flying Squad*, Long, 1938.

Short, Martin, *Lundy*, Grafton, 1992.

Slipper, Jack, *Slipper of the Yard*, Sidgwick and Jackson, 1981.

Thompson, Sir Basil, *The Story of Scotland Yard*, Grayson and Grayson, 1935.

Wensley, Frederick, *40 Years of Scotland Yard*, Garden City, 1930.

Williams, Guy, *The Hidden World of Scotland Yard*, Hutchinson, 1972

Index

243